Taste *of* Home

GRANDMA'S FAVORITES

TASTE OF HOME BOOKS • RDA ENTHUSIAST BRANDS, LLC • MILWAUKEE, WI

© 2022 RDA Enthusiast Brands, LLC.
1610 N. 2nd St., Suite 102,
Milwaukee, WI 53212-3906
All rights reserved. Taste of Home
is a registered trademark of
RDA Enthusiast Brands, LLC.

Visit us at **tasteofhome.com** for other
Taste of Home books and products.

International Standard Book Number:
D 978-1-62145-769-5
U 978-1-62145-770-1
Component Number:
D 117600100H
U 117600102H

Executive Editor: Mark Hagen
Senior Art Director: Raeann Thompson
Editor: Hazel Wheaton
Art Director: Courtney Lovetere
Senior Designer: Jazmin Delgado
Deputy Editor, Copy Desk:
Dulcie Shoener
Copy Editor: Sara Strauss

Cover Photography:
Photographer: Mark Derse
Set Stylist: Stacey Genaw
Food Stylist: Josh Rink

Pictured on front cover:
Strawberry Poke Cake, p. 264

Pattern: Spiderplay/Getty Images

Pictured on back cover:
Honey-Lemon Asparagus, p. 153;
Peppercorn Beef Top Loin Roast, p. 116;
Passover Popovers, p. 79

Printed in USA
1 3 5 7 9 10 8 6 4 2

CONTENTS

STEAMED CARROT
PUDDING, PAGE 307

When we think of finger-licking, stick-to-your-ribs, best-all-time comfort foods, Grandma's cooking springs to mind. From the tempting aroma of freshly baked breads to the satisfaction of a bubbling casserole and the anticipation of a down-home dessert, Grandma's kitchen never disappoints.

Relish much-loved specialties in your home when you explore the hundreds of recipes in *Grandma's Favorites*. You'll delight in forgotten favorites, add heartwarming flair to weeknight suppers, and bring a cherished, old-fashioned touch to holidays and other celebrations.

You'll also enjoy...

• **Grandma's Favorite Breakfasts.** Remember sleepovers at Grandma's? The best food was always waiting in the morning. Relive those moments with this chapter of classics to start the day right.

• **Grandma's Favorite Main Courses.** You can't go wrong with potpies, golden chicken or from-scratch pasta sauces. Don't forget hearty roasts, tasty casseroles and savory stews simmered on the stovetop.

• **Grandma's Favorite Breads, Biscuits & More.** Muffins, biscuits, quick breads, breakfast rolls, braided loaves and more—this chapter has all the tasty breads Grandma created for every meal!

• **Grandma's Favorite Desserts.** Cakes and cobblers, tarts and tortes—here you'll find all the sweets you crave, as well as crispy cookies, decadent brownies and many other beloved treats.

Relive those glorious moments around the table, create new memories in your kitchen and savor the goodness of the home-cooked foods you have always adored. It's easier than ever with this all-new keepsake, *Taste of Home Grandma's Favorites*.

SUNDAY DINNER MENUS

Whether you're new to meal planning or a longtime pro, consider this handy guide
that relies on recipes from this book to create complete meals.

Tangy Pickled Mushrooms,
p. 69 • Peppercorn Beef
Top Loin Roast, p. 116 •
Gruyere Mashed Potatoes,
p. 177 • Baked Custard
with Cinnamon, p. 304

Creamy Carrot Soup,
p. 200 • Chicken Amandine,
p. 147 • Dill Bread, p. 100 •
Sticky Toffee Rice Pudding
with Caramel Cream,
p. 316

Shrimp Salad Appetizers,
p. 47 • Fast Baked Fish,
p. 118 • Asparagus,
Squash & Red Pepper
Saute, p. 182 • Deep-Dish
Apple Pie, p. 287

Grandma's Onion Squares,
p. 90 • Roasted Citrus &
Herb Turkey, p. 125 • Moist
Poultry Dressing, p. 153 •
Rustic Cranberry Tarts,
p. 281

Bacon Cheddar
Potato Skins, p. 71 •
Family-Pleasing Turkey
Chili, p. 195 • Oven-Fried
Cornbread, p. 95 • Mom's
Citrus Buttermilk
Cake, p. 275

Garlic-Dill Deviled Eggs,
p. 69 • Pressure-Cooker
Mini Teriyaki Turkey
Sandwiches, p. 131 •
Cucumbers with Dressing,
p. 156 • Sweet & Tart
Lemon Jell-O, p. 328

Best Ever Stuffed
Mushrooms, p. 63 •
Autumn Lamb Skillet,
p. 132 • Yorkshire Pudding
with Bacon & Sage, p. 76 •
Rich Rum Cake, p. 293

Skillet Herb Bread, p. 81 •
Grandma's Cajun Chicken
& Spaghetti, p. 141 •
Spinach Salad with
Raspberries & Candied
Walnuts, p. 176 • Chocolate
Chess Pie, p. 269

Antipasto Bake, p. 44 •
Great-Grandma's Italian
Meatballs, p. 122 •
Crumb-Topped Macaroni
& Cheese, p. 160 • Orange
Chocolate Ricotta
Pie, p. 271

Heirloom Tomato Galette
with Pecorino, p. 55 • Low
Country Boil, p. 198 •
Baking Powder Drop
Biscuits, p. 105 • Peach
Cobbler, p. 301

Lentil, Bacon & Bean
Soup, p. 204 • Individual
Turkey Potpies, p. 145 •
Blue Cheese & Grape
Coleslaw, p. 157 •
Blueberry Dream
Pie, p. 291

Brie Puff Pastry, p. 48 •
Blue Cheese-Mushroom
Stuffed Tenderloin, p. 142 •
Honey Garlic Green Beans,
p. 180 • Black Forest
Chocolate Torte, p. 278

KAISERSCHMARREN,
PAGE 21

GRANDMA'S FAVORITE
BREAKFASTS

Whether made for a weekend sleepover or a
holiday brunch, Grandma's eye-opening breakfasts
continuously warm hearts and satisfy hungry
tummies. Enjoy those sunny occasions with this
collection of all-time classics.

APPLE SPICE WAFFLES

These apple waffles are cozy and comforting anytime—morning or evening. The smell of toasty waffles with apples is sure to warm you up on even the most blustery of winter days.
—*Jane Pair Sims, De Leon, TX*

TAKES: 30 MIN. • MAKES: 12 WAFFLES

2 cups biscuit/baking mix
2 tsp. ground cinnamon
1 tsp. ground nutmeg
2 large eggs, room temperature
1½ cups 2% milk
6 Tbsp. butter, melted
1 cup chopped peeled apple
Optional: Whipped cream and maple syrup

1. Preheat waffle maker. In a large bowl, combine biscuit mix, cinnamon and nutmeg. In another bowl, whisk eggs, milk and butter; stir into dry ingredients just until moistened; stir in apple.

2. Bake waffles according to manufacturer's directions until golden brown. If desired, serve with whipped cream, syrup and additional chopped apples.

FREEZE OPTION: Arrange waffles in a single layer on sheet pans. Freeze overnight or until frozen. Transfer to a resealable plastic freezer bag. Waffles may be frozen for up to 2 months. To use, reheat frozen waffles in a toaster.

2 WAFFLES: 321 cal., 19g fat (10g sat. fat), 97mg chol., 558mg sod., 34g carb. (6g sugars, 2g fiber), 7g pro.

CORNED BEEF HASH & EGGS

Sunday breakfasts have always been special in our house. It's fun to get in the kitchen and cook with the kids. No matter how many new recipes we try, the kids always rate this No. 1!
—*Rick Skildum, Maple Grove, MN*

PREP: 15 MIN. • BAKE: 20 MIN. • MAKES: 8 SERVINGS

1 pkg. (32 oz.) frozen cubed hash browns
1½ cups chopped onion
½ cup canola oil
4 to 5 cups chopped cooked corned beef
½ tsp. salt
8 large eggs
Salt and pepper to taste
2 Tbsp. minced fresh parsley

1. Preheat oven to 325°. In a large ovenproof skillet, cook hash browns and onion in oil until potatoes are browned and onion is tender. Remove from the heat; stir in corned beef and salt.

2. Make 8 wells in the hash browns. Break 1 egg into each well. Sprinkle with salt and pepper. Cover and bake for 20-25 minutes or until eggs reach desired doneness. Garnish with parsley.

1 SERVING: 442 cal., 30g fat (6g sat. fat), 242mg chol., 895mg sod., 24g carb. (3g sugars, 2g fiber), 20g pro.

APPLE SPICE
WAFFLES

CANADIAN BACON WITH APPLES

At the holidays, I'd rather spend time with family than in the kitchen, so I rely on easy-to-fix recipes like this. No one can resist Canadian bacon and apples coated with a brown sugar glaze.

—*Paula Marchesi, Lenhartsville, PA*

TAKES: 20 MIN. • **MAKES:** 6 SERVINGS

½	cup packed brown sugar	1	large green apple,
1	Tbsp. lemon juice		unpeeled
⅛	tsp. pepper	1	lb. sliced Canadian bacon
1	large red apple, unpeeled		

1. In a large cast-iron or other heavy skillet, mix brown sugar, lemon juice and pepper. Cook and stir over medium heat until the sugar is dissolved. Cut each apple into 16 wedges; add to the brown sugar mixture. Cook over medium heat 5-7 minutes or until apples are tender, stirring occasionally. Remove the apples to a platter with a slotted spoon; keep warm.

2. Add bacon to skillet; cook over medium heat, turning once, until heated through, about 3 minutes. Transfer to platter. Pour the remaining brown sugar mixture over the apples and bacon.

1 SERVING: 199 cal., 4g fat (1g sat. fat), 28mg chol., 744mg sod., 30g carb. (27g sugars, 2g fiber), 12g pro.

FROM GRANDMA'S KITCHEN: Canadian bacon is made of back bacon from the pork loin—it's much leaner than American bacon and is often cured but not smoked. In Canada, it's simply known as back bacon. It's usually precooked, so you only have to cook it until it's warm enough to eat—be careful not to overdo it or you'll end up with dry, tough bacon.

CORNFLAKE-COATED BAKED FRENCH TOAST

We fed a group of hungry Air Force cadets breakfast for dinner with this
go-to baked French toast, along with eggs, sausage, bacon and fresh fruit.
—*Lois Enger, Colorado Springs, CO*

TAKES: 25 MIN. • **MAKES:** 6 SERVINGS (1 CUP SYRUP)

2 **large eggs**
½ **cup 2% milk**
½ **tsp. salt**
½ **tsp. vanilla extract**
1 **cup cornflake crumbs**
6 **slices Texas toast**
¼ **cup butter, melted**

CINNAMON SYRUP
⅔ **cup sugar**
⅓ **cup light corn syrup**
2 **Tbsp. water**
½ **tsp. ground cinnamon**
⅓ **cup evaporated milk or
   2% milk**
1½ **tsp. butter**
¼ **tsp. almond extract**

1. Preheat oven to 450°. In a shallow bowl, whisk eggs, milk, salt and vanilla until blended. Place cornflake crumbs in another shallow bowl. Dip both sides of bread in the egg mixture, then in the cornflake crumbs, patting to help the coating adhere.

2. Place in a greased 15x10x1-in. baking pan. Drizzle with melted butter. Bake 10-12 minutes or until golden brown.

3. For syrup, in a small saucepan, combine sugar, corn syrup, water and cinnamon; bring to a boil. Cook and stir 2 minutes. Remove from heat. Stir in milk, butter and extract. Serve with French toast.

1 PIECE WITH 3 TBSP. SYRUP: 419 cal., 13g fat (7g sat. fat), 91mg chol., 619mg sod., 70g carb. (43g sugars, 1g fiber), 8g pro.

APPLE-SAGE SAUSAGE PATTIES

Apple and sausage naturally go together. Add sage, and you've got a standout patty.
They're freezer-friendly, so I make them ahead and grab when needed.
—*Scarlett Elrod, Newnan, GA*

PREP: 35 MIN. + CHILLING • **COOK:** 10 MIN./BATCH • **MAKES:** 16 SERVINGS

1 **large apple**
1 **large egg, lightly beaten**
½ **cup chopped fresh
   parsley**
3 **to 4 Tbsp. minced fresh
   sage**
2 **garlic cloves, minced**
1¼ **tsp. salt**
½ **tsp. pepper**
½ **tsp. crushed red pepper
   flakes**
1¼ **lbs. lean ground turkey**
6 **tsp. olive oil, divided**

1. Peel and coarsely shred apple; place in a colander over a plate. Let stand 15 minutes. Squeeze and blot dry with paper towels.

2. In a large bowl, combine egg, parsley, sage, garlic, seasonings and apple. Add turkey; mix lightly but thoroughly. Shape into sixteen 2-in. patties. Place patties on waxed paper-lined baking sheets. Refrigerate, covered, 8 hours or overnight.

3. In a large nonstick skillet, heat 2 tsp. oil over medium heat. In batches, cook patties 3-4 minutes on each side or until golden brown and a thermometer reads 165°, adding more oil as needed.

1 PATTY: 79 cal., 5g fat (1g sat. fat), 36mg chol., 211mg sod., 2g carb. (1g sugars, 0 fiber), 8g pro. **DIABETIC EXCHANGES:** 1 lean meat, ½ fat.

AMISH APPLE
SCRAPPLE

AMISH APPLE SCRAPPLE

Just the aroma of this cooking at breakfast takes me back to my days growing up
in Pennsylvania. The recipe was a favorite at home and at church breakfasts.
—*Marion Lowery, Medford, OR*

PREP: 1 HOUR 20 MIN. + CHILLING • COOK: 10 MIN. • MAKES: 8 SERVINGS

¾ lb. bulk pork sausage
½ cup finely chopped onion
4 Tbsp. butter, divided
½ cup diced apple, unpeeled
¾ tsp. dried thyme
½ tsp. ground sage
¼ tsp. pepper
3 cups water, divided
¾ cup cornmeal
1 tsp. salt
2 Tbsp. all-purpose flour
Maple syrup

1. In a large skillet, cook sausage and onion over medium-high heat until sausage is no longer pink and onion is tender. Remove from skillet; set aside.

2. Discard all but 2 Tbsp. drippings. Add 2 Tbsp. butter, apple, thyme, sage and pepper to drippings; cook over low heat until apple is tender, about 5 minutes. Remove from heat; stir in the sausage mixture. Set aside.

3. In a large heavy saucepan, bring 2 cups water to a boil. Combine cornmeal, salt and the remaining 1 cup water; slowly pour into boiling water, stirring constantly. Return to a boil. Reduce heat; simmer, covered, for 1 hour, stirring occasionally. Stir in sausage mixture. Pour into a greased 8x4-in. loaf pan. Refrigerate, covered, for 8 hours or overnight.

4. Slice ½ in. thick. Sprinkle flour over both sides of each slice. In a large skillet, heat remaining 2 Tbsp. butter over medium heat. Add slices; cook until both sides are browned. Serve with syrup.

1 PIECE: 251 cal., 18g fat (7g sat. fat), 44mg chol., 667mg sod., 16g carb. (1g sugars, 1g fiber), 7g pro.

PECAN WAFFLES

I've tried for years to duplicate a delicious waffle I sampled at a restaurant
here in the South. This crisp and nutty version is what I came up with.
Butter and maple syrup are my family's favorite toppings.
—*Susan Elise Jansen, Smyrna, GA*

TAKES: 30 MIN. • MAKES: 10 WAFFLES (4½ IN.)

1¾ cups all-purpose flour
1 Tbsp. baking powder
½ tsp. salt
2 large eggs, separated, room temperature
1¾ cups 2% milk
½ cup canola oil
1 cup chopped pecans
Maple syrup

1. In a bowl, combine flour, baking powder and salt. Combine egg yolks, milk and oil; stir into dry ingredients. Beat egg whites until stiff; fold into batter.

2. Sprinkle hot waffle iron with 2 Tbsp. pecans. Pour ¼ to ⅓ cup of batter over the pecans and bake according to manufacturer's directions until golden brown. Repeat with the remaining pecans and batter. Serve with syrup.

2 WAFFLES: 589 cal., 43g fat (5g sat. fat), 83mg chol., 590mg sod., 41g carb. (5g sugars, 3g fiber), 12g pro.

REUBEN EGGS BENEDICT

When it comes to food, two of my all-time favorites are Reuben sandwiches and eggs Benedict. So naturally I combined them into this incredible breakfast dish. I serve mine with bacon on the side, but hash browns and fresh fruit go well, too!
—*Jessica Rehs, Akron, OH*

PREP: 20 MIN. • COOK: 15 MIN. • MAKES: 4 SERVINGS

4 **large eggs**
  Coarsely ground pepper
⅛ **tsp. salt**
2 **pretzel hamburger buns, split**
4 **slices Swiss cheese (¾ oz. each)**
⅓ **cup sauerkraut, rinsed, drained well and chopped**
¼ **lb. sliced deli corned beef**
  Prepared Thousand Island salad dressing

1. Preheat oven to 350°. Heat a large skillet coated with cooking spray over medium-high heat. Break eggs, 1 at a time, into the pan; sprinkle with coarsely ground pepper. Reduce heat to low. Cook to desired doneness, turning after whites are set, about 2-3 minutes. Sprinkle with salt; keep warm.

2. While eggs are cooking, hollow out split pretzel buns. Toast buns on a baking sheet or oven rack, 3-4 minutes. Top with cheese; return to oven until cheese is melted.

3. To assemble, layer a fourth of the sauerkraut, a fourth of the corned beef and 1 egg on each bun half. Drizzle each with salad dressing.

1 OPEN-FACED SANDWICH: 317 cal., 15g fat (6g sat. fat), 222mg chol., 784mg sod., 25g carb. (2g sugars, 1g fiber), 21g pro.

BREAKFAST LOAF

I love to make this mile-high breakfast sandwich when we have company for the weekend. If you like, add sliced mushrooms and olives.
—*Amy McCuan, Oakley, CA*

PREP: 15 MIN. • BAKE: 25 MIN. + STANDING • MAKES: 6 SERVINGS

6 **large eggs**
¼ **tsp. salt**
⅛ **tsp. pepper**
1 **Tbsp. butter**
1 **round loaf (1 lb.) French bread**
6 **oz. sliced deli ham, divided**
¾ **cup shredded Monterey Jack cheese, divided**
¾ **cup shredded cheddar cheese, divided**
½ **medium sweet red pepper, thinly sliced**
1 **medium tomato, thinly sliced**

1. Preheat oven to 350°. Whisk together eggs, salt and pepper. In a large skillet, heat butter over medium heat. Pour in the egg mixture; cook and stir until thickened and no liquid egg remains. Remove from heat.

2. Cut one-fourth off top of bread loaf. Hollow out both parts, leaving a ½-in. shell (save removed bread for another use).

3. Place a fourth of the ham in bread bottom; top with half of each of the cheeses. Layer with red pepper, scrambled eggs, tomato and the remaining cheeses and ham. Press layers gently; replace bread top. Wrap tightly in foil.

4. Bake until heated through, 25-30 minutes. Let stand 10 minutes before cutting into wedges.

1 PIECE: 439 cal., 18g fat (9g sat. fat), 230mg chol., 1083mg sod., 42g carb. (5g sugars, 2g fiber), 26g pro.

BAKED FRENCH TOAST

Any day is a special day when it starts with
Mom making this do-ahead baked French toast!
—*Jill Baughman, New York, NY*

PREP: 20 MIN. + CHILLING • **BAKE:** 40 MIN. + STANDING • **MAKES:** 8 SERVINGS

8 oz. day-old French bread,
  unsliced
4 large eggs
2 Tbsp. sugar
1 Tbsp. brown sugar
2 tsp. vanilla extract
1 tsp. maple extract
¼ tsp. kosher salt
2 cups whole milk
½ cup heavy whipping
  cream

TOPPING
¼ cup all-purpose flour
3 Tbsp. brown sugar
3 Tbsp. unsalted butter,
  cut into ¼-in. cubes
1 tsp. ground cinnamon
  Freshly grated nutmeg,
  optional
  Fresh blueberries or
  raspberries
  Confectioners' sugar

1. Cut bread into 1-in.-thick slices. Arrange in a single layer in a greased 13x9-in. baking dish. Lightly beat the next 6 ingredients; stir in milk and cream. Pour egg mixture over bread, turning once to coat. Refrigerate, covered, overnight.

2. Preheat oven to 375°. Turn bread again to coat. For topping, combine flour, brown sugar, butter, cinnamon and, if desired, nutmeg. Sprinkle flour mixture over bread.

3. Bake, uncovered, until a knife inserted in center comes out clean and topping is golden brown, 40-45 minutes. Let stand 10 minutes before cutting. Top with blueberries or raspberries; sprinkle with confectioners' sugar.

1 SERVING: 297 cal., 15g fat (8g sat. fat), 128mg chol., 299mg sod., 32g carb. (15g sugars, 1g fiber), 9g pro.

FROM GRANDMA'S KITCHEN: For variety, try changing the fruit or the bread to create a completely different decadent French toast. Use whatever fruit is in season—berries in the spring, stone fruit in summer, apples or pears in fall, and citrus in winter. An egg bread like brioche or challah in place of the French bread will result in a creamier, custardy French toast. Or, go all-out with thick slices of cinnamon-raisin bread!

THE BEST QUICHE LORRAINE

Nestled in a buttery, rustic crust, this quiche is filled with sweet onions,
bacon bits and cheese. It's the perfect addition to brunch.
—*Shannon Norris, Cudahy, WI*

| PREP: 1 HOUR. • BAKE: 1¼ HOURS + COOLING • MAKES: 8 SERVINGS |

Dough for single-crust deep-dish pie
1 **pkg. (12 oz.) thick-sliced bacon strips, coarsely chopped**
3 **large sweet onions, chopped**
1 **Tbsp. minced fresh thyme**
½ **tsp. coarsely ground pepper**
⅛ **tsp. ground nutmeg**
1½ **cups shredded Gruyere cheese**
½ **cup grated Parmesan cheese**
8 **large eggs, room temperature**
2 **cups whole milk**
1 **cup heavy whipping cream**

1. On a lightly floured surface, roll dough to a 14-in. circle. Transfer to a 9-in. springform pan; press firmly against bottom and sides. Refrigerate while preparing filling.

2. In a large skillet, cook bacon over medium heat until crisp, stirring occasionally. Remove with a slotted spoon; drain on paper towels. Discard drippings, reserving 1 Tbsp. in pan. Add onions to drippings; cook and stir over medium heat until caramelized, 20-25 minutes.

3. Stir in thyme, pepper and nutmeg; remove from the heat. Cool slightly. Stir in cheeses and reserved bacon; spoon into crust.

4. Preheat oven to 350°. In a large bowl, whisk eggs, milk, and cream until blended; pour over top. Place springform pan on a rimmed baking sheet.

5. Bake on a lower oven rack until a knife inserted near the center comes out clean, 75-85 minutes. Cool on a wire rack 15 minutes. Loosen side from pan with a knife. Remove rim from pan.

PASTRY FOR SINGLE-CRUST DEEP-DISH PIE (9 IN.): Combine 1½ cups all-purpose flour and ¼ tsp. salt; cut in ⅔ cup cold butter until crumbly. Gradually add 3-6 Tbsp. ice water, tossing with a fork until dough holds together when pressed. Shape into a disk; wrap and refrigerate 1 hour.

1 PIECE: 671 cal., 49g fat (27g sat. fat), 308mg chol., 841mg sod., 33g carb. (10g sugars, 2g fiber), 25g pro.

"Very rich, very delicious, very satisfying. We had this for dinner one night, breakfast the next morning and lunch the day after that."
—RENEEMURBY, TASTEOFHOME.COM

GRANDMA'S SECRET

Splurge on good-quality cheese to get the best flavor. Avoid using low-fat dairy products as these tend to contain more water, so they won't produce the same creamy texture full-fat products give you.

ORANGE MARMALADE BREAKFAST BAKE

When I host brunch, I make something that can be prepared a day ahead so I can spend time making other recipes. Grapefruit or a mixed-fruit marmalade will work just as well as the orange.
—*Judy Wilson, Sun City West, AZ*

PREP: 25 MIN. + CHILLING • **BAKE:** 40 MIN.
MAKES: 12 SERVINGS (1½ CUPS SYRUP)

3 Tbsp. butter, softened
24 slices French bread
 (½ in. thick)
1 jar (12 oz.) orange
 marmalade
6 large eggs
2¾ cups 2% milk
⅓ cup sugar
1 tsp. vanilla extract

¼ tsp. ground nutmeg
⅓ cup finely chopped
 walnuts

SYRUP
1¼ cups maple syrup
⅓ cup orange juice
2 tsp. grated orange zest

1. Spread butter over 1 side of each bread slice. Arrange half of the bread slices overlapping in a greased 3-qt. or 13x9-in. baking dish, buttered side down. Spread marmalade over bread slices; top with the remaining 12 bread slices, buttered side up.

2. In a large bowl, whisk eggs, milk, sugar, vanilla and nutmeg until blended; pour over bread. Refrigerate, covered, several hours or overnight.

3. Preheat oven to 350°. Remove casserole from refrigerator while the oven heats. Sprinkle with walnuts. Bake, uncovered, until golden brown and a knife inserted in the center comes out clean, 40-50 minutes.

4. Let stand 5-10 minutes before serving. In a small saucepan, combine maple syrup, orange juice and zest; heat through. Serve with casserole.

1 PIECE WITH 2 TBSP. SYRUP: 356 cal., 9g fat (4g sat. fat), 105mg chol., 244mg sod., 63g carb. (49g sugars, 1g fiber), 8g pro.

CHERRY CHEESE BLINTZES

You can serve these elegant blintzes as an attractive brunch entree or as a fun dessert.
The bright cherry sauce gives them a pop of fresh flavor. I sometimes substitute other
fruits, such as raspberries, blueberries or peaches.
—*Jessica Vantrease, Anderson, AK*

PREP: 30 MIN. + CHILLING • BAKE: 10 MIN. • MAKES: 9 SERVINGS

1½ cups 2% milk
3 large eggs
2 Tbsp. butter, melted
⅔ cup all-purpose flour
½ tsp. salt

FILLING
1 cup 4% cottage cheese
3 oz. cream cheese,
   softened
¼ cup sugar
½ tsp. vanilla extract

CHERRY SAUCE
1 lb. fresh or frozen pitted
   sweet cherries
⅔ cup plus 1 Tbsp. water,
   divided
¼ cup sugar
1 Tbsp. cornstarch

1. In a small bowl, combine the milk, eggs and butter. Combine flour and salt; add to milk mixture and mix well. Cover and refrigerate for 2 hours.

2. Heat a lightly greased 8-in. nonstick skillet; pour 2 Tbsp. batter into the center of skillet. Lift and tilt pan to evenly coat bottom. Cook until top appears dry; turn and cook 15-20 seconds longer. Remove to a wire rack. Repeat with the remaining batter. When crepes are cool, stack them with waxed paper or paper towels in between. Wrap in foil; refrigerate.

3. In a blender, process cottage cheese until smooth. Transfer to a small bowl; add cream cheese and beat until smooth. Beat in sugar and vanilla. Spread about 1 rounded tablespoonful onto each crepe. Fold opposite sides of crepe over filling, forming a little bundle.

4. Place seam side down in a greased 15x10x1-in. baking pan. Bake, uncovered, at 350° for 10 minutes or until heated through.

5. Meanwhile, for the sauce, in a large saucepan, bring cherries, ⅔ cup water and sugar to a boil over medium heat. Reduce heat; cover and simmer for 5 minutes or until heated through. Combine cornstarch and remaining 1 Tbsp. water until smooth; stir into the cherry mixture. Bring to a boil; cook and stir for 2 minutes or until thickened. Serve with crepes.

2 BLINTZES: 245 cal., 10g fat (6g sat. fat), 97mg chol., 306mg sod., 31g carb. (21g sugars, 1g fiber), 8g pro.

KAISERSCHMARREN

KAISERSCHMARREN

As the story goes, when Austrian Kaiser Franz Josef's chef noticed the monarch always broke his pancake into small pieces before eating it, he began serving it that way.
—*Erika and Peter Durlacher, Whistler, BC*

PREP: 15 MIN. • BAKE: 20 MIN. • MAKES: 8 SERVINGS

2 cups all-purpose flour
1 cup whole milk
   Pinch salt
4 large eggs, separated,
   room temperature
¼ cup unsalted butter,
   melted
¼ cup sugar
½ cup butter
½ cup raisins
2 Tbsp. confectioners'
   sugar
   Stewed plums or
   other fruit

1. Preheat oven to 375°. Mix flour and milk to a thick paste. Add salt. Stir in egg yolks and ¼ cup unsalted butter. Beat egg whites with ¼ cup sugar until stiff and fold into batter.

2. Melt ½ cup butter in a 12-in. round cast-iron skillet or 11x7-in. glass baking dish. Pour in batter. Scatter raisins over top. Bake for 20 minutes.

3. Using two forks, tear pancake into pieces and allow to steam for a moment. Dust with confectioners' sugar and serve with plums or other fruit.

1 SERVING: 379 cal., 21g fat (12g sat. fat), 156mg chol., 183mg sod., 41g carb. (16g sugars, 1g fiber), 8g pro.

HAM & CHEESE EGG BAKE

This make-ahead egg casserole is just the thing when entertaining in the morning. It's loaded with ham, cheese and mushrooms.
—*Susan Miller, North Andover, MA*

PREP: 25 MIN. + CHILLING • BAKE: 35 MIN. • MAKES: 10 SERVINGS

1½ cups shredded cheddar
    cheese
1½ cups shredded part-skim
    mozzarella cheese
2   Tbsp. butter
½   lb. sliced fresh
    mushrooms
1   medium sweet red
    pepper, chopped
6   green onions, chopped
1¾ cups cubed fully cooked
    ham
8   large eggs
1¾ cups 2% milk
¼   cup all-purpose flour
¼   tsp. salt
¼   tsp. pepper

1. Sprinkle cheeses into a greased 13x9-in. baking dish. In a large skillet, heat butter over medium-high heat; saute the mushrooms, red pepper and green onions until tender. Stir in ham; spoon over cheese.

2. In a large bowl, whisk together eggs, milk, flour, salt and pepper; pour over ham mixture. Refrigerate, covered, overnight.

3. Preheat oven to 350°. Remove casserole from refrigerator while oven heats. Bake, uncovered, until a knife inserted in the center comes out clean, 35-45 minutes. Let stand 5 minutes before serving.

1 SERVING: 272 cal., 17g fat (9g sat. fat), 201mg chol., 678mg sod., 8g carb. (4g sugars, 1g fiber), 21g pro.

FROM GRANDMA'S KITCHEN: If your guests don't eat meat, leave out the ham and toss in more veggies. You'll also save 300mg sodium per serving.

CREAMY BAKED EGGS

My husband loves eggs prepared in any way. This recipe is simple but special, and the eggs
come out just as he likes them every time. If you like soft yolks, cook the eggs for
9 minutes; for firmer yolks, cook for about 11 minutes.
—*Macey Allen, Green Forest, AR*

TAKES: 25 MIN. • MAKES: 8 SERVINGS

¼ cup half-and-half cream
8 large eggs
1 cup shredded Jarlsberg
cheese
2 Tbsp. grated Parmesan
cheese
¼ tsp. salt
⅛ tsp. pepper
2 green onions, chopped

1. Preheat oven to 400°. Pour cream into a greased cast-iron or other ovenproof skillet . Gently break an egg into a small bowl; slip egg into skillet. Repeat with the remaining 7 eggs. Sprinkle with cheeses, salt and pepper.

2. Bake until egg whites are completely set and yolks begin to thicken but are not hard, 10-12 minutes. Top with green onions; serve immediately.

1 BAKED EGG: 135 cal., 9g fat (4g sat. fat), 200mg chol., 237mg sod., 2g carb. (1g sugars, 0 fiber), 11g pro.

WHOLE WHEAT PANCAKES

To fix a large batch of tender pancakes for my five children, I rely on this fuss-free recipe.
It calls for whole wheat flour and buttermilk, which make the pancakes filling but also light.
Serve them with hot chocolate for a breakfast that's sure to delight little ones.
—*Line Walter, Wayne, PA*

TAKES: 25 MIN. • MAKES: 20 PANCAKES

2 cups whole wheat flour
½ cup toasted wheat germ
1 tsp. baking soda
½ tsp. salt
2 large eggs, room
temperature
3 cups buttermilk
1 Tbsp. canola oil

1. In a large bowl, combine the flour, wheat germ, baking soda and salt. In another bowl, whisk the eggs, buttermilk and oil. Stir into dry ingredients just until blended.

2. Pour batter by ¼ cupfuls onto a hot griddle coated with cooking spray; turn when bubbles form on top. Cook until the second side is golden brown.

FREEZE OPTION: Freeze cooled pancakes between layers of waxed paper in an airtight freezer container. To use, place pancakes on an ungreased baking sheet, cover with foil and reheat in a preheated 375° oven for 6-10 minutes. Or place a stack of 3 pancakes on a microwave-safe plate and microwave on high until heated through, 45-90 seconds.

2 PANCAKES: 157 cal., 4g fat (1g sat. fat), 45mg chol., 335mg sod., 24g carb. (4g sugars, 4g fiber), 9g pro. DIABETIC EXCHANGES: 1½ starch, 1 fat.

CREAMY STRAWBERRY CREPES

Wrap summer-ripe strawberries and creamy filling into these delicate crepes for an elegant brunch entree.

—*Kathy Kochiss, Huntington, CT*

PREP: 15 MIN. + CHILLING • **COOK:** 25 MIN. • **MAKES:** 7 SERVINGS

4 **large eggs**
1 **cup 2% milk**
1 **cup water**
2 **Tbsp. butter, melted**
2 **cups all-purpose flour**
¼ **tsp. salt**

FILLING
1 **pkg. (8 oz.) cream cheese, softened**
1¼ **cups confectioners' sugar**
1 **Tbsp. lemon juice**
1 **tsp. grated lemon zest**
½ **tsp. vanilla extract**
4 **cups fresh strawberries, sliced, divided**
1 **cup heavy whipping cream, whipped**

1. In a large bowl, whisk eggs, milk, water and butter. In another bowl, mix flour and salt; add to egg mixture and mix well. Refrigerate, covered, 1 hour.

2. Heat a lightly greased 8-in. nonstick skillet over medium heat. Stir batter. Fill a ¼-cup measure halfway with batter; pour into center of pan. Quickly lift and tilt pan to coat bottom evenly. Cook until top appears dry; turn crepe over and cook until bottom is cooked, 15-20 seconds longer. Remove to a wire rack. Repeat with remaining batter, greasing pan as needed. When crepes are cool, stack between pieces of waxed paper or paper towels.

3. For filling, in a small bowl, beat cream cheese, confectioners' sugar, lemon juice, zest and vanilla until smooth. Fold in 2 cups berries and the whipped cream. Spoon about ⅓ cup filling down the center of each crepe; roll up. Garnish with the remaining 2 cups berries and, if desired, additional confectioner's sugar.

2 CREPES: 415 cal., 26g fat (16g sat. fat), 115mg chol., 163mg sod., 40g carb. (28g sugars, 2g fiber), 7g pro.

GRANDMA'S SECRET

These crepes taste best when served immediately after filling. If you're going to have leftovers, refrigerate or freeze the unfilled crepes in an airtight container—filled crepes will get soggy.

APPLE PAN GOODY

I found the recipe for this casserole years ago and adapted it to my family's taste. Dotted with dried cranberries, the tender apple bake is sweetened with brown sugar and a little cinnamon. We enjoy it on breakfast buffets, but it also makes a fun side dish, particularly with a pork entree.
—*Jeanne Bredemeyer, Orient, NY*

PREP: 20 MIN. • BAKE: 20 MIN. • MAKES: 8 SERVINGS

4 to 5 medium tart apples, peeled and sliced
¾ cup dried cranberries
6 Tbsp. brown sugar
1 tsp. ground cinnamon, divided
3 Tbsp. butter
6 large eggs
1½ cups orange juice
1½ cups all-purpose flour
¾ tsp. salt
2 Tbsp. sugar
Maple syrup, optional

1. Preheat oven to 425°. In a large skillet, saute the apples, cranberries, brown sugar and ¾ tsp. cinnamon in butter until apples begin to soften, about 6 minutes. Transfer to a greased 13x9-in. baking dish.

2. Place the eggs, orange juice, flour and salt in a blender; cover and process until smooth. Pour over apple mixture. Sprinkle with sugar and remaining ¼ tsp. cinnamon.

3. Bake, uncovered, until a knife inserted in the center comes out clean, 20-25 minutes. Serve with syrup if desired.

1 CUP: 316 cal., 8g fat (4g sat. fat), 171mg chol., 316mg sod., 54g carb. (32g sugars, 2g fiber), 7g pro.

HAM & EGG SANDWICH

Whenever the whole family gets together for a holiday or long weekend, they request this big breakfast sandwich. I can feed everyone by stacking our favorite breakfast fixings inside a loaf of French bread. Then I simply pop it in the oven to warm up.
—*DeeDee Newton, Toronto, ON*

PREP: 30 MIN. • BAKE: 15 MIN. • MAKES: 8 SERVINGS

1 unsliced loaf (1 lb.) French bread
4 Tbsp. butter, softened, divided
2 Tbsp. mayonnaise
8 thin slices deli ham
1 large tomato, sliced
1 small onion, thinly sliced
8 large eggs, lightly beaten
8 slices cheddar cheese

1. Preheat oven to 375°. Cut bread in half lengthwise; carefully hollow out top and bottom, leaving ½-in. shells (discard removed bread or save for another use). Spread 3 Tbsp. butter and all the mayonnaise inside the bread shells. Line bottom bread shell with ham; top with tomato and onion.

2. In a large skillet, melt the remaining 1 Tbsp. butter; add eggs. Cook over medium heat, stirring occasionally until the edges are almost set.

3. Spoon egg mixture into bottom bread shell; top with cheese. Cover with bread top. Wrap in greased foil. Bake 15-20 minutes or until heated through. Cut into serving-size pieces.

1 SERVING: 543 cal., 31g fat (14g sat. fat), 298mg chol., 1644mg sod., 33g carb. (3g sugars, 2g fiber), 32g pro.

BACON-CHEESE PUFF PIE

This recipe comes from my grandma, and it's one of my family's favorites. We love the combination of bacon, tomatoes and cheese.
—*Sherry Lee, Sheridan, IN*

PREP: 20 MIN. + COOLING • BAKE: 45 MIN. • MAKES: 6 SERVINGS

1 pastry shell, unbaked
1 lb. sliced bacon, cooked and crumbled
1 large tomato, peeled and sliced
1 cup shredded cheddar cheese

3 large eggs, separated
¾ cup sour cream
½ cup all-purpose flour
½ tsp. salt
   Paprika

1. Preheat oven to 450°. Line unpricked pastry shell with a double thickness of heavy-duty foil. Bake for 5 minutes. Remove foil. Bake 5 minutes longer. Cool completely.

2. Sprinkle bacon over the crust. Top with tomato and cheese. In a large bowl, beat the egg yolks, sour cream, flour and salt until smooth. In another large bowl, beat egg whites until stiff. Fold into sour cream mixture; spread over cheese. Sprinkle with paprika.

3. Bake at 350° until a knife inserted in the center comes out clean, about 45 minutes. Let stand 5-10 minutes before cutting.

1 PIECE: 518 cal., 35g fat (17g sat. fat), 176mg chol., 901mg sod., 29g carb. (4g sugars, 1g fiber), 19g pro.

CREAMY SCRAMBLED EGGS WITH HAM

These may just be the creamiest, richest scrambled eggs you've ever had. Pair them with a gourmet sage sausage, and you've got one elegant, yet down home, hearty breakfast.
—*Suzy Horvath, Milwaukie, OR*

TAKES: 20 MIN. • MAKES: 4 SERVINGS

8 large eggs
⅓ cup heavy whipping cream
⅔ cup cubed fully cooked ham
1 green onion, chopped
   Dash salt
   Dash pepper
4 tsp. butter
4 oz. cream cheese, cubed

In a large bowl, whisk eggs and cream; stir in the ham, onion, salt and pepper. In a large skillet, heat butter over medium heat. Add egg mixture; cook and stir until almost set. Stir in cream cheese. Cook and stir until completely set.

⅔ CUP: 383 cal., 33g fat (17g sat. fat), 504mg chol., 594mg sod., 3g carb. (1g sugars, 0 fiber), 20g pro.

EARLY RISER OVEN OMELET

Everyone will rush to the table when you serve this big fluffy omelet. Packed with tomato, broccoli, ham and cheese, it makes a hearty brunch dish that easily serves a crowd.
—*Wendy Fawcett, Gillam, MB*

PREP: 15 MIN. • **BAKE:** 35 MIN. • **MAKES:** 6 SERVINGS

10 large egg whites
5 large eggs
1 cup fat-free milk
¼ tsp. seasoned salt
¼ tsp. pepper
1½ cups cubed fully cooked ham
1 cup chopped fresh broccoli
1 cup shredded reduced-fat cheddar cheese
1 medium tomato, seeded and chopped
3 Tbsp. finely chopped onion

1. Preheat oven to 350°. In a bowl, beat the egg whites, eggs, milk, seasoned salt and pepper. Pour into a greased 10-in. cast-iron or other ovenproof skillet. Sprinkle with the ham, broccoli, cheese, tomato and onion.

2. Bake, uncovered, until eggs are almost set, 30-35 minutes. Broil 4-6 in. from the heat until the eggs are set and top is lightly browned, 1-2 minutes.

1 SERVING: 216 cal., 10g fat (4g sat. fat), 183mg chol., 805mg sod., 6g carb. (4g sugars, 1g fiber), 25g pro. DIABETIC EXCHANGES: 3 medium-fat meat, 1 vegetable.

FRUITY BAKED OATMEAL

This is my husband's favorite breakfast treat and the ultimate comfort food. It's warm, filling and always a hit when I serve it to guests.
—*Karen Schroeder, Kankakee, IL*

PREP: 15 MIN. • **BAKE:** 35 MIN. • **MAKES:** 9 SERVINGS

3 cups quick-cooking oats
1 cup packed brown sugar
2 tsp. baking powder
1 tsp. salt
½ tsp. ground cinnamon
2 large eggs, lightly beaten
1 cup fat-free milk
½ cup butter, melted
¾ cup chopped peeled tart apple
⅓ cup chopped fresh or frozen peaches
⅓ cup fresh or frozen blueberries
   Additional fat-free milk, optional

1. Preheat oven to 350°. In a large bowl, combine oats, brown sugar, baking powder, salt and cinnamon. Combine eggs, milk and butter; add to the dry ingredients. Stir in apple, peaches and blueberries.

2. Pour into an 8-in. square baking dish coated with cooking spray. Bake, uncovered, until a knife inserted in center comes out clean, 35-40 minutes. Cut into squares. Serve with milk if desired.

NOTE: If using frozen blueberries, use without thawing to avoid discoloring the batter.

1 PIECE: 322 cal., 13g fat (7g sat. fat), 75mg chol., 492mg sod., 46g carb. (27g sugars, 3g fiber), 7g pro.

GRANDMA'S SECRET

This recipe makes good use of a mix, but you can use a homemade sausage gravy if you prefer! To add more flavor to your gravy, stir in some fresh herbs like chopped thyme or parsley.

BRUNCH PUFF WITH SAUSAGE GRAVY

BRUNCH PUFF WITH SAUSAGE GRAVY

When company stays overnight, I make this puff with sausage gravy as a hearty breakfast treat. It's meaty, cheesy and delightful with a fresh fruit salad.

—*Danielle Cochran, Grayling, MI*

PREP: 25 MIN. • BAKE: 20 MIN. • MAKES: 9 SERVINGS

7 large eggs, divided use
¼ cup 2% milk
¼ tsp. salt
¼ tsp. plus ⅛ tsp. pepper, divided
1 Tbsp. butter
1 Tbsp. water
1 pkg. (17.3 oz.) frozen puff pastry, thawed
8 oz. sliced deli ham (¼ in. thick)
1 cup shredded cheddar cheese

SAUSAGE GRAVY
¾ lb. bulk pork sausage
1 envelope country gravy mix

1. Preheat oven to 400°. In a small bowl, whisk 6 eggs, milk, salt and ¼ tsp. pepper until blended.

2. In a large nonstick skillet, heat butter over medium heat. Pour in egg mixture; cook and stir just until the eggs are thickened and no liquid egg remains. Remove from heat.

3. In a small bowl, whisk the remaining egg with water. On a lightly floured surface, unfold one sheet of puff pastry and roll to a 10-in. square. Transfer to a parchment-lined baking sheet. Arrange ham over pastry to within 1 in. of edges; top with scrambled eggs. Sprinkle with cheese.

4. Brush beaten egg mixture over edges of pastry (saving some for the top). Roll remaining puff pastry to a 10-in. square; place over filling. Press edges with a fork to seal; cut slits in top. Brush top with remaining egg mixture; sprinkle with remaining ⅛ tsp. pepper. Bake until golden brown, 20-25 minutes.

5. Meanwhile, for the gravy, in a large skillet, cook sausage over medium heat for 6-8 minutes or until no longer pink, breaking into crumbles. Remove with a slotted spoon; drain on paper towels. Discard drippings, wiping skillet clean if necessary. In same pan, prepare gravy mix according to package directions. Stir in sausage. Serve with pastry.

1 PIECE WITH ¼ CUP GRAVY: 546 cal., 35g fat (10g sat. fat), 193mg chol., 1138mg sod., 36g carb. (1g sugars, 4g fiber), 21g pro.

OVERNIGHT PEACH OATMEAL

Hearty oatmeal combined with bright, sweet peaches make this slow-cooker recipe a perfect breakfast or brunch. This is an excellent make-ahead meal for busy mornings.
—*Rachel Lewis, Danville, VA*

PREP: 10 MIN. • COOK: 7 HOURS • MAKES: 6 SERVINGS

4 cups water
1 cup steel-cut oats
1 cup vanilla soy milk or vanilla almond milk
3 Tbsp. brown sugar
¼ tsp. salt
¼ tsp. vanilla or almond extract
2 medium peaches, sliced or 3 cups frozen unsweetened sliced peaches, thawed
Optional toppings: Sliced almonds, brown sugar, cinnamon and additional peaches

In a well-greased 3-qt. slow cooker, combine the first 6 ingredients. Cook, covered, on low until oats are tender, 7-8 hours. Stir in peaches just before serving. If desired, serve with optional toppings.

PRESSURE COOKER OPTION: Decrease water to 3 cups. Add to a 6-qt. electric pressure cooker coated with cooking spray. Stir in oats, soy milk, brown sugar, salt and vanilla. Lock lid; close pressure-release valve. Adjust to pressure-cook on high for 4 minutes. Let pressure release naturally. Stir in peaches just before serving. Oatmeal will thicken upon standing. If desired, serve with optional toppings.

¾ CUP: 163 cal., 2g fat (0 sat. fat), 0 chol., 116mg sod., 31g carb. (13g sugars, 4g fiber), 5g pro. DIABETIC EXCHANGES: 1½ starch, ½ fruit.

FROM GRANDMA'S KITCHEN: Steel-cut oats—also known as Scotch oats or Irish oatmeal—are 100% whole grain. They are slowly absorbed, giving you energy that will last through a day at work or school.

BACON-EGG ENGLISH MUFFIN

I stack cheese, Canadian bacon and poached eggs on an English muffin to make this appealing eye-opener. Perfect for one, this delicious open-faced sandwich is special enough for guests, too.
—*Terry Kuehn, Waunakee, WI*

TAKES: 15 MIN. • MAKES: 2 SERVINGS

1 Tbsp. white vinegar
2 large eggs
1 Tbsp. cream cheese, softened
1 English muffin, split and toasted
2 slices process American cheese
2 slices Canadian bacon

1. Place 2-3 in. of water in a large skillet with high sides; add vinegar. Bring to a boil; reduce heat and simmer gently. Break cold eggs, 1 at a time, into a custard cup or saucer; holding the cup close to the surface of the water, slip egg into water. Cook, uncovered, until whites are completely set, about 4 minutes.

2. Meanwhile, spread cream cheese over muffin halves. Top with cheese slices and Canadian bacon. Using a slotted spoon, lift eggs out of water and place over bacon.

1 SERVING: 273 cal., 15g fat (7g sat. fat), 247mg chol., 828mg sod., 16g carb. (3g sugars, 1g fiber), 19g pro.

CRISPY FRENCH TOAST

Cornflakes add irresistible crunch to this easy baked French toast recipe. My light version uses egg substitute and skim milk, but still gets plenty of flavor from vanilla, spice and a kiss of orange.
—*Flo Burtnett, Gage, OK*

PREP: 20 MIN. • BAKE: 15 MIN. • MAKES: 6 SERVINGS

½ cup egg substitute
½ cup fat-free milk
¼ cup orange juice
1 tsp. vanilla extract
Dash ground nutmeg

12 slices day-old French bread (¾ in. thick)
1½ cups crushed cornflakes
Maple syrup, optional

1. Preheat oven to 425°. In a shallow dish, combine the egg substitute, milk, orange juice, vanilla and nutmeg. Add bread; soak for 5 minutes, turning once. Coat both sides of each slice with cornflake crumbs.

2. Place in a 15x10x1-in. baking pan coated with cooking spray. Bake for 10 minutes; turn. Bake 5-8 minutes longer or until golden brown. Serve with maple syrup, if desired.

FREEZE OPTION: Remove French toast from pan to wire racks to cool. Freeze between layers of waxed paper in an airtight container. To use, place frozen French toast on a greased baking sheet. Bake at 425° for 5-7 minutes or microwave each piece on high for 30-60 seconds or until heated through.

2 PIECES (WITHOUT SYRUP): 200 cal., 1g fat (0 sat. fat), 0 chol., 421mg sod., 40g carb. (4g sugars, 1g fiber), 7g pro. DIABETIC EXCHANGES: 3 starch.

CUBAN BREAKFAST SANDWICHES

Grab hold of breakfast time by serving these warm energy-boosting sandwiches. They travel well for hectic mornings, and the hearty helping of protein will help keep hunger at bay.
—*Lacie Griffin, Austin, TX*

TAKES: 20 MIN. • MAKES: 4 SERVINGS

1 loaf (1 lb.) Cuban or French bread
4 large eggs
16 pieces thinly sliced hard salami
8 slices deli ham
8 slices Swiss cheese

1. Split bread loaf in half lengthwise; cut into 4 pieces. Fry eggs in a large non-stick skillet coated with cooking spray until yolks are set. Layer bread bottoms with salami, ham, egg and cheese; replace tops.

2. Cook sandwiches on a panini maker or indoor grill for 2 minutes or until bread is browned and cheese is melted.

1 SANDWICH: 697 cal., 29g fat (12g sat. fat), 280mg chol., 1949mg sod., 61g carb. (1g sugars, 3g fiber), 43g pro.

BACON HASH BROWN BAKE

This tasty dish has wonderful from-scratch flavor that makes it a great choice for brunch. It's very popular with guests at my bed-and-breakfast.
—*Mark Clark, Twin Mountain, NH*

| PREP: 10 MIN. • BAKE: 35 MIN. • MAKES: 8 SERVINGS |

4 cups refrigerated or frozen hash brown potatoes, thawed
12 bacon strips, cooked and crumbled
½ cup 2% milk
⅓ cup chopped onion
½ tsp. salt
¼ tsp. pepper
¼ tsp. garlic powder
1 Tbsp. butter, melted
½ tsp. paprika

Preheat oven to 350°. Combine the first 7 ingredients. Transfer to a greased 9-in. pie plate. Drizzle with butter; sprinkle with paprika. Bake until lightly browned, 35-45 minutes.

½ CUP: 159 cal., 7g fat (3g sat. fat), 14mg chol., 372mg sod., 19g carb. (1g sugars, 2g fiber), 6g pro.

CHEESY HAM & EGG SANDWICHES

I turned classic breakfast sandwiches into something heartier that you could even enjoy for dinner. We pile toppings like salsa and avocado—mayo and ketchup, too—on the homemade biscuits.
—*Fay Moreland, Wichita Falls, TX*

| TAKES: 30 MIN. • MAKES: 10 SERVINGS |

4 cups biscuit/baking mix
1 cup shredded cheddar cheese
1 cup finely chopped fully cooked ham
1 tsp. coarsely ground pepper, divided
1 cup 2% milk
3 Tbsp. butter, melted

EGGS
8 large eggs
½ cup 2% milk
¼ tsp. coarsely ground pepper
⅛ tsp. salt
2 Tbsp. butter
1 cup shredded cheddar cheese
Optional: Salsa, sliced tomato, red onion and avocado

1. Preheat oven to 425°. In a large bowl, combine biscuit mix, cheese, ham and ½ tsp. pepper. Add milk; mix just until moistened.

2. Turn onto a lightly floured surface; knead gently 8-10 times. Pat or roll dough to 1-in. thickness; cut with a floured 2½-in. biscuit cutter. Place 2 in. apart on an ungreased baking sheet. Brush with melted butter; sprinkle with remaining pepper. Bake 12-14 minutes or until golden brown.

3. Meanwhile, in a bowl, whisk eggs, milk, pepper and salt. In a large nonstick skillet, heat butter over medium heat. Pour in egg mixture; cook and stir until eggs are thickened and no liquid egg remains. Stir in cheese; remove from heat.

4. Split warm biscuits in half. Layer bottoms with egg mixture and toppings as desired. Replace tops.

1 SANDWICH: 430 cal., 25g fat (12g sat. fat), 198mg chol., 1058mg sod., 34g carb. (3g sugars, 1g fiber), 18g pro.

GRANDMA'S SECRET

This hash brown recipe is a great main-course option for brunch, but also makes a good side dish at dinner time. Try serving this up with a meaty main dish like glazed ham or steak.

BACON HASH
BROWN BAKE

RED PEPPER CORNMEAL SOUFFLE

I use the vegetables from our garden in all my cooking. Doing so adds a freshness that just can't be beat. Dotted with parsley and red pepper, this souffle is a favorite.
—*Janet Eckhoff, Woodland, CA*

PREP: 20 MIN. • BAKE: 35 MIN. • MAKES: 10 SERVINGS

1 **large onion, chopped**
1 **cup chopped sweet red pepper**
¼ **cup butter**
3 **cups whole milk**
⅔ **cup cornmeal**
1 **cup shredded sharp cheddar cheese**
2 **Tbsp. minced fresh parsley**
1 **tsp. salt, divided**
½ **tsp. white pepper**
2 **large egg yolks, beaten**
7 **large egg whites**
½ **tsp. cream of tartar**

1. Preheat oven to 375°. In a large saucepan, saute the onion and red pepper in butter until tender. Add the milk. Bring to a boil. Gradually whisk in cornmeal; whisk constantly until thickened, about 5 minutes.

2. Add the cheese, parsley, ½ tsp. salt and the pepper. Add 1 cup cornmeal mixture to the egg yolks; mix well. Return all to the saucepan.

3. In a large bowl, beat egg whites, cream of tartar and remaining ½ tsp. salt until stiff peaks form. Fold into the cornmeal mixture. Transfer to a greased 2-qt. souffle dish. Bake until golden brown, for 35-40 minutes.

1 SERVING: 193 cal., 11g fat (7g sat. fat), 77mg chol., 427mg sod., 14g carb., 1g fiber, 9g pro.

THE BEST FRENCH TOAST

There's no question that this is the best French toast recipe. The caramelized exterior meets a soft, custardlike center that practically melts in your mouth. Not only that, but it's quick and easy, too!
—*Audrey Rompon, Milwaukee, WI*

TAKES: 15 MIN. • MAKES: 4 SERVINGS

1½ cups half-and-half cream
3 large egg yolks
3 Tbsp. brown sugar
2 tsp. vanilla extract
¾ tsp. ground cinnamon
½ tsp. salt
¼ tsp. ground nutmeg
8 slices day-old brioche bread (1 in. thick)
Optional: Butter, maple syrup, fresh berries, whipped cream and confectioners' sugar

1. In a shallow dish, whisk together the first 7 ingredients. Preheat a greased griddle over medium heat.

2. Dip bread in egg mixture, letting it soak 5 seconds on each side. Cook on griddle until golden brown on both sides. Serve with toppings as desired.

2 PIECES: 546 cal., 24g fat (15g sat. fat), 263mg chol., 786mg sod., 64g carb. (25g sugars, 2g fiber), 13g pro.

FROM GRANDMA'S KITCHEN: Using day-old bread from a bakery helps the French toast to be more stable. If using commercially produced brioche, be sure to allow the bread to become slightly stale for best results.

PORK SAUSAGE PATTIES

With savory pork sausage patties, any breakfast gets a boost. These little beauties will certainly have them coming back for seconds.
—*Carole Thomson, Komarno, MB*

TAKES: 25 MIN. • MAKES: 6 SERVINGS

1 large egg, beaten
⅓ cup milk
½ cup chopped onion
2 Tbsp. all-purpose flour
⅛ tsp. salt
Dash pepper
1 lb. sage bulk pork sausage

1. In a large bowl, combine the first 6 ingredients. Crumble sausage over mixture and mix well. Shape into 6 patties.

2. In a large skillet, cook patties over medium heat for 6 minutes on each side or until meat is no longer pink, turning occasionally.

FREEZE OPTION: Prepare uncooked patties and freeze, covered, on a plastic wrap-lined baking sheet until firm. Transfer patties to an airtight container; return to freezer. To use, cook frozen patties as directed, increasing time as necessary for a thermometer to read 160°.

1 PATTY: 219 cal., 18g fat (6g sat. fat), 73mg chol., 527mg sod., 5g carb. (1g sugars, 0 fiber), 10g pro.

CORNFLAKE-COATED
CRISPY BACON

CORNFLAKE-COATED CRISPY BACON

I've loved my aunt's crispy-coated bacon ever since I was a child. Now I've shared the super simple recipe with my own children. We still enjoy a big panful every Christmas morning—and on many other days throughout the year!
—Brenda Severson, Norman, OK

PREP: 20 MIN. • BAKE: 25 MIN. • MAKES: 9 SERVINGS

½ cup evaporated milk
2 Tbsp. ketchup
1 Tbsp. Worcestershire sauce
Dash pepper
18 bacon strips (1 lb.)
3 cups crushed cornflakes

1. Preheat oven to 375°. In a large bowl, combine the first 4 ingredients. Add bacon strips, turning to coat. Dip strips in crushed cornflakes, patting to help coating adhere.

2. Place bacon on 2 racks; place each rack on an ungreased 15x10x1-in. baking pan. Bake until golden and crisp, rotating pans halfway through baking, 25-30 minutes.

2 BACON STRIPS: 198 cal., 7g fat (3g sat. fat), 20mg chol., 547mg sod., 26g carb. (4g sugars, 0 fiber), 8g pro.

SPICED APPLE OATMEAL

These easy, apple-y oats let your family have a warm and cozy breakfast no matter how busy you are.
—Teri Rasey, Cadillac, MI

PREP: 15 MIN. • COOK: 4½ HOURS. • MAKES: 10 SERVINGS

½ cup packed brown sugar
2 Tbsp. lemon juice
2 Tbsp. molasses
3 tsp. ground cinnamon
1 tsp. ground nutmeg
½ tsp. ground ginger
½ tsp. ground allspice
¼ tsp. salt
4 medium apples, peeled and cut into 1-in. slices
2 cups steel-cut oats
2 large eggs
2½ cups water
2 cups 2% milk
1 cup refrigerated vanilla dairy creamer
Optional: Chopped pecans and additional milk

1. Mix the first 8 ingredients. Place apples in a greased 4-qt. slow cooker. Top with brown sugar mixture, then with oats.

2. Whisk together eggs, water, milk and creamer; pour over the oats. Cook, covered, on low until oats are tender, 4½ to 5 hours. If desired, serve with pecans and additional milk.

NOTE: This recipe was tested with Coffee-mate Natural Bliss vanilla coffee creamer.

1 CUP: 290 cal., 7g fat (3g sat. fat), 49mg chol., 109mg sod., 53g carb. (30g sugars, 5g fiber), 7g pro.

FROM GRANDMA'S KITCHEN: Steel-cut oats give this oatmeal more texture than old-fashioned or quick-cooking oats. Pay attention to the time. If you start this before going to bed and cook it longer than 5 hours, you'll risk burning the outside edges of the oatmeal mixture.

SHIRRED EGG CORN MUFFINS

When hosting a brunch or taking a dish to a potluck, I bake eggs in little cornbread cups—they're more portable that way. With cheddar sauce and more cheese on top, they're a tasty little meal.
—*Lisa Speer, Palm Beach, FL*

PREP: 15 MIN. • **BAKE:** 20 MIN. • **MAKES:** 1 DOZEN

1   pkg. (8½ oz.) cornbread/
    muffin mix
½   cup buttermilk
2   Tbsp. sour cream
½   cup shredded sharp
    cheddar cheese
½   cup crumbled cooked
    bacon
12 large eggs
¼   tsp. salt
⅛   tsp. coarsely ground
    pepper

TOPPING
4   tsp. butter
4   tsp. all-purpose flour
1   cup 2% milk
1¼ cups shredded sharp
    cheddar cheese, divided
⅛   tsp. dried thyme
¼   tsp. seasoned salt,
    divided

1. Preheat oven to 375°. In a small bowl, combine muffin mix, buttermilk and sour cream just until moistened; fold in cheese and bacon. Spoon into 12 greased muffin cups. Crack an egg into each cup; sprinkle with salt and pepper.

2. Bake until egg whites are completely set and yolks are still soft, 18-22 minutes. Cool 5 minutes before removing from pan.

3. Meanwhile, in a small saucepan, melt butter over medium-low heat. Stir in flour until smooth; gradually whisk in milk. Bring to a boil, stirring constantly; cook and stir until thickened, 1-2 minutes. Remove from heat. Stir in 1 cup cheese, the thyme and ⅛ tsp. seasoned salt until cheese is melted.

4. Serve muffins with sauce; sprinkle with the remaining ¼ cup cheese and ⅛ tsp. seasoned salt. Serve immediately.

1 MUFFIN: 262 cal., 15g fat (7g sat. fat), 244mg chol., 598mg sod., 18g carb. (7g sugars, 0 fiber), 14g pro.

FAMILY-FAVORITE OATMEAL WAFFLES

These healthful, tasty waffles are a tried-and-true family favorite—even with our two children. My husband and I have a small herd of beef cattle and some pigs. A hearty breakfast really gets us going!
—*Marna Heitz, Farley, IA*

TAKES: 30 MIN. • **MAKES:** 6 WAFFLES

1½ cups all-purpose flour
1   cup quick-cooking oats
3   tsp. baking powder
½   tsp. ground cinnamon
¼   tsp. salt
2   large eggs, lightly beaten,
    room temperature
1½ cups whole milk
6   Tbsp. butter, melted
2   Tbsp. brown sugar
    Assorted fresh fruit and
    yogurt of your choice

1. In a large bowl, combine flour, oats, baking powder, cinnamon and salt; set aside. In a small bowl, whisk eggs, milk, butter and brown sugar. Add to flour mixture; stir until blended.

2. Pour batter into a lightly greased waffle iron (amount will vary with size of waffle iron). Close lid quickly. Bake according to manufacturer's directions; do not open during baking. Use fork to remove baked waffle. Top with fresh fruit and yogurt.

1 WAFFLE: 344 cal., 16g fat (9g sat. fat), 99mg chol., 482mg sod., 41g carb. (8g sugars, 2g fiber), 9g pro.

APPLE-HONEY DUTCH BABY

I love to make this treat on Sunday morning. It's so impressive when it's served warm right out of the oven, and the honey and apple filling is yummy.
—*Kathy Fleming, Lisle, IL*

TAKES: 30 MIN. • **MAKES:** 4 SERVINGS

3 large eggs,
 room temperature
¾ cup 2% milk
¾ cup all-purpose flour
1 Tbsp. sugar
2 Tbsp. butter

TOPPING
1 Tbsp. butter
2 large apples, sliced
½ cup honey
2 to 3 tsp. lemon juice
½ tsp. ground cardamom
1 tsp. cornstarch
2 tsp. cold water

1. Preheat oven to 400°. In a large bowl, whisk together the first 4 ingredients until smooth. Place butter in a 10-in. ovenproof skillet; heat in oven until melted, 2-3 minutes.

2. Tilt pan to coat bottom and sides. Pour batter into hot skillet. Bake until puffed and edges are lightly browned, 16-20 minutes.

3. Meanwhile, in a large saucepan, heat butter for topping over medium heat; saute apples until lightly browned. Stir in honey, lemon juice and cardamom. Mix cornstarch and water until smooth; stir into apple mixture. Bring to a boil; cook and stir until thickened, 1-2 minutes. Spoon into pancake; serve immediately.

1 SERVING: 429 cal., 14g fat (7g sat. fat), 166mg chol., 146mg sod., 72g carb. (50g sugars, 3g fiber), 9g pro.

PUMPKIN CREAM OF WHEAT

This autumn-inspired breakfast tastes like pumpkin pie—without the guilt! Double the recipe if you feel like sharing.
—*Amy Bashtovoi, Sidney, NE*

TAKES: 10 MIN. • **MAKES:** 1 SERVING

½ cup 2% milk
¼ cup half-and-half cream
3 Tbsp. Cream of Wheat
¼ cup canned pumpkin
2 tsp. sugar
⅛ tsp. ground cinnamon
 Additional 2% milk

In a small microwave-safe bowl, combine the milk, cream and Cream of Wheat. Microwave, uncovered, on high for 1 minute; stir until blended. Cover and cook for 1-2 minutes or until thickened, stirring every 30 seconds. Stir in the pumpkin, sugar and cinnamon. Serve with additional milk.

1 CUP: 314 cal., 9g fat (6g sat. fat), 39mg chol., 96mg sod., 46g carb. (18g sugars, 4g fiber), 10g pro.

BUFFET
MEATBALLS,
PAGE 55

GRANDMA'S FAVORITE

SNACKS

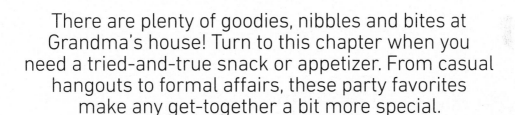

There are plenty of goodies, nibbles and bites at
Grandma's house! Turn to this chapter when you
need a tried-and-true snack or appetizer. From casual
hangouts to formal affairs, these party favorites
make any get-together a bit more special.

CHAMPION CHICKEN PUFFS

My guests peeled rubber getting to the table to munch on these chicken puffs. These tender bites are made with hassle-free refrigerated crescent rolls and a flavorful chicken and cream cheese filling.
—*Amber Kimmich, Powhatan, VA*

TAKES: 30 MIN. • MAKES: 32 SERVINGS

4 oz. cream cheese, softened
½ tsp. garlic powder
½ cup shredded cooked chicken
2 tubes (8 oz. each) refrigerated crescent rolls

1. Preheat oven to 375°. In a small bowl, beat cream cheese and garlic powder until smooth. Stir in chicken.

2. Unroll crescent dough; separate into 16 triangles. Cut each triangle in half lengthwise, forming 2 triangles. Place 1 tsp. of chicken mixture in the center of each. Fold short side over filling; press sides to seal and roll up.

3. Place 1 in. apart on greased baking sheets. Bake until golden brown, 12-14 minutes. Serve warm.

1 PUFF: 67 cal., 4g fat (1g sat. fat), 6mg chol., 119mg sod., 6g carb. (2g sugars, 0 fiber), 2g pro.

INSIDE-OUT VEGGIE DIP

Cherry tomatoes and cucumber slices transform into fresh, cool, bite-sized treats ideal for any gathering.
—*Judie Thurstenson, Colcord, OK*

PREP: 35 MIN. + CHILLING • MAKES: 3½ DOZEN

2 large cucumbers
16 cherry tomatoes
1 pkg. (8 oz.) cream cheese, softened
¼ cup finely chopped sweet red pepper
2 Tbsp. finely chopped celery
2 Tbsp. finely chopped green onion
1 Tbsp. finely chopped carrot
1 tsp. garlic powder
½ tsp. salt
½ tsp. onion powder

1. Peel strips from cucumbers to create decorative edges if desired; cut cucumbers into ½-in. slices. Finely chop 2 slices; set aside. With a small spoon, scoop out some of the seeds from the remaining slices.

2. Cut a thin slice from bottoms of the tomatoes to allow them to rest flat. Cut a thin slice from tops of the tomatoes; scoop out the pulp, leaving a ¼-in. shell. Invert onto paper towels to drain.

3. In a large bowl, combine the cream cheese, red pepper, celery, onion, carrot, seasonings and chopped cucumber.

4. Fill the tomatoes and cucumber slices with the cream cheese mixture, about 1 tsp. in each. Refrigerate for at least 1 hour.

1 PIECE: 23 cal., 2g fat (1g sat. fat), 6mg chol., 45mg sod., 1g carb. (1g sugars, 0 fiber), 1g pro.

CHAMPION
CHICKEN PUFFS

ANTIPASTO BAKE

Stuffed with savory meats and cheeses, this hearty bake would satisfy a crowd! It comes together quickly and bakes in under an hour, making it the perfect potluck bring-along.
—*Brea Barclay, Green Bay, WI*

PREP: 20 MIN. • **BAKE:** 45 MIN. + STANDING • **MAKES:** 20 SERVINGS

- 2 tubes (8 oz. each) refrigerated crescent rolls
- ¼ lb. thinly sliced hard salami
- ¼ lb. thinly sliced Swiss cheese
- ¼ lb. thinly sliced pepperoni
- ¼ lb. thinly sliced Colby-Monterey Jack cheese
- ¼ lb. thinly sliced prosciutto
- ¼ lb. thinly sliced provolone cheese
- 2 large eggs
- ½ tsp. garlic powder
- ½ tsp. pepper
- 1 jar (12 oz.) roasted sweet red peppers, drained
- 1 large egg yolk, beaten

1. Preheat oven to 350°. Unroll 1 tube of crescent dough into a long rectangle; press perforations to seal. Press onto the bottom and up sides of an ungreased 11x7-in. baking dish.

2. Layer meats and cheeses on dough in the order listed. Whisk eggs and seasonings until well blended; pour into dish. Top with roasted pepper.

3. Unroll the remaining tube of dough into a long rectangle; press perforations to seal. Place over filling; pinch seams tight. Brush with beaten egg yolk; cover with foil. Bake for 30 minutes; remove foil and bake until golden brown, 15-20 minutes longer. Let stand 20 minutes.

1 PIECE: 229 cal., 15g fat (7g sat. fat), 58mg chol., 662mg sod., 10g carb. (2g sugars, 0 fiber), 11g pro.

GRANDMA'S SECRET
You can adapt this recipe by using different meats—turkey, ham, or classic Italian options like capocollo, mortadella or pancetta. Just keep an eye on the salt level, as deli meats can be quite salty.

SENSATIONAL CRABMEAT FONDUE

We entertain a lot, and this luxurious crab fondue makes our guests feel pampered.
—Debbie Obert, Middleburg, FL

TAKES: 30 MIN. • MAKES: 8 CUPS

½ cup butter, cubed
3 green onions,
 finely chopped
2 pkg. (8 oz. each)
 imitation crabmeat,
 coarsley chopped
2 cups whole milk
½ cup white wine or
 chicken broth
¼ tsp. pepper
2 cups shredded Monterey
 Jack cheese
2 cups shredded Swiss
 cheese
2 cups shredded Gruyere
 or additional shredded
 Swiss cheese
1 cup cubed Velveeta
 Cubed French bread

1. In a 6-qt. stockpot, cook butter over medium-high heat. Add onions: cook and stir until tender. Add crab; cook 2-3 minutes longer or until heated through. Stir in milk, wine and pepper; heat until bubbles form around sides of pan.

2. Reduce heat to medium-low. Add ½ cup Monterey Jack cheese; stir constantly until almost completely melted. Continue adding the cheeses, ½ cup at a time, allowing cheese to almost melt completely between additions. Cook and stir until mixture is thickened and smooth.

3. Transfer to a heated fondue pot; keep fondue bubbling gently. Serve with bread cubes.

¼ CUP: 144 cal., 11g fat (6g sat. fat), 34mg chol., 257mg sod., 3g carb. (1g sugars, 0 fiber), 8g pro.

CHEESY SNACK MIX

Our love for Mexican food inspired me to add taco seasoning to my party mix. The flavor is so mild that it's even kid-friendly.
—Elizabeth Wynne, Aztec, NM

PREP: 10 MIN. • COOK: 5 MIN. + COOLING • MAKES: 2½ QT.

3 cups Corn Chex
3 cups Rice Chex
3 cups cheddar miniature
 pretzels
¼ cup butter, melted
1 envelope cheesy taco
 seasoning
2 cups white cheddar
 popcorn

1. In a large microwave-safe bowl, combine cereal and pretzels. In a small bowl, mix melted butter and taco seasoning; drizzle over cereal mixture and toss to coat.

2. Microwave, uncovered, on high 3-3½ minutes or until heated through, stirring once every minute. Stir in popcorn. Transfer to a baking sheet to cool completely. Store in an airtight container.

¾ CUP: 151 cal., 5g fat (3g sat. fat), 11mg chol., 362mg sod., 23g carb. (2g sugars, 1g fiber), 3g pro. DIABETIC EXCHANGES: 1½ starch, 1 fat.

SHRIMP SALAD
APPETIZERS

SHRIMP SALAD APPETIZERS

This refreshing hors d'oeuvre has gained a big following since a friend shared her family recipe with me. My son says it best: The celery and shrimp are so good together.
—*Solie Kimble, Kanata, ON*

TAKES: 15 MIN. • MAKES: 2 DOZEN

1 lb. peeled and deveined cooked shrimp, chopped
1 can (6 oz.) lump crabmeat, drained
2 celery ribs, finely chopped
¼ cup Dijon-mayonnaise blend
24 Belgian endive leaves (3 to 4 heads) or small Bibb lettuce leaves
Chopped fresh parsley, optional

In a large bowl, combine shrimp, crab and celery. Add the mayonnaise blend; toss to coat. To serve, top each lettuce leaf with about 2 Tbsp. of the shrimp mixture. If desired, top with chopped parsley.

1 APPETIZER: 31 cal., 0 fat (0 sat. fat), 35mg chol., 115mg sod., 1g carb. (0 sugars, 0 fiber), 5g pro.

"Not only delicious but it is super simple to prepare. The lettuce leaf makes a nice presentation but I baked French bread in a scalloped bread tube yesterday and sliced it for the salad. It made a very pretty appetizer."
—MARINEMOM_TEXAS, TASTEOFHOME.COM

CHOCOLATY FRUIT DIP

My grandma helped me experiment with chocolate sauce and yogurt combinations to create this fruit dip for a tea party we had. Our guests said it was yummy!
—*Abigail Sims, Terrell, TX*

PREP: 10 MIN. + CHILLING • COOK: 5 MIN. + COOLING • MAKES: 1 CUP

1½ cups plain yogurt
2 Tbsp. fat-free milk
10 miniature marshmallows
2 Tbsp. semisweet chocolate chips
Assorted fresh fruit

1. Line a strainer with 4 layers of cheesecloth or 1 coffee filter and place over a bowl. Place yogurt in prepared strainer; cover yogurt with edges of cheesecloth. Refrigerate for 8 hours or overnight.

2. In a small heavy saucepan, combine the milk, marshmallows and chocolate chips. Cook and stir until the chips are melted and the mixture is smooth. Transfer to a small bowl; cool to room temperature.

3. Remove yogurt from cheesecloth and discard liquid from bowl. Gradually stir yogurt into milk mixture. Refrigerate until serving. Serve with fruit.

¼ CUP: 88 cal., 5g fat (3g sat. fat), 12mg chol., 47mg sod., 9g carb. (8g sugars, 0 fiber), 4g pro. **DIABETIC EXCHANGES:** 1 fat, ½ starch.

BRIE PUFF PASTRY

My husband was in the Air Force, so we've entertained guests all over the United States.
I acquired this recipe while in California. It's one of my favorite special appetizers.
—Sandra Twait, Tampa, FL

PREP: 15 MIN. • BAKE: 20 MIN. + STANDING • MAKES: 10 SERVINGS

1 round (13.2 oz.) Brie cheese
½ cup crumbled blue cheese
1 sheet frozen puff pastry, thawed
¼ cup apricot jam
½ cup slivered almonds, toasted
1 large egg, lightly beaten
Assorted crackers

1. Preheat oven to 400°. Cut Brie horizontally in half. Sprinkle bottom half with blue cheese; replace top.

2. On a lightly floured surface, roll pastry into a 14-in. square. Trim corners to make a circle. Spoon jam onto the center of pastry; sprinkle with almonds. Top with Brie.

3. Lightly brush edges of pastry with beaten egg. Fold pastry over cheese, pinching edges to seal; trim excess pastry as desired.

4. Transfer to an ungreased baking sheet, seam side down. Brush pastry with beaten egg. Bake until golden brown, 20-25 minutes.

5. Immediately remove from pan to a serving plate; let stand for 45 minutes before serving. Serve with crackers.

NOTE: To toast nuts, bake in a shallow pan in a 350° oven for 5-10 minutes or cook in a skillet over low heat until lightly browned, stirring occasionally.

1 SERVING: 328 cal., 22g fat (10g sat. fat), 64mg chol., 424mg sod., 20g carb. (3g sugars, 2g fiber), 13g pro.

EGGNOG DIP

I put together a cookbook of my grandma's Christmas recipes that includes this classic eggnog appetizer. Serve it as a dip with fresh fruit or drizzle it over cake for dessert.
—Sharon MacDonnell, Lantzville, BC

PREP: 10 MIN. + CHILLING • COOK: 10 MIN. + COOLING • MAKES: ABOUT 2½ CUPS

1½ cups eggnog
2 Tbsp. cornstarch
½ cup sour cream
½ cup heavy whipping cream
1 Tbsp. sugar
½ tsp. rum extract, optional
Assorted fruit and pound cake cubes

1. In a small saucepan, combine the eggnog and cornstarch until smooth. Bring to a boil; boil and stir for 2 minutes. Remove from heat; stir in sour cream. Cool completely.

2. In a small bowl, beat whipping cream and sugar until stiff peaks form. Fold into eggnog mixture with extract if desired. Cover and refrigerate overnight. Serve with fruit and cake cubes.

2 TBSP.: 64 cal., 5g fat (3g sat. fat), 23mg chol., 16mg sod., 4g carb. (4g sugars, 0 fiber), 1g pro.

LEFTOVER TURKEY TURNOVERS

I came up with this dish in 1993 while putting together a booklet called "Totally Turkey" for leftover turkey recipes. My children gobble them up in no time.
—*Renee Murby, Johnston, RI*

PREP: 40 MIN. + CHILLING • COOK: 5 MIN./BATCH • MAKES: 1 DOZEN

1¼ cups all-purpose flour
¼ tsp. salt
½ cup shortening
1 large egg
2 Tbsp. ice water, divided

FILLING
2 Tbsp. canola oil
⅓ cup finely chopped onion

¼ tsp. ground turmeric
¼ tsp. ground cinnamon
1 garlic clove, minced
1 cup finely chopped cooked turkey
¼ cup raisins
¼ tsp. salt
⅛ tsp. pepper
Oil for frying

1. In a large bowl, mix flour and salt; cut in shortening until crumbly. Whisk egg and 1 Tbsp. ice water; gradually add to flour with the remaining water as needed, tossing with a fork until the dough holds together when pressed. Turn onto a lightly floured surface; knead gently 6-8 times. Shape into a disk; wrap and refrigerate for 1 hour or overnight.

2. In a large skillet, heat oil over medium-high heat. Add onion, turmeric and cinnamon; cook and stir 1-2 minutes or until tender. Add garlic; cook 30 seconds longer. Stir in turkey, raisins, salt and pepper.

3. On a lightly floured surface, roll dough to ⅛-in. thickness. Cut with a floured 4-in. round cookie cutter. Place a heaping tablespoon of filling in the center of each circle. Moisten edges with water; fold in half and press edges with a fork to seal. Repeat with the remaining dough and filling.

4. In a deep skillet or electric skillet, heat ½ in. oil to 375°. Fry turnovers, a few at a time, 2-3 minutes on each side or until golden brown. Drain on paper towels.

1 TURNOVER: 212 cal., 15g fat (3g sat. fat), 27mg chol., 117mg sod., 13g carb. (2g sugars, 1g fiber), 5g pro.

GRANDMA'S SECRET

If you like, you can make these in an air fryer instead. Place turnovers in a single layer, spritz with cooking spray and cook in an air fryer set to 400° until golden brown, 10-15 minutes.

MARINATED OLIVE & CHEESE RING

We love to make Italian meals into celebrations, and an antipasto always kicks off the party.
This one is almost too pretty to eat, especially when sprinkled with pimientos, fresh basil and parsley.
—*Patricia Harmon, Baden, PA*

PREP: 25 MIN. + CHILLING • MAKES: 16 SERVINGS

1 pkg. (8 oz.) cream cheese, cold
1 pkg. (10 oz.) sharp white cheddar cheese, cut into ¼-in. slices
⅓ cup pimiento-stuffed olives
⅓ cup pitted Greek olives
¼ cup balsamic vinegar
¼ cup olive oil
1 Tbsp. minced fresh parsley
1 Tbsp. minced fresh basil or 1 tsp. dried basil
2 garlic cloves, minced
1 jar (2 oz.) pimiento strips, drained and chopped
  Toasted French bread baguette slices

1. Cut cream cheese lengthwise in half; cut each half into ¼-in. slices. On a serving plate, arrange cheeses upright in a ring, alternating cheddar and cream cheese slices. Place olives in the center of the ring.

2. In a small bowl, whisk vinegar, oil, parsley, basil and garlic until blended; drizzle over cheeses and olives. Sprinkle with pimientos. Refrigerate, covered, at least 8 hours or overnight. Serve with baguette slices.

1 SERVING: 168 cal., 16g fat (7g sat. fat), 34mg chol., 260mg sod., 2g carb. (1g sugars, 0 fiber), 6g pro.

FROM GRANDMA'S KITCHEN: This stylish appetizer is super adaptable. Any cheeses will work in place of the cream cheese and sharp cheddar. Just keep the overall weight the same. For more variety, fold thin slices of deli cuts such as pepperoni and salami in half and tuck them between the cheese slices.

BEER CHEESE IN A BREAD BOWL

My entire family loves this cheese dip, and my friends always request I bring it to gatherings.
It's also quite attractive thanks to the bread bowl. Chopped scallions make a pretty garnish.
—*Julie Koch, Delaware, OH*

TAKES: 15 MIN. • MAKES: 20 SERVINGS (2½ CUPS DIP)

1 round loaf (1 lb.) pumpernickel bread
2 jars (5 oz. each) sharp American cheese spread
1 pkg. (8 oz.) cream cheese, softened
¼ cup beer or nonalcoholic beer
½ cup bacon bits

1. Cut top fourth off loaf of bread; carefully hollow out bottom, leaving a ½-in. shell. Cube the removed bread; set aside.

2. In a microwave-safe bowl, combine cheese spread and cream cheese. Microwave, uncovered, on high for 2 minutes, stirring every 30 seconds. Stir in beer. Microwave, uncovered, 20 seconds longer. Stir in bacon.

3. Fill bread shell with cheese dip. Serve with the reserved bread cubes.

2 TBSP. DIP: 147 cal., 9g fat (5g sat. fat), 26mg chol., 506mg sod., 12g carb. (0 sugars, 1g fiber), 6g pro.

MARINATED OLIVE
& CHEESE RING

BACON CHEESEBURGER SLIDER BAKE

I created this dish to fill two pans because these sliders disappear fast. Just cut the recipe in half to make a single batch.
—*Nick Iverson, Denver, CO*

PREP: 20 MIN. • BAKE: 25 MIN. • MAKES: 2 DOZEN

- 2 pkg. (17 oz. each) Hawaiian sweet rolls
- 4 cups shredded cheddar cheese, divided
- 2 lbs. ground beef
- 1 cup chopped onion
- 1 can (14½ oz.) diced tomatoes with garlic and onion, drained
- 1 Tbsp. Dijon mustard
- 1 Tbsp. Worcestershire sauce
- ¾ tsp. salt
- ¾ tsp. pepper
- 24 bacon strips, cooked and crumbled

GLAZE
- 1 cup butter, cubed
- ¼ cup packed brown sugar
- 4 tsp. Worcestershire sauce
- 2 Tbsp. Dijon mustard
- 2 Tbsp. sesame seeds

1. Preheat oven to 350°. Without separating rolls, cut each package of rolls horizontally in half; arrange bottom halves in 2 greased 13x9-in. baking pans. Sprinkle each pan of rolls with 1 cup cheese. Bake until cheese is melted, 3-5 minutes.

2. In a large skillet, cook beef and onion over medium heat until beef is no longer pink and onion is tender, breaking beef into crumbles, 6-8 minutes; drain. Stir in tomatoes, mustard, Worcestershire sauce, salt and pepper. Cook and stir until combined, 1-2 minutes.

3. Spoon the beef mixture evenly over rolls; sprinkle with remaining 2 cups cheese. Top with bacon. Replace tops.

4. For glaze, in a microwave-safe bowl, combine butter, brown sugar, Worcestershire sauce and mustard. Microwave, covered, on high until butter is melted, stirring occasionally. Pour over rolls; sprinkle with sesame seeds. Bake, uncovered, until golden brown and heated through, 20-25 minutes.

FREEZE OPTION: Cover and freeze unbaked sandwiches; prepare and freeze glaze. To use, partially thaw in refrigerator overnight. Remove from refrigerator 30 minutes before baking. Pour glaze over buns and sprinkle with sesame seeds. Bake sandwiches at 350° as directed, increasing time by 10-15 minutes, until cheese is melted and a thermometer inserted in center reads 165°.

1 SLIDER: 380 cal., 24g fat (13g sat. fat), 86mg chol., 628mg sod., 21g carb. (9g sugars, 2g fiber), 18g pro.

SHRIMP APPETIZER SPREAD

There's no secret to this creamy seafood appetizer—it's simply delicious! I originally tasted it at a friend's house and liked it so much, I requested the recipe.
—*Brenda Buhler, Abbotsford, BC*

TAKES: 20 MIN. • MAKES: 20 SERVINGS

1 pkg. (8 oz.) cream cheese, softened
½ cup sour cream
¼ cup mayonnaise
1 cup seafood cocktail sauce
12 oz. frozen cooked salad shrimp, thawed
2 cups shredded mozzarella cheese
1 medium green pepper, chopped
1 small tomato, chopped
3 green onions with tops, sliced
   Assorted crackers

1. In a large bowl, beat the cream cheese, sour cream and mayonnaise until smooth.

2. Spread mixture on a round 12-in. serving platter. Top with seafood sauce. Sprinkle with shrimp, mozzarella, green pepper, tomato and onions. Refrigerate until serving. Serve with crackers.

2 TBSP.: 136 cal., 10g fat (5g sat. fat), 62mg chol., 372mg sod., 4g carb. (3g sugars, 1g fiber), 8g pro.

LITTLE PIGS IN A HAMMOCK

Pigs in a blanket aren't just for kids! Dijon and Camembert transform this children's favorite into a version that's perfect for grown-ups.
—*Crystal Schlueter, Northglenn, CO*

TAKES: 30 MIN. • MAKES: 1½ DOZEN

1 pkg. (17.3 oz.) frozen puff pastry, thawed
3 Tbsp. seedless raspberry jam
1 Tbsp. Dijon mustard
1 round (8 oz.) Camembert cheese
18 miniature smoked sausages
1 large egg
1 Tbsp. water

1. Preheat oven to 425°. Unfold puff pastry. Cut each pastry into 9 squares. Cut each square into 2 triangles. In a small bowl, mix jam and mustard; spread over triangles. Cut cheese in half crosswise; cut each half into 9 wedges.

2. Top each triangle with a cheese piece and a sausage. Fold pastry over sausage and cheese; press to seal. Place on a parchment-lined baking sheet. In a small bowl, whisk egg with water. Brush over pastries. Bake until pastry is golden brown, 15-17 minutes.

1 APPETIZER: 211 cal., 13g fat (5g sat. fat), 25mg chol., 312mg sod., 18g carb. (2g sugars, 2g fiber), 6g pro.

HEIRLOOM TOMATO GALETTE
WITH PECORINO

HEIRLOOM TOMATO GALETTE WITH PECORINO

I found beautiful heirloom tomatoes and had to show them off. In this easy galette,
the tomatoes are tangy and the crust is beyond buttery.
—*Jessica Chang, Playa Vista, CA*

PREP: 10 MIN. + CHILLING • BAKE: 25 MIN. + COOLING • MAKES: 6 SERVINGS

1 **cup all-purpose flour**
1 **tsp. baking powder**
¾ **tsp. kosher salt, divided**
½ **cup cold unsalted butter,
   cubed**
½ **cup sour cream**
2 **cups heirloom cherry
   tomatoes, halved**
3 **oz. pecorino Romano
   cheese, thinly sliced**

1. Whisk flour, baking powder and ½ tsp. salt; cut in butter until mixture resembles coarse crumbs. Stir in sour cream until dough forms a ball. Shape into a disk; cover and refrigerate until firm enough to roll, about 2 hours.

2. Meanwhile, place tomatoes in a colander; toss with remaining ¼ tsp. salt. Let stand 15 minutes.

3. Preheat oven to 425°. On a floured sheet of parchment, roll dough into a 12-in. circle. Transfer to a baking sheet.

4. Place cheese slices over crust to within 2 in. of edge; arrange tomatoes over cheese. Fold crust edges over filling, pleating as you go and leaving center uncovered. Bake until crust is golden brown and cheese is bubbly, about 25 minutes. Cool 10 minutes before slicing.

1 PIECE: 317 cal., 23g fat (15g sat. fat), 68mg chol., 559mg sod., 19g carb. (2g sugars, 1g fiber), 9g pro.

BUFFET MEATBALLS

I need only five ingredients to fix these easy appetizers. Grape juice and apple jelly are the
secrets behind the sweet yet tangy sauce that complements convenient packaged meatballs.
—*Janet Anderson, Carson City, NV*

PREP: 10 MIN. • COOK: 4 HOURS • MAKES: ABOUT 10½ DOZEN

1 **cup grape juice**
1 **cup apple jelly**
1 **cup ketchup**
1 **can (8 oz.) tomato sauce**
1 **pkg. (64 oz.) frozen fully
   cooked Italian meatballs
   Minced fresh parsley,
   optional**

1. In a small saucepan, combine juice, jelly, ketchup and tomato sauce. Cook and stir over medium heat until jelly is melted.

2. Place meatballs in a 5-qt. slow cooker. Pour sauce over the top and gently stir to coat. Cover and cook on low for 4-5 hours or until heated through. If desired, sprinkle with parsley.

1 MEATBALL: 147 cal., 9g fat (4g sat. fat), 20mg chol., 411mg sod., 10g carb. (7g sugars, 1g fiber), 7g pro.

FROM GRANDMA'S KITCHEN: Skip packaged and opt for homemade meatballs instead. This recipe is among our favorite Christmas buffet ideas, as well as a popular Thanksgiving appetizer.

SWEET CEREAL TREATS

It doesn't take long to mix up a batch of these yummy snacks since they have only four ingredients and don't need to bake. As a small child, I helped my grandma make them. Now my three children enjoy helping me. We all love this crunchy treat.
—*Barri VanderHulst, Allegan, MI*

TAKES: 20 MIN. • MAKES: ABOUT 5 DOZEN

5⅓ cups Cap'n Crunch's Peanut Butter Crunch cereal
1 cup dry roasted peanuts
1 pkg. (10 to 12 oz.) white baking chips
1 Tbsp. butter

1. In a large bowl, combine cereal and peanuts; set aside. In a microwave or double boiler, melt the baking chips and butter; stir until smooth.

2. Pour over cereal mixture and stir to coat. Drop by rounded tablespoonfuls onto waxed paper-lined baking sheets. Refrigerate until firm.

2 TREATS: 119 cal., 7g fat (3g sat. fat), 3mg chol., 101mg sod., 13g carb. (2g sugars, 1g fiber), 2g pro.

ROAST BEEF FINGER SANDWICHES

These simple sandwiches are ideal for a bridal shower, brunch or high tea, when the menu is a bit more substantial. The mustard adds a nice kick without being overly spicy.
—*Anndrea Bailey, Huntington Beach, CA*

TAKES: 15 MIN. • MAKES: 1½ DOZEN

½ cup butter, softened
½ cup chopped pitted Greek olives
¼ cup spicy brown mustard
¼ tsp. pepper
6 slices whole wheat bread, crusts removed
6 oz. thinly sliced deli roast beef
6 slices white bread, crusts removed

Place butter, olives, mustard and pepper in a food processor; pulse until chopped. Spread butter mixture over wheat bread; top with roast beef and white bread. Cut each sandwich crosswise into thirds.

1 SANDWICH: 98 cal., 7g fat (4g sat. fat), 19mg chol., 240mg sod., 5g carb. (1g sugars, 1g fiber), 3g pro.

REUBEN ROUNDS

Fans of the classic Reuben sandwich will go crazy for baked pastry spirals of corned beef, Swiss and sauerkraut. They're a breeze to make, and bottled Thousand Island dressing makes the perfect dipping sauce.
—*Cheryl Snavely, Hagerstown, MD*

TAKES: 30 MIN. • MAKES: 16 APPETIZERS

1 sheet frozen puff pastry, thawed
6 slices Swiss cheese
5 slices deli corned beef
½ cup sauerkraut, rinsed and well drained
1 tsp. caraway seeds
¼ cup Thousand Island salad dressing

1. Preheat oven to 400°. Unfold puff pastry; layer with Swiss cheese, corned beef and sauerkraut to within ½-in. of edges. Roll up jelly-roll style. Trim ends and cut crosswise into 16 slices. Place on greased baking sheets, cut side down. Sprinkle with caraway seeds.

2. Bake until golden brown, 18-20 minutes. Serve with Thousand Island dressing.

1 APPETIZER: 114 cal., 7g fat (2g sat. fat), 8mg chol., 198mg sod., 10g carb. (1g sugars, 1g fiber), 3g pro.

SWEET & SAVORY CHEESE PIE

It looks like a pie, but serves like a spread! Layer ruby red preserves on top of this savory appetizer as the crowning touch.
—*Annette Whitmarsh, Lincoln, NE*

PREP: 15 MIN. + CHILLING • MAKES: 32 SERVINGS

1 cup chopped pecans
1 pkg. (8 oz.) cream cheese, softened
½ cup mayonnaise
4 cups shredded sharp cheddar cheese
6 green onions, chopped
½ lb. bacon strips, cooked and crumbled
1 jar (10 oz.) seedless raspberry or strawberry preserves
Sliced green onions, optional
Assorted crackers

1. Spread pecans evenly over bottom of a greased 9-in. springform pan. In a large bowl, beat cream cheese and mayonnaise until smooth. Stir in the cheddar cheese, green onions and bacon. Carefully spread over pecans. Refrigerate, covered, overnight.

2. Loosen sides from pan with a knife; remove rim from pan. Spread preserves over top. If desired, top with sliced onions. Serve with crackers.

2 TBSP.: 161 cal., 13g fat (5g sat. fat), 27mg chol., 170mg sod., 7g carb. (6g sugars, 0 fiber), 5g pro.

HAM & CHEESE BISCUIT STACKS

These finger sandwiches are a pretty addition to any spread, yet filling enough to satisfy hearty appetites. I've served them at holidays, showers and tailgate parties.

—*Kelly Williams, Forked River, NJ*

PREP: 1 HOUR • **BAKE:** 10 MIN. + COOLING • **MAKES:** 40 APPETIZERS

4 tubes (6 oz. each) small refrigerated flaky biscuits (5 count each)
¼ cup stone-ground mustard

ASSEMBLY
½ cup butter, softened
¼ cup chopped green onions
½ cup stone-ground mustard
¼ cup mayonnaise
¼ cup honey
10 thick slices deli ham, quartered
10 slices Swiss cheese, quartered
2½ cups shredded romaine
20 pitted ripe olives, drained and patted dry
20 pimiento-stuffed olives, drained and patted dry
40 party toothpicks

1. Preheat oven to 400°. Cut biscuits in half to make half-circles; place 2 in. apart on ungreased baking sheets. Spread mustard over tops. Bake until golden brown, 8-10 minutes. Cool completely on wire racks.

2. Mix butter and green onions. In another bowl, mix mustard, mayonnaise and honey.

3. Split each biscuit into 2 layers. Spread biscuit bottoms with butter mixture; top with ham, cheese, romaine and biscuit tops. Spoon mustard mixture over tops. Thread 1 olive onto each toothpick; insert into stacks. Serve immediately.

1 APPETIZER: 121 cal., 7g fat (3g sat. fat), 16mg chol., 412mg sod., 11g carb. (2g sugars, 0 fiber), 4g pro.

GRANDMA'S SECRET
Stone-ground mustard, made with brown mustard seeds, is spicier and less acidic than yellow mustard, which is made with white seeds. For a substitute, use spicy brown mustard, Dijon or even horseradish!

RISOTTO BALLS (ARANCINI)

My Italian grandma made these for me. I still ask for them when I visit her, and so do my children. Arancini freeze well, so I make them ahead of time. They're the perfect combination of crispy and creamy.
—*Gretchen Whelan, San Francisco, CA*

PREP: 35 MIN. • BAKE: 25 MIN. • MAKES: ABOUT 3 DOZEN

1½ cups water
1 cup uncooked arborio rice
1 tsp. salt
2 large eggs, lightly beaten
⅔ cup sun-dried tomato pesto
2 cups panko bread crumbs, divided
Marinara sauce, warmed

1. Preheat oven to 375°. In a large saucepan, combine water, rice and salt; bring to a boil. Reduce heat; simmer, covered, until liquid is absorbed and rice is tender, 18-20 minutes. Let stand, covered, 10 minutes. Transfer to a large bowl; cool slightly. Add eggs and pesto; stir in 1 cup bread crumbs.

2. Place remaining 1 cup bread crumbs in a shallow bowl. Shape rice mixture into 1¼-in. balls. Roll in bread crumbs, patting to help coating adhere. Place on greased 15x10x1-in. baking pans. Bake until golden brown, 25-30 minutes. Serve with marinara sauce.

1 APPETIZER: 42 cal., 1g fat (0 sat. fat), 10mg chol., 125mg sod., 7g carb. (1g sugars, 0 fiber), 1g pro. DIABETIC EXCHANGES: ½ starch.

FROM GRANDMA'S KITCHEN: You can serve risotto balls with many Italian dishes, including carbonara, manicotti and grilled veggies. Arancini will last 3-4 days in the fridge and about a month in the freezer. To cook frozen risotto balls, bake at 375° for 20 minutes, turning halfway through.

FRESH FROM THE GARDEN WRAPS

We moved into a house with a garden that needed tending. Using the herbs
we found, we made these freshtastic wraps for our first dinner there.
—*Chris Bugher, Fairview, NC*

PREP: 20 MIN. + STANDING • **MAKES:** 8 SERVINGS

1 medium ear sweet corn
1 medium cucumber,
  chopped
1 cup shredded cabbage
1 medium tomato, chopped
1 small red onion, chopped
1 jalapeno pepper, seeded
  and minced
1 Tbsp. minced fresh basil
1 Tbsp. minced fresh
  cilantro
1 Tbsp. minced fresh mint
⅓ cup Thai chili sauce
3 Tbsp. rice vinegar
2 tsp. reduced-sodium
  soy sauce
2 tsp. creamy peanut butter
8 Bibb or Boston lettuce
  leaves

1. Cut corn from cob and place in a large bowl. Add cucumber,
cabbage, tomato, onion, jalapeno and herbs.

2. Whisk together chili sauce, vinegar, soy sauce and peanut
butter. Pour over vegetable mixture; toss to coat. Let stand for
20 minutes.

3. Using a slotted spoon, place ½ cup salad in each lettuce leaf.
Fold lettuce over filling.

NOTE: Wear disposable gloves when cutting hot peppers; the oils
can burn skin. Avoid touching your face.

1 FILLED LETTUCE WRAP: 64 cal., 1g fat (0 sat. fat), 0 chol., 319mg
sod., 13g carb. (10g sugars, 2g fiber), 2g pro. DIABETIC EXCHANGES:
1 vegetable, ½ starch.

DEVILED EGG SPREAD

I tried this egg salad at a luncheon and had to have it. I punched it up with pickled
banana peppers. It's a hit both with my kids and my picky mother!
—*Lisa Easley, Longview, TX*

TAKES: 20 MIN. • **MAKES:** 16 SERVINGS

10 hard-boiled large eggs
1 cup Miracle Whip
1 cup finely shredded
  cheddar cheese
½ lb. bacon strips,
  cooked and crumbled
¼ cup finely chopped
  pickled banana peppers
2 tsp. juice from pickled
  banana peppers
¼ tsp. salt
¼ tsp. pepper
  Ritz crackers and
  assorted fresh
  vegetables

Place eggs in a large bowl; mash with a fork. Stir in the Miracle
Whip, cheese, bacon, banana peppers, juice from the peppers,
salt and pepper. Refrigerate until serving. Serve with Ritz
crackers and vegetables.

¼ CUP: 149 cal., 12g fat (4g sat. fat), 134mg chol., 383mg sod.,
3g carb. (2g sugars, 0 fiber), 7g pro.

LEMON-HERB
SALMON TOASTS

LEMON-HERB SALMON TOASTS

Quick, light and tasty, my salmon toasts make irresistible finger food.

—*Christie Wells, Lake Villa, IL*

TAKES: 20 MIN. • MAKES: 2 DOZEN

1 pkg. (8 oz.) cream cheese, softened
4 green onions, chopped
2 Tbsp. snipped fresh dill or 2 tsp. dill weed
¾ tsp. sea salt
½ tsp. pepper
¼ tsp. cayenne pepper
¼ tsp. grated lemon zest
2 tsp. lemon juice
24 slices snack rye bread
8 oz. smoked salmon or lox
   Optional: Grated lemon zest, coarsely ground pepper and fresh dill sprigs

Preheat broiler. In a small bowl, beat the first 8 ingredients. Place bread slices on baking sheets. Broil 4-5 in. from heat for 1-2 minutes on each side or until lightly toasted. Spread each piece of toast with cream cheese mixture; top with lox. Serve with toppings as desired.

1 APPETIZER: 63 cal., 4g fat (2g sat. fat), 12mg chol., 196mg sod., 4g carb. (1g sugars, 0 fiber), 3g pro.

BEST EVER STUFFED MUSHROOMS

Every Christmas Eve, I bring out a platter of my fresh-from-the-oven mushrooms. They have become a much-anticipated family tradition!

—*Debby Beard, Eagle, CO*

PREP: 20 MIN. • BAKE: 15 MIN. • MAKES: 2½ DOZEN

1 lb. bulk pork sausage
¼ cup finely chopped onion
1 garlic clove, minced
1 pkg. (8 oz.) reduced-fat cream cheese
¼ cup shredded Parmesan cheese
⅓ cup seasoned bread crumbs
3 tsp. dried basil
1½ tsp. dried parsley flakes
30 large fresh mushrooms (about 1½ lbs.), stems removed
3 Tbsp. butter, melted

1. Preheat oven to 400°. In a large skillet, cook sausage, onion and garlic over medium heat until the sausage is no longer pink and onion is tender, 6-8 minutes, breaking up sausage into crumbles; drain. Add cream cheese and Parmesan cheese; cook and stir until melted. Stir in bread crumbs, basil and parsley.

2. Meanwhile, place mushroom caps in a greased 15x10x1-in. baking pan, bottom side up. Brush with butter. Spoon sausage mixture into mushroom caps. Bake, uncovered, until the mushrooms are tender, 12-15 minutes.

1 APPETIZER: 79 cal., 6g fat (3g sat. fat), 17mg chol., 167mg sod., 2g carb. (1g sugars, 0 fiber), 3g pro.

FROM GRANDMA'S KITCHEN: When you want a change, consider fixing the filling on its own instead of having stuffed mushrooms. It's a good spread all by itself on baguette slices and crackers.

THREE-CHEESE FONDUE

I got this easy recipe from my daughter, who lives in France.
It's become my go-to fondue, and I make it often for our family.
—*Betty Mangas, Toledo, OH*

TAKES: 30 MIN. • MAKES: 4 CUPS

½ lb. each Emmenthaler, Gruyere and Jarlsberg cheeses, shredded
2 Tbsp. cornstarch, divided
4 tsp. cherry brandy
2 cups dry white wine
⅛ tsp. ground nutmeg
⅛ tsp. paprika
Dash cayenne pepper
Cubed French bread baguette, boiled red potatoes and/or tiny whole pickles

1. In a large bowl, combine cheeses and 1 Tbsp. cornstarch. In a small bowl, combine remaining 1 Tbsp. cornstarch and the brandy; set aside. In a large saucepan, heat wine over medium heat until bubbles form around sides of pan.

2. Reduce heat to medium-low; add a handful of cheese mixture. Stir constantly, using a figure-8 motion, until the cheese is almost completely melted. Continue adding cheese, a handful at a time, allowing cheese to almost completely melt between additions.

3. Stir brandy mixture; gradually stir into cheese mixture. Add spices; cook and stir until mixture is thickened and smooth.

4. Transfer to a fondue pot and keep warm. Serve with bread cubes, potatoes and/or pickles.

¼ CUP: 191 cal., 12g fat (7g sat. fat), 37mg chol., 151mg sod., 3g carb. (1g sugars, 0 fiber), 12g pro.

ITALIAN MEATBALL BUNS

These soft little rolls come with a surprise inside—savory Italian meatballs. They're wonderful dipped in marinara sauce, making them fun for my grandkids—and adults, too. I love how easy they are to put together.
—*Trina Linder-Mobley, Clover, SC*

PREP: 30 MIN. + RISING • BAKE: 15 MIN. • MAKES: 2 DOZEN

12 frozen bread dough dinner rolls
1 pkg. (12 oz.) frozen fully cooked Italian meatballs, thawed
2 Tbsp. olive oil
¼ cup grated Parmesan cheese
¼ cup minced fresh basil
1½ cups marinara sauce, warmed

1. Let dough stand at room temperature until softened, 25-30 minutes.

2. Cut each roll in half. Wrap each portion around a meatball, enclosing meatball completely; pinch dough firmly to seal. Place on greased baking sheets, seam side down. Cover with kitchen towel; let rise in a warm place until dough has almost doubled, 1½-2 hours.

3. Preheat oven to 350°. Bake buns until crust is golden brown, 12-15 minutes. Brush tops with oil; sprinkle with cheese and basil. Serve with marinara sauce.

1 BUN WITH 1 TBSP. SAUCE: 98 cal., 4g fat (1g sat. fat), 13mg chol., 253mg sod., 12g carb. (2g sugars, 1g fiber), 5g pro.

RICOTTA SAUSAGE TRIANGLES

Stuffed with cheese, sausage and seasonings, these pockets are hard to put down! They freeze well, so go ahead and make a big batch for future parties.
—*Virginia C. Anthony, Jacksonville, FL*

PREP: 1 HOUR • BAKE: 15 MIN./BATCH • MAKES: 12 DOZEN

1 carton (15 oz.) part-skim ricotta cheese
1 pkg. (10 oz.) frozen chopped spinach, thawed and squeezed dry
1 jar (8 oz.) roasted sweet red peppers, drained and chopped
⅓ cup grated Parmesan cheese
3 Tbsp. chopped ripe olives
1 large egg

1 Tbsp. minced fresh basil or 1 tsp. dried basil
1 tsp. Italian seasoning
¼ tsp. salt
¼ tsp. pepper
1 lb. bulk Italian sausage
1 medium onion, chopped
96 sheets phyllo dough (14x9-in. size)
Olive oil-flavored cooking spray
Warm marinara sauce, optional

1. Preheat oven to 375°. In a large bowl, combine the first 10 ingredients. In a large skillet, cook sausage and onion over medium heat until meat is no longer pink; drain. Stir into the cheese mixture.

2. Place 1 sheet of phyllo dough on a work surface with a short end facing you; spray with cooking spray. Top with a second sheet of phyllo; spray again with cooking spray. Cut layered sheets into three 14x3-in. strips.

3. Place a rounded teaspoonful of filling on lower corner of each strip. Fold dough over filling, forming a triangle. Fold triangle up, then fold triangle over, forming another triangle. Continue folding, like a flag, until you come to the end of the strip.

4. Spritz end of dough with spray and press onto triangle to seal. Turn triangle and spritz top with spray. Repeat with remaining phyllo and filling.

5. Place triangles on baking sheets coated with cooking spray. Bake until golden brown, 15-20 minutes. Serve warm and, if desired, with marinara sauce.

FREEZE OPTION: Freeze unbaked triangles in freezer containers, separating layers with waxed paper. To use, bake triangles as directed, increasing time as necessary until triangles are golden and heated through.

1 APPETIZER: 42 cal., 2g fat (0 sat. fat), 4mg chol., 64mg sod., 5g carb. (0 sugars, 0 fiber), 2g pro.

GRANDMA'S SECRET

Pre-made phyllo dough is a wonderful convenience, but it is vulnerable to drying out. Always keep unused phyllo covered with a damp towel while you're working with the other layers.

OYSTER CHEESE APPETIZER LOG

Every winter, I make lots of these cheese logs and freeze them for when I'm expecting company or need to take food to a party. The blend of smoked oysters, chili powder, nuts and cream cheese tastes so good—even people who don't like oysters enjoy this interesting appetizer.
—*William Tracy, Jerseyville, IL*

TAKES: 20 MIN. • **MAKES:** 32 SERVINGS (2 LOGS)

3 **pkg. (8 oz. each) cream cheese, softened**
2 **Tbsp. steak sauce**
¼ **cup Miracle Whip**
1 **garlic clove, peeled and minced, or 1 tsp. garlic powder**
1 **small onion, finely chopped**
2 **cans (3¾ oz. each) smoked oysters, well-drained and chopped**
3 **cups chopped pecans, divided**
3 **Tbsp. chili powder**
  Minced fresh parsley

Combine the cheese, steak sauce, Miracle Whip, garlic and onion. Stir in oysters and 1 cup of pecans. Shape into two 9-in. logs. Roll logs in mixture of chili powder, remaining pecans and parsley.

2 TBSP.: 117 cal., 12g fat (2g sat. fat), 10mg chol., 62mg sod., 3g carb. (1g sugars, 1g fiber), 2g pro.

"Outrageously good! This has a perfect balance of savory taste with a spicy kick from the raw onion and chili powder. My guests raved about this appetizer, including the picky eaters. Thanks, Bill, this one is a keeper!"
—METROCOOKBOOKDIVANY, TASTEOFHOME.COM

HERB-ROASTED OLIVES & TOMATOES

Eat these roasted veggies with a crunchy baguette or a couple of cheeses. You can also double or triple the amounts and have leftovers to toss with spaghetti the next day.
—*Anndrea Bailey, Huntington Beach, CA*

TAKES: 25 MIN. • **MAKES:** 4 CUPS

2 **cups cherry tomatoes**
1 **cup garlic-stuffed olives**
1 **cup Greek olives**
1 **cup pitted ripe olives**
8 **garlic cloves, peeled**
3 **Tbsp. olive oil**
1 **Tbsp. herbes de Provence**
¼ **tsp. pepper**

Preheat oven to 425°. Combine the first 5 ingredients on a greased 15x10x1-in. baking pan. Add oil and seasonings; toss to coat. Roast until tomatoes are softened, 15-20 minutes, stirring occasionally.

¼ CUP: 71 cal., 7g fat (1g sat. fat), 0 chol., 380mg sod., 3g carb. (1g sugars, 1g fiber), 0 pro.

OYSTER CHEESE
APPETIZER LOG

HOMEMADE GUACAMOLE

Nothing is better than freshly made guacamole when you're eating something spicy. It's easy to whip together in a matter of minutes and quickly tames anything that's too hot.
—*Joan Hallford, North Richland Hills, TX*

TAKES: 10 MIN. • MAKES: 2 CUPS

- 3 **medium ripe avocados, peeled and cubed**
- 1 **garlic clove, minced**
- ¼ **to ½ tsp. salt**
- 1 **small onion, finely chopped**
- 1 **to 2 Tbsp. lime juice**
- 1 **Tbsp. minced fresh cilantro**
- 2 **medium tomatoes, seeded and chopped, optional**
- ¼ **cup mayonnaise, optional**

Mash avocados with garlic and salt. Stir in remaining ingredients, adding tomatoes and mayonnaise if desired.

¼ CUP: 90 cal., 8g fat (1g sat. fat), 0 chol., 78mg sod., 6g carb. (1g sugars, 4g fiber), 1g pro. DIABETIC EXCHANGES: 1½ fat.

FROM GRANDMA'S KITCHEN: Avocado is high in monounsaturated fat, a so-called "good fat" that can lower your blood cholesterol along with the risk of stroke and heart disease. You can use lemon juice in place of the lime to achieve a different flavor.

PASTRAMI ROLL-UPS

For a book club event, I created pastrami roll-ups with cream cheese and a pickle. Those tasty bites quickly pulled a disappearing act.
—*Merritt Heinrich, Oswego, IL*

TAKES: 15 MIN. • MAKES: 4 DOZEN

- ¾ **cup spreadable cream cheese**
- ½ **cup crumbled blue cheese**
- 12 **slices lean deli pastrami**
- 12 **dill pickle spears**

1. In a small bowl, mix cream cheese and blue cheese until blended. If necessary, pat pastrami and pickles dry with paper towels.

2. Spread about 1 Tbsp. cheese mixture over each pastrami slice; top with a pickle spear. Roll up tightly. Cut each roll into 4 slices. Refrigerate leftovers.

1 APPETIZER: 25 cal., 2g fat (1g sat. fat), 8mg chol., 158mg sod., 0 carb. (0 sugars, 0 fiber), 2g pro.

TANGY PICKLED MUSHROOMS

Home-canned pickled mushrooms are a great addition to your pantry.
They're ideal for cocktails, appetizers, salads and relish trays.
—Jill Hihn, West Grove, PA

PREP: 50 MIN. • PROCESS: 20 MIN./BATCH • MAKES: 8 PINTS

5 lbs. small fresh
   mushrooms
2 large onions,
   halved and sliced
2 cups white vinegar
1½ cups canola oil
¼ cup sugar
2 Tbsp. canning salt
3 garlic cloves, minced
1½ tsp. pepper
¼ tsp. dried tarragon

1. Place all ingredients in a stockpot. Bring to a boil. Reduce heat; simmer, uncovered, 10 minutes. Carefully ladle hot mixture into 8 hot 1-pint jars, leaving ½-in. headspace.

2. Remove air bubbles and adjust headspace, if necessary, by adding hot mixture. Wipe rims. Center lids on jars; screw on bands until fingertip tight. Place jars into canner, ensuring that they are completely covered with water. Bring to a boil. Process for 20 minutes. Remove jars and cool.

NOTE: The processing time listed is for altitudes of 1,000 feet or less. For altitudes up to 3,000 feet, add 5 minutes; 6,000 feet, add 10 minutes; 8,000 feet, add 15 minutes; 10,000 feet, add 20 minutes.

¼ CUP: 18 cal., 1g fat (0 sat. fat), 0 chol., 35mg sod., 2g carb. (1g sugars, 1g fiber), 1g pro. DIABETIC EXCHANGES: 1 free food.

GARLIC-DILL DEVILED EGGS

In my family, Easter isn't complete without deviled eggs. Fresh dill and garlic perk
up the flavor of these irresistible appetizers you'll want to eat on every occasion.
—Kami Horch, Calais, ME

PREP: 20 MIN. + CHILLING • MAKES: 2 DOZEN

12 hard-boiled large eggs
⅔ cup mayonnaise
4 tsp. dill pickle relish
2 tsp. snipped fresh dill
2 tsp. Dijon mustard
1 tsp. coarsely ground
   pepper
¼ tsp. garlic powder
⅛ tsp. paprika or
   cayenne pepper

1. Cut eggs lengthwise in half. Remove yolks, reserving whites. In a bowl, mash yolks. Stir in all remaining ingredients except paprika. Spoon or pipe yolk mixture into egg whites.

2. Refrigerate, covered, at least 30 minutes before serving. Sprinkle with paprika.

1 FILLED EGG HALF: 81 cal., 7g fat (1g sat. fat), 94mg chol., 81mg sod., 1g carb. (0 sugars, 0 fiber), 3g pro.

BACON CHEDDAR POTATO SKINS

Both crisp and hearty, this restaurant-quality snack is one that my family requests often.

—Trish Perrin, Keizer, OR

TAKES: 30 MIN. • MAKES: 8 SERVINGS

4   **large baking potatoes, baked**
3   **Tbsp. canola oil**
1   **Tbsp. grated Parmesan cheese**
½   **tsp. salt**
¼   **tsp. garlic powder**
¼   **tsp. paprika**
⅛   **tsp. pepper**
8   **bacon strips, cooked and crumbled**
1½   **cups shredded cheddar cheese**
½   **cup sour cream**
4   **green onions, sliced**

1. Preheat oven to 475°. Cut potatoes in half lengthwise; scoop out pulp, leaving a ¼-in. shell (save pulp for another use). Place potato skins on a greased baking sheet.

2. Combine oil with next 5 ingredients; brush over both sides of the potato skins.

3. Bake until crisp, about 7 minutes on each side. Sprinkle bacon and cheddar cheese inside skins. Bake until cheese is melted, about 2 minutes longer. Top with sour cream and onions. Serve immediately.

1 POTATO SKIN: 350 cal., 19g fat (7g sat. fat), 33mg chol., 460mg sod., 34g carb. (2g sugars, 4g fiber), 12g pro.

FROM GRANDMA'S KITCHEN: In Europe, Parmigiano-Reggiano and Parmesan are considered the same cheese. But in the U.S., "Parmesan" is a generic term that may not come from Italy's Parmigiano-Reggiano region. If you can, use the authentic Italian cheese—its full flavor lets you use a little less than the 1 cup called for to get the same cheesy richness, resulting in less fat and fewer calories.

CHICKEN TAMALES

I love making tamales from scratch for my husband and our four children. Look for dried corn husks and masa harina in the international foods aisle at the grocery store.
—*Cindy Pruitt, Grove, OK*

PREP: 2½ HOURS + SOAKING • COOK: 50 MIN. • MAKES: 20 TAMALES

24 dried corn husks
1 broiler/fryer chicken (3 to 4 lbs.), cut up
1 medium onion, quartered
2 tsp. salt
1 garlic clove, crushed
3 qt. water

DOUGH
1 cup shortening
3 cups masa harina

FILLING
6 Tbsp. canola oil
6 Tbsp. all-purpose flour
¾ cup chili powder
½ tsp. salt
¼ tsp. garlic powder
¼ tsp. pepper
2 cans (2¼ oz. each) sliced ripe olives, drained
Hot water

1. Cover corn husks with cold water; soak until softened, at least 2 hours.

2. Place chicken, onion, salt and garlic in a 6-qt. stockpot. Add water; bring to a boil. Reduce heat; simmer, covered, until chicken is tender, 45-60 minutes. Remove chicken from broth. When cool enough to handle, remove bones and skin; discard. Shred chicken. Strain cooking juices; skim fat. Reserve 6 cups stock.

3. For dough, beat shortening until light and fluffy, about 1 minute. Beat in small amounts of masa harina alternately with small amounts of the reserved stock, using no more than 2 cups stock. Drop a small amount of dough into a cup of cold water; the dough should float. If it doesn't, continue beating, rechecking every 1-2 minutes.

4. For filling, heat oil in a Dutch oven; stir in flour until blended. Cook and stir over medium heat until mixture is lightly browned, 7-9 minutes. Stir in the seasonings, chicken and the remaining stock; bring to a boil. Reduce heat; simmer, uncovered, stirring occasionally, until thickened, about 45 minutes.

5. Drain corn husks and pat dry. To prevent husks from drying out, cover with a damp towel until ready to use. Tear 4 husks to make 20 strips for tying tamales. On the wide end of each remaining husk, spread 3 Tbsp. dough to within ½ in. of side edges; top each with 2 Tbsp. chicken filling and 2 tsp. olives. Fold long sides of husk over filling, overlapping slightly. Fold over the narrow end of husk; tie with a strip of husk to secure.

6. Place a large steamer basket in the stockpot over water; place tamales upright in basket. Bring water to a boil; steam, covered, adding hot water as needed, until dough peels away from husk, about 45 minutes.

2 TAMALES: 564 cal., 35g fat (7g sat. fat), 44mg chol., 835mg sod., 43g carb. (2g sugars, 7g fiber), 20g pro.

FROM GRANDMA'S KITCHEN: Tamales are most commonly associated with Mexican cuisine, but you can find them all over Latin America. It's traditional for friends and family to come together for a *tamalada*—a tamale-making party—to help assemble the savory treats.

MUSTARD PRETZEL NUGGETS

This quick and fun snack is similar to the mustard pretzels you can buy at the store, but you can make it for a fraction of the price. It's a killer recipe for all kinds of parties and gatherings.
—*Sarah Mathews, Ava, MO*

PREP: 10 MIN. • BAKE: 15 MIN. + COOLING • MAKES: 6 CUPS

6 cups sourdough pretzel nuggets
⅓ cup prepared mustard
2 Tbsp. honey
1 Tbsp. cider vinegar
½ tsp. onion powder
½ tsp. garlic powder
½ tsp. ground mustard

1. Preheat oven to 350°. Place pretzels in a bowl. In another bowl, mix the remaining ingredients. Drizzle over pretzels; toss to coat.

2. Spread mixture in a greased 15x10-in. pan. Bake until lightly browned and crisp, 15-20 minutes, stirring every 5 minutes. Cool completely in pan on a wire rack. Store in an airtight container.

¾ CUP: 204 cal., 0 fat (0 sat. fat), 0 chol., 411mg sod., 43g carb. (6g sugars, 2g fiber), 5g pro.

PINA COLADA FRUIT DIP

A taste of the tropics is always welcome and refreshing. This cool and creamy dip works as an appetizer, but is also terrific to munch on after dinner when you need a light and sweet dessert.
—*Shelly Bevington, Hermiston, OR*

TAKES: 15 MIN. • MAKES: 10 SERVINGS (2½ CUPS)

1 pkg. (8 oz.) cream cheese, softened
1 jar (7 oz.) marshmallow creme
1 can (8 oz.) crushed pineapple, drained
½ cup sweetened shredded coconut
  Assorted fresh fruit or cubed pound cake

In a small bowl, beat cream cheese and marshmallow creme until fluffy. Fold in pineapple and coconut. Cover and chill until serving. Serve with fruit, pound cake or both.

¼ CUP: 186 cal., 10g fat (6g sat. fat), 25mg chol., 96mg sod., 24g carb. (19g sugars, 0 fiber), 2g pro.

PRALINE-TOPPED
APPLE BREAD, PAGE 84

GRANDMA'S FAVORITE

BREADS, BISCUITS & MORE

Dinner rolls and doughnuts, sweet muffins and
herb loaves—let the aroma of these freshly baked
delights usher in heartwarming memories
of Grandma's kitchen and the amazing,
magic treats she pulled from her oven.

YORKSHIRE PUDDING WITH BACON & SAGE

These savory bites are a nice change from traditional dinner rolls. The flavorful popovers are tastefully topped with crumbled bacon and fresh sage.
—*Melissa Jelinek, Apple Valley, MN*

PREP: 15 MIN. • BAKE: 20 MIN. • MAKES: 1 DOZEN

- 5 bacon strips, chopped
- 2 Tbsp. butter, melted
- 1½ cups all-purpose flour
- 3 Tbsp. minced fresh sage, divided
- ½ tsp. salt
- 1½ cups 2% milk
- 3 large eggs, room temperature

1. Preheat oven to 450°. In a large skillet, cook bacon over medium heat until crisp. Remove to paper towels with a slotted spoon; drain, reserving drippings.

2. Transfer drippings to a measuring cup; add enough melted butter to measure ¼ cup. Pour into 12 ungreased muffin cups. Place in oven until hot.

3. Meanwhile, in a small bowl, combine flour, 2 Tbsp. sage and the salt; beat in milk and eggs until smooth. Fold in two-thirds of the bacon. Divide batter among prepared muffin cups.

4. Bake for 10 minutes. Reduce heat to 350° (do not open oven door). Bake 10-12 minutes longer or until popovers are puffed and golden brown. Sprinkle with remaining bacon and 1 Tbsp. sage.

1 PUDDING: 150 cal., 8g fat (3g sat. fat), 67mg chol., 224mg sod., 14g carb. (2g sugars, 0 fiber), 5g pro.

HONEY CORNBREAD

Serving this moist cornbread to family and guests is a pleasure. Honey gives the bread a slightly sweet taste, and most people find it difficult to eat just one piece.
—*Adeline Piscitelli, Sayreville, NJ*

TAKES: 30 MIN. • MAKES: 9 SERVINGS

- 1 cup all-purpose flour
- 1 cup yellow cornmeal
- ¼ cup sugar
- 3 tsp. baking powder
- ½ tsp. salt
- 2 large eggs, room temperature
- 1 cup heavy whipping cream
- ¼ cup canola oil
- ¼ cup honey

1. Preheat oven to 400°. Combine the flour, cornmeal, sugar, baking powder and salt. In a small bowl, beat the eggs. Add cream, oil and honey; beat well. Stir into dry ingredients just until moistened. Pour into a greased 9-in. square baking pan.

2. Bake for 20-25 minutes or until a toothpick inserted in the center comes out clean. Serve warm.

1 PIECE: 318 cal., 17g fat (7g sat. fat), 83mg chol., 290mg sod., 37g carb. (14g sugars, 2g fiber), 5g pro.

YORKSHIRE PUDDING
WITH BACON & SAGE

DELICIOUS ALMOND BRAIDS

Similar to an almond crescent, this coffee cake is light and flaky with a rich almond center. It's versatile, so you can serve it for dessert, breakfast or brunch. It tastes as if it came from a high-end bakery, but packaged puff pastry dough makes it easy.
—*Gina Idone, Staten Island, NY*

PREP: 25 MIN. • **BAKE:** 30 MIN. + COOLING
MAKES: 2 BRAIDS (6 SERVINGS EACH)

1   **pkg. (7 oz.) almond paste**
½   **cup butter**
½   **cup sugar**
1   **large egg,**
    room temperature
2   **Tbsp. all-purpose flour**
1   **pkg. (17.3 oz.) frozen**
    puff pastry, thawed

GLAZE
¾   **cup plus 1 Tbsp.**
    confectioners' sugar
2   **Tbsp. 2% milk**
½   **tsp. almond extract**
¼   **cup sliced almonds,**
    toasted

1. Preheat oven to 375°. Place the almond paste, butter and sugar in a food processor; cover and pulse until chopped. Add egg and flour; process until smooth.

2. Place puff pastry sheets onto a greased baking sheet. Spread half the filling mixture down the center third of 1 pastry sheet. On each side, cut 8 strips about 3½ in. into the center. Starting at 1 end, fold alternating strips at an angle across filling. Pinch ends to seal. Repeat with the remaining pastry and filling.

3. Bake until golden brown, 30-35 minutes. Remove to a wire rack to cool completely.

4. For the glaze, combine the confectioners' sugar, milk and almond extract. Drizzle over braids; sprinkle with almonds. Cut into slices to serve.

1 SERVING: 430 cal., 25g fat (8g sat. fat), 38mg chol., 197mg sod., 49g carb. (22g sugars, 4g fiber), 6g pro.

PASSOVER POPOVERS

Popovers have an important role at the Passover table as a substitute
for bread. When puffed and golden brown, they're ready to share.
—*Gloria Mezikofsky, Wakefield, MA*

PREP: 25 MIN. • BAKE: 20 MIN. + STANDING • MAKES: 1 DOZEN

1   cup water
½   cup safflower oil
⅛ to ¼ tsp. salt
1   cup matzo cake meal
7   large eggs,
    room temperature

1. Preheat oven to 450°. Generously grease 12 muffin cups. In a large saucepan, bring water, oil and salt to a rolling boil. Add cake meal all at once and beat until blended. Remove from heat; let stand 5 minutes.

2. Transfer mixture to a blender. Add 2 eggs; process, covered, until blended. Continue adding 1 egg at a time and processing until incorporated. Process until mixture is smooth, about 2 minutes longer.

3. Fill prepared muffin cups three-fourths full. Bake until puffed, very firm and golden brown, 18-22 minutes. Turn off oven (do not open oven door); leave popovers in oven 10 minutes. Immediately remove popovers from pan to a wire rack. Serve hot.

NOTE: This recipe was tested with Manischewitz cake meal. Look for it in the baking aisle or kosher foods section.

1 POPOVER: 174 cal., 12g fat (2g sat. fat), 109mg chol., 66mg sod., 11g carb. (0 sugars, 0 fiber), 5g pro.

NO-FUSS ROLLS

With only four ingredients, these delicious rolls are ready in no time.
They're fantastic with herb butter or jam.
—*Glenda Trail, Manchester, TN*

TAKES: 25 MIN. • MAKES: 6 ROLLS

1   cup self-rising flour
½   cup 2% milk
2   Tbsp. mayonnaise
½   tsp. sugar

Preheat oven to 450°. In a small bowl, combine all ingredients. Spoon batter into 6 muffin cups coated with cooking spray. Bake until a toothpick comes out clean, 12-14 minutes. Cool for 5 minutes before removing from pan to a wire rack. Serve warm.

1 ROLL: 111 cal., 4g fat (1g sat. fat), 3mg chol., 275mg sod., 16g carb. (1g sugars, 0 fiber), 3g pro. DIABETIC EXCHANGES: 1 starch, 1 fat.

FROM GRANDMA'S KITCHEN: As a substitute for 1 cup of self-rising flour, place 1½ tsp. baking powder and ½ tsp. salt in a measuring cup. Add all-purpose flour to measure 1 cup.

SKILLET
HERB BREAD

SKILLET HERB BREAD

We had a lot of family get-togethers while I was growing up. My grandmother, aunts and mom were all good cooks, and each had her own specialty when it came to bread. Mom's was my favorite—she created this recipe more than 40 years ago. The flavors call to mind the taste of cornbread stuffing!
—*Shirley Smith, Yorba Linda, CA*

PREP: 10 MIN. • BAKE: 35 MIN. • MAKES: 10 SERVINGS

1½ cups all-purpose flour
2 Tbsp. sugar
4 tsp. baking powder
1½ tsp. salt
1 tsp. rubbed sage
1 tsp. dried thyme
1½ cups yellow cornmeal
1½ cups chopped celery
1 cup chopped onion
1 jar (2 oz.) chopped pimientos, drained
3 large eggs, room temperature, beaten
1½ cups fat-free milk
⅓ cup vegetable oil

1. Preheat oven to 400°. In a large bowl, combine the flour, sugar, baking powder, salt, sage and thyme. Combine cornmeal, celery, onion and pimientos; add to the dry ingredients and mix well. Add eggs, milk and oil; stir just until moistened.

2. Pour into a greased 10- or 11-in. ovenproof skillet. Bake for 35-45 minutes or until bread tests done. Serve warm.

1 PIECE: 275 cal., 9g fat (2g sat. fat), 57mg chol., 598mg sod., 40g carb. (6g sugars, 2g fiber), 7g pro.

WELSH CAKES

My grandfather was Welsh and liked to make Welsh cakes on the griddle. Our whole family loves them. Sometimes he would make them for Christmas and wrap them in little bundles for each family. It's a very special memory for us.
—*Wendy Masters, East Garafraxa, ON*

PREP: 20 MIN. • COOK: 5 MIN./BATCH • MAKES: ABOUT 4½ DOZEN

3½ cups all-purpose flour
1 cup sugar
1½ tsp. baking powder
1 tsp. salt
½ tsp. baking soda
1 cup cold butter, cubed
¾ cup 2% milk
1 large egg, beaten
1¼ cups dried currants or raisins

1. In a large bowl, whisk flour, sugar, baking powder, salt and baking soda. Cut in butter until the mixture resembles coarse crumbs. Add milk and egg; stir just until moistened. Fold in the currants.

2. Pat or roll dough to ¼-in. thickness; cut with a floured 2-in. biscuit cutter. Preheat griddle over medium heat. In batches, place cakes on griddle; cook until tops puff and bottoms are golden brown, 1-2 minutes. Turn; cook until second side is golden brown. Cool on wire racks.

1 CAKE: 87 cal., 4g fat (2g sat. fat), 13mg chol., 99mg sod., 13g carb. (6g sugars, 0 fiber), 1g pro.

SWEET ITALIAN HOLIDAY BREAD

This is authentic ciambellotto, a sweet loaf my great-grandmother used to bake in Italy.
I still use her traditional recipe—the only update I made was for modern appliances.
—*Denise Perrin, Vancouver, WA*

PREP: 15 MIN. • BAKE: 45 MIN. • MAKES: 1 LOAF (20 SLICES)

4 **cups all-purpose flour**
1 **cup sugar**
2 **Tbsp. grated orange zest**
3 **tsp. baking powder**
3 **large eggs,**
   room temperature
½ **cup 2% milk**
½ **cup olive oil**
1 **large egg yolk,**
   lightly beaten
1 **Tbsp. coarse sugar**

1. Preheat oven to 350°. In a large bowl, whisk flour, sugar, orange zest and baking powder. In another bowl, whisk eggs, milk and oil until blended. Add to flour mixture; stir just until moistened.

2. Shape dough into a 6-in. round loaf on a greased baking sheet. Brush top with egg yolk; sprinkle with coarse sugar. Bake until a toothpick inserted in center comes out clean, 45-50 minutes. Cover loosely with foil during the last 10 minutes if needed to prevent overbrowning. Remove from pan to a wire rack to cool slightly; serve warm.

1 SLICE: 197 cal., 7g fat (1g sat. fat), 38mg chol., 87mg sod., 30g carb. (11g sugars, 1g fiber), 4g pro.

HERB QUICK BREAD

This simple bread is especially good with soups and stews, but slices are also tasty
alongside fresh green salads. The herbs make it a flavorful treat any time of the year.
—*Donna Roberts, Manhattan, KS*

PREP: 15 MIN. • BAKE: 40 MIN. + COOLING • MAKES: 1 LOAF (16 PIECES)

3 **cups all-purpose flour**
3 **Tbsp. sugar**
1 **Tbsp. baking powder**
3 **tsp. caraway seeds**
½ **tsp. salt**
½ **tsp. ground nutmeg**
½ **tsp. dried thyme**
1 **large egg,**
   room temperature
1 **cup fat-free milk**
⅓ **cup canola oil**

1. Preheat oven to 350°. In a large bowl, whisk together the first 7 ingredients. In another bowl, whisk together the egg, milk and oil. Add to the flour mixture; stir just until moistened.

2. Transfer batter to a 9x5-in. loaf pan coated with cooking spray. Bake until a toothpick inserted in the center comes out clean, 40-50 minutes. Cool in pan 10 minutes before removing to a wire rack to cool completely.

1 PIECE: 147 cal., 5g fat (1g sat. fat), 12mg chol., 160mg sod., 21g carb. (3g sugars, 1g fiber), 3g pro. DIABETIC EXCHANGES: 1½ starch, 1 fat.

FROM GRANDMA'S KITCHEN: For skillet bread, prepare batter as directed. Spoon batter into a greased 8-in. cast-iron skillet and bake at 350° until a toothpick inserted in center comes out clean, 45-50 minutes. For muffins, prepare batter as directed. Spoon into 9 greased muffin tins and bake at 350° until a toothpick inserted in center comes out clean, 25-30 minutes.

JELLY DOUGHNUTS

There's no need to run to the bakery for delicious jelly doughnuts! These sweet treats are lighter than air. I've been fixing them for my family for many years. They disappear almost as fast as I make them.

—*Kathy Westendorf, Westgate, IA*

PREP: 30 MIN. + RISING • COOK: 10 MIN. • MAKES: 16 DOUGHNUTS

2 pkg. (¼ oz. each) active dry yeast	3 large egg yolks, room temperature
½ cup warm water (110° to 115°)	1 tsp. salt
½ cup warm 2% milk (110° to 115°)	3 to 3¾ cups all-purpose flour
⅓ cup butter, softened	3 Tbsp. jelly or jam
1⅓ cups sugar, divided	1 large egg white, lightly beaten
	Oil for deep-fat frying

1. In a small bowl, dissolve yeast in warm water. In a large bowl, combine milk, butter, ⅓ cup sugar, egg yolks, salt, the yeast mixture and 3 cups flour; beat until smooth. Stir in enough remaining flour to form a soft dough (do not knead).

2. Place in a greased bowl, turning once to grease top. Cover and let rise in a warm place until doubled, about 45 minutes.

3. Punch down dough. Turn onto a lightly floured surface; knead about 10 times. Divide dough in half.

4. Roll each portion to ¼-in. thickness; cut with a floured 2½-in. round cutter. Place about ½ tsp. jelly in the center of half the circles; brush edges with egg white. Top with remaining circles; press edges to seal tightly.

5. Place on greased baking sheet. Cover and let rise until doubled, about 45 minutes.

6. In an electric skillet or deep-fat fryer, heat oil to 375°. Fry doughnuts, a few at a time, 1-2 minutes on each side or until golden brown. Drain on paper towels. Roll warm doughnuts in remaining 1 cup sugar.

1 DOUGHNUT: 270 cal., 12g fat (3g sat. fat), 45mg chol., 188mg sod., 38g carb. (19g sugars, 1g fiber), 4g pro.

PRALINE-TOPPED APPLE BREAD

Apples and candied pecans make this bread so much better
than the usual coffee cakes you see at brunches.

—Sonja Blow, Nixa, MO

PREP: 30 MIN. • **BAKE:** 50 MIN. + COOLING • **MAKES:** 1 LOAF (16 SLICES)

2 cups all-purpose flour
2 tsp. baking powder
½ tsp. baking soda
½ tsp. salt
1 cup sugar
1 cup sour cream
2 large eggs,
　room temperature
3 tsp. vanilla extract
1½ cups chopped peeled
　Granny Smith apples
1¼ cups chopped pecans,
　toasted, divided
½ cup butter, cubed
½ cup packed brown sugar

1. Preheat oven to 350°. In a large bowl, mix flour, baking powder, baking soda and salt. In another bowl, beat sugar, sour cream, eggs and vanilla until well blended. Stir into flour mixture just until moistened. Fold in apples and 1 cup pecans.

2. Transfer to a greased 9x5-in. loaf pan. Bake until a toothpick inserted in center comes out clean, 50-55 minutes. Cool in pan 10 minutes. Remove to a wire rack to cool completely.

3. In a small saucepan, combine butter and brown sugar. Bring to a boil, stirring constantly to dissolve sugar; boil 1 minute. Working quickly, pour over bread. Sprinkle with remaining ¼ cup pecans; let stand until set.

NOTE: To toast nuts, bake in a shallow pan in a 350° oven 5-10 minutes or cook in a skillet over low heat until lightly browned, stirring occasionally.

1 PIECE: 288 cal., 16g fat (6g sat. fat), 42mg chol., 235mg sod., 34g carb. (21g sugars, 1g fiber), 4g pro.

GRANDMA'S SECRET

For a southern spin on this bread, you can make it with peaches instead of apples. Peaches and praline make a delicious combination, especially in summer when peaches are ripe.

ONION & GARLIC SODA BREAD

This is one of my favorite recipes for soda bread. It's versatile, so you can make endless sweet or savory variations. I serve it as an appetizer, sliced alongside assorted spreads and cheeses.
—*Theresa Vujosevic, Hamburg, NJ*

PREP: 20 MIN. • **BAKE:** 35 MIN. + COOLING • **MAKES:** 1 LOAF (12 PIECES)

1 Tbsp. olive oil	1 tsp. baking soda
1 medium onion, chopped	¼ cup cold butter, cubed
5 garlic cloves, minced	1 large egg,
4 cups all-purpose flour	room temperature
1 tsp. salt	1½ cups buttermilk

1. Preheat oven to 425°. In a small skillet, heat oil over medium-high heat. Add onion; cook and stir until light golden brown, 3-5 minutes. Add garlic; cook and stir 30 seconds longer. Cool.

2. In a large bowl, whisk flour, salt and baking soda. Cut in butter until mixture resembles coarse crumbs. Stir in the cooled onion mixture, then make a well in center.

3. In a small bowl, whisk egg and buttermilk; pour into well. Using a wooden spoon, mix dough until it is too stiff to stir. Turn dough onto a lightly floured surface; knead gently 10 times. Shape into a round loaf.

4. Transfer loaf to a large greased cast-iron skillet or baking sheet. Using a sharp knife, cut a shallow "X" on the top of the loaf. Bake until golden brown, 35-40 minutes.

5. Remove from pan to a wire rack; serve warm.

1 PIECE: 219 cal., 6g fat (3g sat. fat), 27mg chol., 398mg sod., 35g carb. (2g sugars, 1g fiber), 6g pro.

GRANDMA'S SWEET POTATO BISCUITS

The recipe for these mild biscuits was my grandmother's. They're
a family favorite that we always serve at holidays.

—*Nancy Daugherty, Cortland, OH*

TAKES: 30 MIN. • **MAKES:** 1½ DOZEN

2½ cups all-purpose flour
1 Tbsp. baking powder
1 tsp. salt
⅓ cup shortening
1 can (15¾ oz.)
   sweet potatoes, drained
¾ cup 2% milk

1. Preheat oven to 425°. In a large bowl, combine flour, baking powder and salt. Cut in shortening until mixture resembles coarse crumbs. In another bowl, mash the sweet potatoes and milk. Add to the crumb mixture just until combined.

2. Turn dough onto a floured surface; knead 8-10 times. Roll out to ½-in. thickness; cut with a 2½-in. biscuit cutter. Place on ungreased baking sheets.

3. Bake until golden brown, 8-10 minutes. Remove to wire racks. Serve warm.

1 BISCUIT: 124 cal., 4g fat (1g sat. fat), 1mg chol., 214mg sod., 19g carb. (4g sugars, 1g fiber), 2g pro.

WILD BLUEBERRY MUFFINS

Nothing is better than a warm blueberry muffin in the morning, and these muffins are
the best I have ever made. The wild blueberries make them extra special.

—*Dewey Grindle, Blue Hill, ME*

PREP: 15 MIN. • **BAKE:** 20 MIN. • **MAKES:** 1 DOZEN

¼ cup butter, softened
⅓ cup sugar
1 large egg,
   room temperature
2⅓ cups all-purpose flour
4 tsp. baking powder
½ tsp. salt
1 cup 2% milk
1 tsp. vanilla extract
1½ cups fresh or frozen
   wild blueberries or 1 can
   (15 oz.) water-packed
   wild blueberries,
   well drained

STREUSEL TOPPING

½ cup sugar
⅓ cup all-purpose flour
½ tsp. ground cinnamon
¼ cup cold butter, cubed

1. Preheat oven to 375°. In a bowl, cream butter and sugar. Add egg; mix well. Combine dry ingredients; add to creamed mixture alternately with milk. Stir in vanilla. Gently fold in blueberries. Fill greased or paper-lined muffin cups two-thirds full.

2. For streusel topping, in a small bowl, combine sugar, flour and cinnamon; cut in the butter until crumbly. Sprinkle over muffins. Bake for 20-25 minutes.

1 MUFFIN: 252 cal., 9g fat (5g sat. fat), 41mg chol., 325mg sod., 39g carb. (17g sugars, 1g fiber), 4g pro.

"I loved that these were so light and fluffy, not too sweet, and we could taste the blueberries. Excellent recipe—I'm freezing some to have homemade goodies on hand when friends drop in!"

—TAMARACHRONISTER, TASTEOFHOME.COM

RUSTIC RYE BREAD

This gorgeous rye bread has just a touch of sweetness and the perfect amount of caraway seeds. With a crusty top and firm texture, it holds up well for sandwiches.
—*Holly Wade, Harrisonburg, VA*

PREP: 25 MIN. + RISING • **BAKE:** 30 MIN. • **MAKES:** 2 LOAVES (12 PIECES EACH)

1 pkg. (¼ oz.) active dry yeast
1¾ cups warm water (110° to 115°), divided
¼ cup packed brown sugar
¼ cup light molasses
3 Tbsp. caraway seeds
2 Tbsp. canola oil
1 Tbsp. salt
1¾ cups rye flour
¾ cup whole wheat flour
2½ to 3 cups all-purpose flour

GRANDMA'S SECRET
For a caraway topping, before baking brush loaves with an egg white beaten lightly with water; sprinkle with caraway seeds.

1. In a large bowl, dissolve yeast in ¼ cup warm water. Stir in brown sugar, molasses, caraway seeds, oil, salt and remaining water. Add rye flour, whole wheat flour and 1 cup all-purpose flour; beat on medium speed until smooth. Stir in enough remaining all-purpose flour to form a firm dough.

2. Turn dough onto a floured surface; knead until smooth and elastic, 6-8 minutes. Place in a greased bowl, turning once to grease the top. Cover and let rise in a warm place until doubled, about 1½ hours.

3. Punch down dough. Turn onto a lightly floured surface; divide in half. Shape each into a round loaf; place on a baking sheet coated with cooking spray. Cover with kitchen towels; let rise in a warm place until almost doubled, about 1½ hours. Preheat oven to 350°.

4. Bake until golden brown, 30-35 minutes. Remove from pan to wire racks to cool.

1 PIECE: 118 cal., 2g fat (0 sat. fat), 0 chol., 298mg sod., 24g carb. (5g sugars, 2g fiber), 3g pro.

GRANDMA'S ONION SQUARES

My grandma brought this recipe with her when she emigrated from
Italy as a young wife and mother. It is still a family favorite.
—*Janet Eddy, Stockton, CA*

PREP: 40 MIN. • BAKE: 35 MIN. • MAKES: 9 SERVINGS

2 Tbsp. olive oil
2 cups sliced onions
1 tsp. salt, divided
¼ tsp. pepper
2 cups all-purpose flour
3 tsp. baking powder
5 Tbsp. shortening
⅔ cup 2% milk
1 large egg,
   room temperature
¾ cup sour cream

1. Preheat oven to 400°. In a large skillet, heat oil over medium heat. Add onions; cook and stir until softened, 8-10 minutes. Reduce heat to medium-low; cook until deep golden brown, 30-40 minutes, stirring occasionally. Stir in ½ tsp. salt and the pepper.

2. In a large bowl, combine flour, baking powder and remaining ½ tsp. salt. Cut in shortening until mixture resembles coarse crumbs. Stir in milk just until moistened. Press into a greased 9-in. square baking pan; top with onions.

3. Combine egg and sour cream; spread over onion layer. Bake until golden brown, 35-40 minutes. Cut into squares. Serve warm.

1 PIECE: 256 cal., 15g fat (5g sat. fat), 27mg chol., 447mg sod., 25g carb. (3g sugars, 1g fiber), 5g pro.

LEMON POUND CAKE MUFFINS

I make these lemony muffins for all kinds of occasions. My family is always asking for them.
They have a rich cakelike taste and a sweet, tangy flavor. All I can say is: They're so unbelievably good!
—*Lola Baxter, Winnebago, MN*

PREP: 15 MIN. • BAKE: 20 MIN. • MAKES: 1 DOZEN

½ cup butter, softened
1 cup sugar
2 large eggs,
   room temperature
½ cup sour cream
1 tsp. vanilla extract
½ tsp. lemon extract
1¾ cups all-purpose flour
½ tsp. salt
¼ tsp. baking soda

GLAZE
2 cups confectioners' sugar
3 Tbsp. lemon juice

1. In a large bowl, cream the butter and sugar until light and fluffy, 5-7 minutes. Add eggs, 1 at a time, beating well after each addition. Beat in the sour cream and extracts. Combine the flour, salt and baking soda; add to creamed mixture just until moistened.

2. Fill 12 greased or paper-lined muffin cups three-fourths full. Bake at 400° until a toothpick inserted in the center comes out clean, 18-20 minutes. Cool for 5 minutes before removing from pan to a wire rack.

3. Combine glaze ingredients; drizzle over muffins. Serve warm.

1 MUFFIN: 311 cal., 10g fat (6g sat. fat), 63mg chol., 218mg sod., 51g carb. (36g sugars, 1g fiber), 3g pro.

CHOCOLATE CHIP CARAMEL ROLLS

As a teenager, I keep active with sports and friends, but baking is my favorite hobby. My five older brothers eat these delicious breakfast rolls right out of the oven!

—*Julia Holm, Northfield, MN*

PREP: 40 MIN. + RISING • BAKE: 30 MIN. • MAKES: 1 DOZEN

1 pkg. (¼ oz.) active dry yeast
¾ cup warm water (110° to 115°)
¾ cup warm 2% milk (110° to 115°)
3 Tbsp. canola oil
¼ cup sugar
1½ tsp. salt
3¾ to 4½ cups all-purpose flour
¾ cup miniature semisweet chocolate chips

FILLING
¼ cup butter, softened
⅓ cup sugar
2 Tbsp. ground cinnamon
1 cup miniature semisweet chocolate chips

SYRUP
1 cup packed brown sugar
¾ cup heavy whipping cream

1. In a large bowl, dissolve yeast in warm water. Add the milk, oil, sugar, salt and 3 cups flour; beat on medium speed for 3 minutes. Stir in enough remaining flour to form a firm dough.

2. Turn onto a floured surface; knead in chocolate chips until dough is smooth and elastic, 6-8 minutes. Place in a greased bowl, turning once to grease top. Cover and let rise in a warm place until doubled, about 1 hour.

3. Punch down dough. Turn onto a lightly floured surface. Roll into an 18x12-in. rectangle. Spread butter over dough to within ½ in. of edges. Combine sugar and cinnamon; sprinkle over butter. Sprinkle with chocolate chips; gently press into dough. Roll up jelly-roll style, starting with a long side; pinch seam to seal. Cut into 12 slices.

4. In a small bowl, combine brown sugar and cream; pour into a greased 13x9-in. baking dish. Arrange rolls cut side up over the syrup. Cover and let rise until doubled, about 50 minutes.

5. Bake at 375° for 30-35 minutes or until golden brown. Cool for 10 minutes before removing to a serving platter. Serve warm.

1 ROLL: 499 cal., 21g fat (11g sat. fat), 33mg chol., 358mg sod., 76g carb. (43g sugars, 3g fiber), 6g pro.

LEFSE

Lefse is a Scandinavian flatbread made with potatoes. We traditionally make
these delicious breads during the holiday season. Serve them topped with butter
and a sprinkle of sugar or jelly, then roll them up. It's hard to eat just one.
—*Donna Goutermont, Sequim, WA*

PREP: 1 HOUR • COOK: 5 MIN./BATCH • MAKES: 12 SERVINGS

2 lbs. potatoes,
    peeled and cubed
⅓ cup heavy
    whipping cream, warmed
¼ cup shortening or butter,
    softened
1 tsp. sugar
¾ tsp. salt
2 cups all-purpose flour

1. Place potatoes in a large saucepan; add water to cover. Bring to
a boil. Reduce heat; simmer, covered, until tender, 10-12 minutes.
Drain. Press through a potato ricer or strainer into a large bowl.
Stir in cream, shortening, sugar and salt. Cool completely.

2. Preheat griddle over medium-high heat. Stir flour into potato
mixture. Turn onto a lightly floured surface; knead 6-8 times
or until smooth and combined. Divide into 12 portions. Roll each
portion between 2 sheets of waxed paper into an 8-in. circle.

3. Place on griddle; cook until lightly browned, 2-3 minutes on
each side. Remove to a platter; cover loosely with a kitchen towel.
Repeat with remaining portions. When each lefse is cool, stack
them between pieces of waxed paper or paper towels and
store in an airtight container.

1 PIECE: 180 cal., 7g fat (3g sat. fat), 8mg chol., 151mg sod.,
27g carb. (1g sugars, 1g fiber), 3g pro.

MAPLE BACON FRENCH TOAST BAKE

Our family loves Sunday brunch. Each season I try to bring a little different flavor
to the table. This French toast bake reminds us of fall. Whole or 2% milk is best,
but I use regular almond milk because I can't have dairy and it works, too!
—*Peggie Brott, Milford, KS*

PREP: 35 MIN. + CHILLING • BAKE: 50 MIN. • MAKES: 12 SERVINGS

8 cups cubed bread
8 large eggs
2 cups 2% milk
½ cup packed brown sugar
⅓ cup maple syrup
½ tsp. ground cinnamon
1 lb. bacon strips,
    cooked and crumbled

1. Place bread in a greased 13x9-in. baking dish. In a large bowl,
whisk eggs, milk, brown sugar, syrup and cinnamon. Pour over
the bread. Sprinkle with bacon. Refrigerate, covered, 4 hours
or overnight.

2. Remove casserole from the refrigerator 30 minutes before
baking. Preheat oven to 350°. Bake, uncovered, until a knife
inserted in center comes out clean, 50-60 minutes. Let stand
5-10 minutes before serving.

1 PIECE: 256 cal., 10g fat (3g sat. fat), 141mg chol., 426mg sod.,
29g carb. (18g sugars, 1g fiber), 12g pro.

LEFSE

PECAN COFFEE CAKE MUFFINS

These moist, cakelike muffins with heaps of crumb topping are to die for! They're wonderful for company, entertaining, brunch or anytime.
—*Shannon Saltsman, Olmsted Falls, OH*

PREP: 25 MIN. • BAKE: 20 MIN. • MAKES: 15 MUFFINS

STREUSEL
- ½ cup butter, softened
- 1 cup packed brown sugar
- 1 cup all-purpose flour
- 1 tsp. ground cinnamon
- ½ cup chopped pecans

BATTER
- 1 cup butter, softened
- ¾ cup packed brown sugar
- ½ cup sugar
- 2 large eggs, room temperature
- ⅓ cup half-and-half cream
- 1½ tsp. vanilla extract
- 2 cups all-purpose flour
- 2 tsp. baking powder
- ½ tsp. salt
- Confectioners' sugar, optional

1. Preheat oven to 350°. For the streusel, in a small bowl, combine the butter, brown sugar, flour and cinnamon until crumbly. Stir in pecans; set aside.

2. In a large bowl, cream butter and sugars until light and fluffy, 5-7 minutes. Add eggs, 1 at a time, beating well after each addition. Beat in cream and vanilla. Combine the flour, baking powder and salt; add to creamed mixture just until moistened.

3. Fill greased or paper-lined muffin cups one-fourth full. Drop 1 Tbsp. streusel into the center of each muffin cup; cover with batter. Sprinkle tops with remaining streusel.

4. Bake until a toothpick inserted in muffin comes out clean, 20-22 minutes. Cool in pan 5 minutes, then remove to wire racks to cool completely. Dust with confectioners' sugar. Serve warm.

1 MUFFIN: 420 cal., 22g fat (12g sat. fat), 79mg chol., 284mg sod., 52g carb. (32g sugars, 1g fiber), 4g pro.

WHOLE WHEAT BREAD

I'm 12 years old and make this bread with my mother, who got the
recipe from her mother. I usually prepare the dough, and my mom bakes it.
—*Freida Stutman, Fillmore, NY*

PREP: 20 MIN. + RISING • BAKE: 40 MIN. • MAKES: 2 LOAVES (16 PIECES EACH)

1 pkg. (¼ oz.) active
   dry yeast
3 cups warm water
   (110° to 115°), divided
¾ cup canola oil
¼ cup sugar
¼ cup molasses
1 Tbsp. salt
7 to 7½ cups
   all-purpose flour
3 cups whole wheat flour

1. In a large bowl, dissolve yeast in ¾ cup warm water. Add oil, sugar, molasses, salt and the remaining 2¼ cups water. Combine flours; add 4-5 cups flour to mixture. Beat until smooth. Add enough remaining flour to form a firm dough.

2. Turn onto a floured surface; knead until smooth and elastic, 6-8 minutes. Place in a greased bowl, turning once to grease top. Cover and let rise in a warm place until doubled, about 1 hour.

3. Punch down dough. Turn onto a lightly floured surface; divide in half. Shape each portion into a loaf. Place in 2 greased 9x5-in. loaf pans. Cover and let rise until doubled, about 30 minutes.

4. Bake at 350° until golden brown, 40-45 minutes. Remove from pans to cool on wire racks.

1 PIECE: 168 cal., 6g fat (1g sat. fat), 0 chol., 223mg sod., 26g carb. (4g sugars, 2g fiber), 4g pro.

OVEN-FRIED CORNBREAD

Nothing says good southern cooking like a crisp cornbread baked in a cast-iron skillet.
This old family recipe has been passed down to each generation.
—*Emory Doty, Jasper, GA*

PREP: 20 MIN. • BAKE: 15 MIN. • MAKES: 8 SERVINGS

4 Tbsp. canola oil, divided
1½ cups finely ground
   white cornmeal
¼ cup sugar
2 tsp. baking powder
1 tsp. baking soda
1 tsp. salt
2 large eggs,
   room temperature
2 cups buttermilk

1. Place 2 Tbsp. oil in a 10-in. cast-iron skillet; place in oven. Preheat oven to 450°. Whisk together cornmeal, sugar, baking powder, baking soda and salt. In another bowl, whisk together eggs, buttermilk and remaining 2 Tbsp. oil. Add to the cornmeal mixture; stir just until moistened.

2. Carefully remove hot skillet from oven. Add batter; bake until golden brown and a toothpick inserted in center comes out clean, 15-20 minutes. Cut into wedges; serve warm.

1 WEDGE: 238 cal., 9g fat (1g sat. fat), 49mg chol., 709mg sod., 33g carb. (10g sugars, 1g fiber), 6g pro.

GRANDMA'S ROSEMARY DINNER ROLLS

My grandma (I called her Baba) made these in her coal oven. How she regulated the temperature is beyond me! She always made extra rolls for the neighbors to bake in their own ovens. My mom and aunts would deliver the formed rolls at lunchtime.
—*Charlotte Hendershot, Hudson, PA*

PREP: 35 MIN. + RISING • BAKE: 20 MIN. • MAKES: 1 DOZEN

1 pkg. (¼ oz.) active
   dry yeast
¼ cup warm water
   (110° to 115°)
3 cups bread flour
2 Tbsp. sugar
1 Tbsp. minced
   fresh rosemary, divided
¾ tsp. salt
⅔ cup warm 2% milk
   (110° to 115°)
1 large egg,
   room temperature
¼ to ⅓ cup canola oil

EGG WASH
1 large egg yolk
2 Tbsp. 2% milk

GRANDMA'S SECRET

"Punching down" dough sounds violent, but the action isn't an actual fast punch—just press down firmly with your knuckles to remove some of the air.

1. In a small bowl, dissolve yeast in warm water. Place the flour, sugar, 2 tsp. rosemary and salt in a food processor; pulse until blended. Add the warm milk, egg and yeast mixture; cover and pulse 10 times or until almost blended.

2. While processing, gradually add oil just until dough pulls away from sides and begins to form a ball. Process 2 minutes longer to knead dough (dough will be very soft).

3. Transfer dough to a greased bowl, turning once to grease the top. Cover and let rise in a warm place until doubled, about 1 hour.

4. Punch down dough. Turn onto a lightly floured surface; divide and shape into 12 balls. Roll each into a 15-in. rope. Starting at 1 end, loosely wrap dough around itself to form a coil. Tuck end under; pinch to seal.

5. Place 2 in. apart on greased baking sheets. Cover and let rise until doubled, about 30 minutes.

6. For egg wash, in a small bowl, whisk egg yolk and milk; brush over rolls. Sprinkle with remaining 1 tsp. rosemary. Bake at 350° until golden brown, 18-22 minutes. Remove from pans to wire racks; serve warm.

1 ROLL: 194 cal., 6g fat (1g sat. fat), 32mg chol., 163mg sod., 28g carb. (3g sugars, 1g fiber), 6g pro.

GRANDMA'S OATMEAL BREAD

The aroma from this old-fashioned oat bread will draw your
family members to the kitchen so they can sample it fresh from the oven.
—*Marcia Hostetter, Canton, NY*

PREP: 20 MIN. + RISING • BAKE: 30 MIN. • MAKES: 2 LOAVES (8 PIECES EACH)

1½ cups boiling water
1 Tbsp. butter
2 tsp. salt
½ cup sugar
1 cup old-fashioned oats
2 pkg. (¼ oz. each) active
   dry yeast
¾ cup warm water
   (110° to 115°)
¼ cup molasses
¼ cup packed brown sugar
6 to 6½ cups all-purpose
   flour, divided

1. In a small bowl, combine the boiling water, butter, salt and sugar. Stir in oats; cool to lukewarm. In a large bowl, dissolve yeast in warm water. Stir in the molasses, brown sugar and 1 cup flour. Beat until smooth. Stir in oat mixture and enough remaining flour to make a stiff dough.

2. Turn out onto a floured surface; knead until smooth and elastic, 6-8 minutes. Place in a greased bowl, turning once to grease top. Cover and let rise in a warm place until doubled, about 1½ hours.

3. Punch down dough. Turn onto a lightly floured surface; divide in half. Shape each portion into a ball. Cover and let rest for 10 minutes. Shape into loaves. Place in 2 greased 9x5-in. loaf pans. Cover and let rise until nearly doubled, about 1 hour.

4. Bake at 375° for 30-35 minutes (cover loosely with foil if top browns too quickly). Remove from pans to wire racks to cool.

1 PIECE: 247 cal., 2g fat (1g sat. fat), 2mg chol., 307mg sod., 52g carb. (13g sugars, 2g fiber), 6g pro.

GRANDMA'S BISCUITS

Homemade biscuits add a warm and comforting touch to any meal.
My grandmother makes these tender biscuits to go with her seafood chowder.
—*Melissa Obernesser, Oriskany, NY*

TAKES: 25 MIN. • MAKES: 10 BISCUITS

2 cups all-purpose flour
3 tsp. baking powder
1 tsp. salt
⅓ cup shortening
⅔ cup 2% milk
1 large egg, lightly beaten

1. Preheat oven to 450°. In a large bowl, whisk flour, baking powder and salt. Cut in shortening until mixture resembles coarse crumbs. Add milk; stir just until moistened.

2. Turn onto a lightly floured surface; knead gently 8-10 times. Pat dough into a 10x4-in. rectangle. Cut rectangle lengthwise in half; cut crosswise to make 10 squares.

3. Place 1 in. apart on an ungreased baking sheet; brush tops with egg. Bake until golden brown, 8-10 minutes. Serve warm.

1 BISCUIT: 165 cal., 7g fat (2g sat. fat), 20mg chol., 371mg sod., 20g carb. (1g sugars, 1g fiber), 4g pro.

CHERRY-GO-ROUND

This fancy coffee cake is surprisingly easy to prepare.
It makes a delightful gift during the holidays or year-round.
—*Kathy McCreary, Wichita, KS*

PREP: 30 MIN. + CHILLING • BAKE: 20 MIN.
MAKES: 2 COFFEE CAKES (12 PIECES EACH)

1 pkg. (¼ oz.) active
dry yeast
¼ cup warm water
(110° to 115°)
1 cup warm whole milk
(110° to 115°)
½ cup sugar
½ cup butter, softened
1 large egg,
room temperature
1 tsp. salt
4½ to 5 cups
all-purpose flour

FILLING
2 cans (16 oz. each)
pitted tart cherries,
well drained and
roughly chopped
½ cup all-purpose flour
½ cup packed brown sugar
½ cup chopped pecans

ICING
1 cup confectioners' sugar
¼ tsp. vanilla extract
1 to 2 Tbsp. whole milk

1. In a large bowl, dissolve yeast in warm water. Add the milk, sugar, butter, egg, salt and 2 cups flour. Beat until smooth. Stir in enough remaining flour to form a soft dough.

2. Turn onto a lightly floured surface; knead until smooth and elastic, 6-8 minutes. Place in a greased bowl, turning once to grease top. Cover and refrigerate overnight.

3. Line 2 baking sheets with parchment; set aside. Punch down dough. Turn onto a lightly floured surface; divide in half. Roll each portion into a 14x7-in. rectangle. Spread cherries over dough to within ½ in. of edges. Combine flour, brown sugar and pecans; sprinkle over cherries.

4. Roll up each rectangle jelly-roll style, starting with a long side; pinch seams and tuck ends under. Place each seam side down on a prepared baking sheet; pinch ends together to form a ring. With a kitchen scissors, cut from outside edge two-thirds of the way toward center of ring at 1-in. intervals. Separate strips slightly and twist to allow filling to show. Cover and let rise until doubled, about 1 hour.

5. Bake at 350° until golden brown, 20-25 minutes. Remove from pans to wire racks.

6. Combine the confectioners' sugar, vanilla and enough milk to reach desired consistency; drizzle over warm coffee cakes.

1 PIECE: 223 cal., 6g fat (3g sat. fat), 21mg chol., 149mg sod., 38g carb. (18g sugars, 1g fiber), 4g pro.

DILL BREAD

This golden-brown loaf is moist and flavorful. Dill weed gives each wedge an herbed zest, making it a nice complement to most any meal. What's more, this easy yeast bread requires no kneading!
—*Corky Huffsmith, Salem, OR*

PREP: 10 MIN. + RISING • **BAKE:** 35 MIN. + COOLING • **MAKES:** 12 SERVINGS

1 pkg. (¼ oz.) active
  dry yeast
¼ cup warm water
  (110° to 115°)
1 cup 2% cottage cheese
¼ cup snipped fresh dill
  or 4 tsp. dill weed
1 Tbsp. butter, melted
1½ tsp. salt
1 tsp. sugar
1 tsp. dill seed
1 large egg,
  room temperature,
  lightly beaten
2¼ to 2¾ cups
  all-purpose flour

1. In a large bowl, dissolve yeast in warm water. In a small saucepan, heat cottage cheese to 110°-115°; add to the yeast mixture. Add fresh dill, butter, salt, sugar, dill seed, egg and 1 cup flour; beat until smooth. Stir in enough remaining flour to form a soft dough. Do not knead. Cover and let rise in a warm place until doubled, about 1 hour.

2. Punch down dough. Turn onto a lightly floured surface; shape into a 6-in. circle. Transfer to a greased 9-in. round baking pan. Cover and let rise in a warm place until doubled, about 45 minutes.

3. Bake at 350° until crust is golden brown and bread sounds hollow when tapped, 35-40 minutes. Remove from pan to a wire rack to cool. Cut into wedges.

1 PIECE: 118 cal., 2g fat (1g sat. fat), 19mg chol., 364mg sod., 19g carb., (1g sugars, 1g fiber), 5g pro. DIABETIC EXCHANGES: 1 starch, ½ fat.

ZUCCHINI MUFFINS

These yummy zucchini, currant and walnut muffins are an excellent and tasty way to use up surplus zucchini from your garden.
—*Peg Gausz, Watchung, NJ*

PREP: 20 MIN. • **BAKE:** 25 MIN. • **MAKES:** 6 MUFFINS

¾ cup all-purpose flour
½ cup sugar
¼ tsp. baking powder
¼ tsp. baking soda
¼ tsp. salt
¼ tsp. ground cinnamon
1 large egg,
  room temperature
¼ cup canola oil
1 cup finely shredded
  unpeeled zucchini
½ cup chopped walnuts
¼ cup dried currants or
  chopped raisins

1. Preheat oven to 350°. Coat muffin cups with cooking spray or use paper liners; set aside.

2. In a bowl, combine the first 6 ingredients. Combine egg and oil; stir into the dry ingredients just until moistened. Fold in the zucchini, walnuts and currants.

3. Fill muffin cups three-fourths full with batter. Bake until a toothpick in center comes out clean, 22-25 minutes. Cool for 5 minutes in pan before removing from pan to a wire rack.

1 MUFFIN: 318 cal., 16g fat (1g sat. fat), 35mg chol., 180mg sod., 40g carb. (25g sugars, 2g fiber), 6g pro.

DILL BREAD

SUGAR PLUM BREAD

I grew up with my Grandma Mitchell's irresistible plum bread.
We slathered it with butter and ate it with cottage cheese
and fresh fruit for a simple breakfast. It still always
makes an appearance during the holidays!
—*Emily Tyra, Lake Ann, MI*

PREP: 15 MIN. + STANDING • **BAKE:** 40 MIN. + COOLING
MAKES: 1 LOAF (12 SLICES)

1 cup pitted dried
  plums (prunes),
  coarsely chopped
¾ cup water
2 Tbsp. plus ¾ cup sugar,
  divided
2 Tbsp. shortening

1 large egg,
  room temperature
2 cups all-purpose flour
2 tsp. baking powder
1 tsp. baking soda
½ tsp. salt
2 Tbsp. coarse sugar

1. Preheat oven to 350°. In a small saucepan, combine dried
plums, water and 2 Tbsp. sugar. Bring to a simmer over medium
heat for 1 minute. Remove from heat; let stand until plumped,
about 10 minutes. Drain plums, reserving fruit and liquid.
Measure liquid, adding enough water to yield ½ cup.

2. Cream shortening and remaining ¾ cup sugar until light and
fluffy, 5-7 minutes. Beat in egg. In another bowl, whisk together
flour, baking powder, baking soda and salt. Add to creamed
mixture alternately with reserved cooking liquid; fold in
cooled dried plums (batter will be thick).

3. Transfer batter to a greased 8x4-in. loaf pan. Sprinkle with
coarse sugar. Bake until a toothpick inserted in center comes
out with moist crumbs, 40-45 minutes. Cool in pan 10 minutes
before removing to a wire rack to cool completely.

1 PIECE: 202 cal., 3g fat (1g sat. fat), 16mg chol., 291mg sod.,
41g carb. (21g sugars, 1g fiber), 3g pro.

FROM GRANDMA'S KITCHEN: If dried plums (prunes) aren't to
your liking, try substituting dried apricots. Add a little lemon
zest to some softened butter and slather it on top.

BACON DATE BREAD

Friends joke that whenever I'm asked to bring a dish to a party, my contribution always contains bacon. This recipe has the sweet and salty flavors of date-nut bread and bacon-wrapped dates.
—*Terrie Gammon, Eden Prairie, MN*

PREP: 25 MIN. • BAKE: 45 MIN. + COOLING • MAKES: 1 LOAF (16 PIECES)

8 **bacon strips, chopped**
8 **green onions,**
thinly sliced
2 **cups all-purpose flour**
3 **tsp. baking powder**
1 **tsp. sugar**
¼ **tsp. salt**
⅛ **tsp. cayenne pepper**
2 **large eggs,**
room temperature
1 **cup sour cream**
¼ **cup butter, melted**
1½ **cups shredded**
Asiago cheese, divided
⅔ **cup pitted dates, chopped**

1. Preheat oven to 350°. In a large skillet, cook bacon over medium heat until crisp, stirring occasionally. Remove with a slotted spoon; drain on paper towels. Discard drippings, reserving 2 Tbsp. in pan.

2. Add green onions to drippings; cook and stir over medium-high heat until tender, 1-2 minutes. Cool slightly.

3. In a large bowl, whisk flour, baking powder, sugar, salt and cayenne. In another bowl, whisk eggs, sour cream and melted butter until blended. Add to the flour mixture; stir just until moistened. Fold in 1 cup cheese, the dates, bacon and green onions (batter will be thick).

4. Transfer to a greased 9x5-in. loaf pan; sprinkle with remaining ½ cup cheese. Bake until a toothpick inserted in the center comes out clean, 45-50 minutes. Cool in pan 10 minutes before removing to a wire rack. Serve warm.

1 PIECE: 211 cal., 13g fat (7g sat. fat), 49mg chol., 267mg sod., 17g carb. (4g sugars, 1g fiber), 7g pro.

FLAKY CHEDDAR-CHIVE BISCUITS

These buttery biscuits will complement just about any dinner.
Speckled with cheese and chives, they look wonderful—and taste even better!
—*Elizabeth King, Duluth, MN*

TAKES: 25 MIN. • MAKES: 10 BISCUITS

2¼ **cups all-purpose flour**
2½ **tsp. baking powder**
2 **tsp. sugar**
½ **tsp. baking soda**
½ **tsp. salt**
½ **cup cold butter, cubed**
1 **cup shredded**
cheddar cheese
3 **Tbsp. minced**
fresh chives
1 **cup buttermilk**

1. Preheat oven to 425°. In a large bowl, whisk the first 5 ingredients. Cut in butter until mixture resembles coarse crumbs; stir in cheese and chives. Add buttermilk; stir just until moistened. Turn onto a lightly floured surface; knead gently 8-10 times.

2. Pat or roll dough to ¾-in. thickness; cut with a floured 2½-in. biscuit cutter. Place 2 in. apart on a greased baking sheet. Bake 10-12 minutes or until golden brown. Serve warm.

1 BISCUIT: 236 cal., 13g fat (8g sat. fat), 37mg chol., 440mg sod., 24g carb. (3g sugars, 1g fiber), 6g pro.

BAKING POWDER
DROP BISCUITS

BAKING POWDER DROP BISCUITS

One day I had company coming and realized I had run out of biscuit mix. I'd never made biscuits from scratch before, but I decided to give this recipe a try. Now this is the only way I make them!
—*Sharon Evans, Clear Lake, IA*

TAKES: 20 MIN. • MAKES: 1 DOZEN

2 cups all-purpose flour
2 Tbsp. sugar
4 tsp. baking powder
½ tsp. cream of tartar
½ tsp. salt
½ cup shortening
⅔ cup 2% milk
1 large egg,
   room temperature

1. Preheat oven to 450°. In a large bowl, combine the first 5 ingredients. Cut in shortening until the mixture resembles coarse crumbs. In a small bowl, whisk milk and egg. Stir into the crumb mixture just until moistened.

2. Drop by ¼ cupfuls 2 in. apart onto an ungreased baking sheet. Bake until golden brown, 10-12 minutes. Serve warm.

1 BISCUIT: 170 cal., 9g fat (2g sat. fat), 17mg chol., 271mg sod., 19g carb. (3g sugars, 1g fiber), 3g pro.

AMISH POTATO BREAD

A tasty mix of whole wheat and all-purpose flour, plus a small amount of mashed potatoes, combine to give this golden bread its wonderful texture. The loaf is very moist and stays that way for days.
—*Sue Violette, Neillsville, WI*

PREP: 30 MIN. + RISING • BAKE: 40 MIN. + COOLING • MAKES: 1 LOAF (16 PIECES)

1 pkg. (¼ oz.) active
   dry yeast
¼ cup warm water
   (110° to 115°)
1¾ cups warm fat-free milk
   (110° to 115°)
⅓ cup butter, softened
¼ cup mashed potatoes
   (without added milk
   and butter)
3 Tbsp. sugar
1½ tsp. salt
1½ cups whole wheat flour
3½ to 4 cups
   all-purpose flour

1. In a large bowl, dissolve yeast in warm water. Add milk, butter, mashed potatoes, sugar, salt, whole wheat flour and ½ cup all-purpose flour. Beat until smooth. Stir in enough remaining flour to form a firm dough.

2. Turn dough onto a lightly floured surface; knead until smooth and elastic, 6-8 minutes. Place in a bowl coated with cooking spray, turning once to coat the top. Cover and let rise in a warm place until doubled, about 1 hour.

3. Punch down dough and turn onto a floured surface; shape into a loaf. Place in a 9x5-in. loaf pan coated with cooking spray. Cover and let rise until doubled, about 30 minutes.

4. Bake at 350° for 40-45 minutes or until golden brown. Remove from pan to wire rack to cool.

1 PIECE: 193 cal., 4g fat (2g sat. fat), 11mg chol., 276mg sod., 33g carb. (4g sugars, 2g fiber), 6g pro.

APPLESAUCE MUFFINS

These are such a popular item at the restaurant I own that
I had the recipe printed on a card to share with guests.
—Linda Williams, LaFayette, AL

PREP: 10 MIN. • BAKE: 20 MIN. • MAKES: ABOUT 2 DOZEN

1 cup butter, softened
2 cups sugar
2 large eggs,
   room temperature
1 tsp. vanilla extract
2 cups applesauce
4 cups all-purpose flour
1 tsp. baking soda
1 tsp. ground cinnamon
1 tsp. ground allspice
¼ tsp. ground cloves
1 cup chopped walnuts,
   optional
   Cinnamon sugar, optional

1. Preheat oven to 350°. In a bowl, cream butter and sugar until light and fluffy, 5-7 minutes. Beat in eggs and vanilla. Stir in applesauce. Combine flour, baking soda and spices; stir into the creamed mixture. If desired, fold in nuts.

2. Fill greased or paper-lined muffin cups three-fourths full. Bake until a toothpick comes out clean, 20-25 minutes. Cool 5 minutes before removing from pans to wire racks. If desired, sprinkle with cinnamon sugar.

1 MUFFIN: 224 cal., 8g fat (5g sat. fat), 36mg chol., 120mg sod., 35g carb. (19g sugars, 1g fiber), 3g pro. DIABETIC EXCHANGES: 2 starch, 1½ fat.

CRUSTY FRENCH BREAD

I love to treat guests to these crusty loaves. Don't hesitate to try this recipe even if you are
not an accomplished bread baker. It's easy because there's no kneading required!
—Christy Freeman, Central Point, OR

PREP: 30 MIN. + RISING • BAKE: 20 MIN. + COOLING • MAKES: 2 LOAVES (10 PIECES EACH)

1 pkg. (¼ oz.) active
   dry yeast
1½ cups warm water
   (110° to 115°), divided
1 Tbsp. sugar
2 tsp. salt
1 Tbsp. shortening, melted
4 to 5 cups
   all-purpose flour
   Cornmeal

1. In a large bowl, dissolve yeast in ½ cup water. Add sugar, salt, shortening, the remaining 1 cup water and 3½ cups flour. Beat until smooth. Stir in enough remaining flour to form a soft dough. Do not knead. Cover and let rise in a warm place until doubled, about 1 hour.

2. Turn dough onto a floured surface. Divide in half; let rest for 10 minutes. Roll each half into a 10x8-in. rectangle. Roll up each rectangle, starting from a long side; pinch to seal. Place seam side down on 2 greased baking sheets sprinkled with cornmeal. Sprinkle the tops with cornmeal. Cover and let rise until doubled, about 45 minutes.

3. With a very sharp knife, make 5 diagonal cuts across the top of each loaf. Bake at 400° until lightly browned, 20-30 minutes. Remove from pans to wire rack to cool.

1 PIECE: 100 cal., 1g fat (0 sat. fat), 0 chol., 237mg sod., 20g carb. (1g sugars, 1g fiber), 3g pro.

SKILLET CORNBREAD

This skillet bread looks like a puffy pancake but has
the easy-to-cut texture of conventional cornbread.
It complements everything from chicken to chili.
—*Kathy Teela, Tucson, AZ*

TAKES: 15 MIN. • **MAKES:** 4 SERVINGS

¼ cup all-purpose flour	1 large egg,
¼ cup cornmeal	room temperature
½ tsp. baking powder	¼ cup 2% milk
¼ tsp. salt	4 tsp. vegetable oil, divided

1. In a small bowl, combine flour, cornmeal, baking powder and salt. In another small bowl, whisk egg, milk and 3 tsp. oil; stir into the dry ingredients just until moistened.

2. Heat the remaining 1 tsp. oil in a heavy 8-in. skillet over low heat. Carefully pour the batter into the hot skillet; cover and cook for 4-5 minutes. Turn and cook 4 minutes longer or until golden brown.

1 SERVING: 127 cal., 6g fat (1g sat. fat), 54mg chol., 222mg sod., 13g carb. (1g sugars, 1g fiber), 4g pro.

FROM GRANDMA'S KITCHEN: How can you spice up cornbread? Boost the spice and flavor of cornbread by adding diced jalapenos, a sprinkling of red pepper flakes or any of your favorite herbs to the batter. Cornbread is a wonderful canvas for experimentation.

PEPPERCORN BEEF TOP
LOIN ROAST, PAGE 116

GRANDMA'S FAVORITE

MAIN COURSES

Pull up a chair and get ready for a mouthwatering
meal that stars one of Grandma's longtime favorites.
Featuring the savory goodness of recipes that have
stood the test of time, these entrees combine
the convenience today's cooks need with
the flavors they love.

PRIME RIB WITH FRESH HERB SAUCE

Nothing says special occasion like a perfectly seasoned prime rib. Savory, succulent, tender, it's the perfect choice when you want to share something truly divine.

—Tonya Burkhard, Palm Coast, FL

PREP: 40 MIN. • BAKE: 3¼ HOURS + STANDING • MAKES: 10 SERVINGS (1½ CUPS SAUCE)

1 **bone-in beef rib roast (6 to 8 lbs.)**
1 **tsp. kosher salt**
1 **tsp. freshly ground pepper**
3 **cups water**
2 **small onions, halved**
7 **garlic cloves, crushed**
5 **fresh sage sprigs**
5 **fresh thyme sprigs**
2 **bay leaves**

SAUCE
2 **Tbsp. butter**
2 **shallots, thinly sliced**
4 **garlic cloves, thinly sliced**
5 **fresh sage sprigs**
5 **fresh thyme sprigs**
2 **bay leaves**
1 **Tbsp. all-purpose flour**
2 **Tbsp. cracked black pepper**
¼ **tsp. kosher salt**
1½ **to 2½ cups beef stock, divided**
½ **cup dry red wine or beef stock**
½ **tsp. red wine vinegar Fresh thyme sprigs, optional**

1. Preheat oven to 450°. Place roast in a shallow roasting pan, fat side up; rub with salt and pepper. Add 1 cup water, onions, garlic and herbs to roasting pan. Roast 15 minutes.

2. Reduce oven setting to 325°. Roast 3-3½ hours longer or until meat reaches desired doneness (for medium-rare, a thermometer should read 135°; medium, 140°; medium-well, 145°), adding 1 cup water every hour.

3. For sauce, in a large saucepan, heat butter over medium-high heat. Add shallots; cook and stir 5-6 minutes or until tender. Add garlic and herbs; cook 1 minute longer. Stir in flour, pepper and salt until blended. Gradually stir in 1½ cups of stock. Remove from heat.

4. Remove roast to a serving platter; tent with foil. Let stand 15 minutes before carving. Meanwhile, strain any pan juices through a sieve into a measuring cup; discard onions and herbs. Skim fat from pan juices. If necessary, add additional stock to pan juices to measure 1 cup. Add to the shallot mixture for the sauce.

5. Place roasting pan over 2 burners; add wine. Bring to a boil; cook 2-3 minutes, stirring to loosen browned bits from pan. Add to sauce. Bring to a boil, stirring occasionally; cook until mixture is reduced to about 1½ cups, 10-15 minutes.

6. Stir in vinegar; strain, discarding shallots and herbs. Serve with roast and, if desired, garnish with thyme.

5 OZ. COOKED BEEF WITH 2 TBSP. SAUCE: 353 cal., 20g fat (9g sat. fat), 6mg chol., 430mg sod., 2g carb. (1g sugars, 0g fiber), 37g pro.

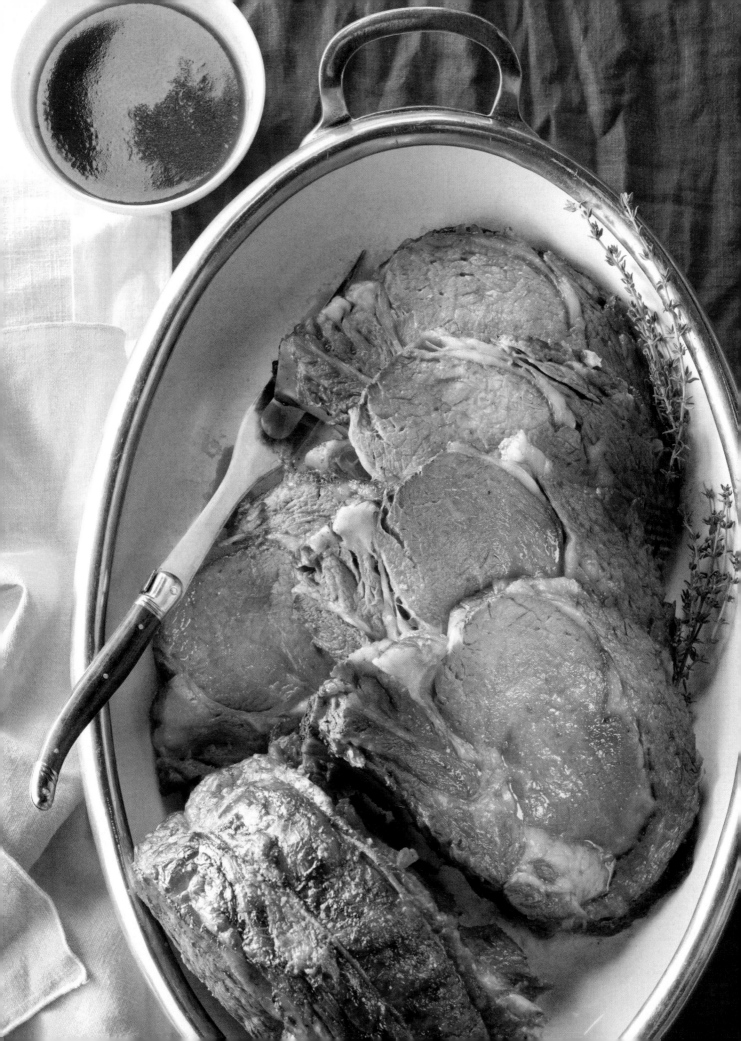

GRANDMA'S SECRET
If you want to get cheesy richness with less fat and fewer calories, use authentic Italian Parmigiano-Reggiano (in a lesser amount than the original recipe's ½ cup). The more intense flavor will make up the difference.

PARMESAN CHICKEN

PARMESAN CHICKEN

The savory coating on this chicken has the satisfying flavor of Parmesan cheese. It's easy enough to be a family weekday meal yet impressive enough to serve to guests. When I make this chicken for dinner, we never have leftovers.
—*Schelby Thompson, Camden Wyoming, DE*

PREP: 10 MIN. • BAKE: 25 MIN. • MAKES: 6 SERVINGS

½ cup butter, melted
2 tsp. Dijon mustard
1 tsp. Worcestershire sauce
½ tsp. salt
1 cup dry bread crumbs
½ cup grated Parmesan cheese
6 boneless skinless chicken breast halves (7 oz. each)

1. Preheat oven to 350°. In a shallow bowl, combine the butter, mustard, Worcestershire sauce and salt. Combine the bread crumbs and cheese in another shallow bowl. Dip chicken in the butter mixture, then in bread crumb mixture, patting to help the coating adhere.

2. Place in an ungreased 15x10x1-in. baking pan. Drizzle with any remaining butter mixture. Bake, uncovered, until a thermometer inserted in chicken reads 165°, 25-30 minutes.

1 CHICKEN BREAST HALF : 270 cal., 16g fat (9g sat. fat), 82mg chol., 552mg sod., 10g carb. (1g sugars, 0 fiber), 21g pro.

OLD-WORLD CORNED BEEF & VEGETABLES

This traditional corned beef dinner is a winner with my husband, family and friends. It's a nice meal in one.
—*Ruth Burrus, Zionsville, IN*

PREP: 25 MIN. • COOK: 8 HOURS • MAKES: 8 SERVINGS

2½ lbs. red potatoes, quartered
2 cups fresh baby carrots
1 pkg. (10 oz.) frozen pearl onions
1 corned beef brisket with spice packet (3 to 3½ lbs.)
½ cup water
1 Tbsp. marinade for chicken
⅛ tsp. pepper
3 Tbsp. cornstarch
¼ cup cold water

1. In a 5-qt. slow cooker, combine the potatoes, carrots and onions. Add beef; discard spice packet from corned beef or save for another use. Combine the water, marinade and pepper; pour over meat. Cover and cook on low for 8-10 hours or until the meat and vegetables are tender.

2. Remove meat and vegetables to a serving platter; keep warm. Skim fat from cooking juices; transfer to a small saucepan. Bring liquid to a boil. Combine cornstarch and cold water until smooth. Gradually stir into the pan. Bring to a boil; cook and stir for 1-2 minutes or until thickened. Serve with meat and vegetables.

NOTE: This recipe was tested with Lea & Perrins Marinade for Chicken.

1 SERVING: 446 cal., 23g fat (8g sat. fat), 117mg chol., 1419mg sod., 34g carb. (5g sugars, 3g fiber), 25g pro.

GLAZED CORNISH HENS
WITH PECAN-RICE STUFFING

Cornish hens bake up with a lovely golden brown shine when they are basted with my sweet and tangy glaze. The traditional rice stuffing has added interest with crunchy pecans and sweet golden raisins.

—*Agnes Ward, Stratford, ON*

PREP: 1 HOUR • **BAKE:** 1 HOUR 25 MIN. + STANDING • **MAKES:** 8 SERVINGS

8 **Cornish game hens
(20 to 24 oz. each)**
¼ **cup butter, softened**
½ **tsp. salt**
½ **tsp. pepper**
2 **cups unsweetened
apple juice**
1 **Tbsp. honey**
1 **Tbsp. Dijon mustard**

PECAN RICE

2 **Tbsp. butter**
1½ **cups uncooked long grain
rice**
2 **tsp. ground cumin**
1 **tsp. curry powder**
4 **cups reduced-sodium
chicken broth**
1 **cup chopped pecans,
toasted**
3 **green onions, thinly
sliced**
½ **cup golden raisins**

1. Preheat oven to 350°. Tuck wings under hens; tie drumsticks together. Rub skin with butter; sprinkle with salt and pepper. Place hens breast side up in a shallow roasting pan. Bake, uncovered, for 1 hour.

2. Meanwhile, place apple juice in a small saucepan. Bring to a boil; cook until reduced by half. Remove from heat. Stir in honey and mustard. Set aside ½ cup for serving.

3. Brush hens with apple mixture. Bake, basting occasionally with pan drippings, until a thermometer reads 180°, 25-35 minutes longer. Cover hens loosely with foil if they brown too quickly.

4. For pecan rice, heat butter in a large saucepan over medium heat. Add rice, cumin and curry; cook and stir until the rice is lightly browned, 2-3 minutes. Stir in broth. Bring to a boil. Reduce heat; simmer, covered, until the rice is tender, 15-20 minutes. Stir in pecans, onions and raisins.

5. Remove hens from oven and cover; let stand 10 minutes before serving. Serve with rice and reserved sauce.

1 HEN WITH 1 TBSP. SAUCE: 1075 cal., 68g fat (20g sat. fat), 371mg chol., 905mg sod., 48g carb. (16g sugars, 3g fiber), 65g pro.

FROM GRANDMA'S KITCHEN: If all eight hens won't fit in your roasting pan, you can bake them on two 15x10x1-in. baking pans with wire racks. Rotate the baking pans occasionally to make sure the hens cook evenly.

PEPPERCORN BEEF TOP LOIN ROAST

A red wine sauce complements the caramelized brown sugar coating on the crust of this special-occasion roast. The down-home flavor makes it the ultimate Christmas entree.

—Taste of Home *Test Kitchen*

PREP: 30 MIN. • BAKE: 1 HOUR + STANDING • MAKES: 10 SERVINGS (1½ CUPS SAUCE)

1 beef top round roast (4 lbs.)
⅓ cup packed brown sugar
3 Tbsp. whole peppercorns, crushed
4 garlic cloves, minced
¾ tsp. salt
1 large onion, finely chopped
1 Tbsp. olive oil
2 Tbsp. tomato paste
2 tsp. Worcestershire sauce
1½ cups port wine
1½ cups dry red wine

1. Preheat oven to 325° Trim fat from roast. If desired, tie roast with kitchen twine every 1½-2 in. to help the beef maintain its shape while cooking. In a small bowl, combine brown sugar, peppercorns, garlic and salt. Rub over meat. Place in a shallow roasting pan.

2. Bake until meat reaches desired doneness (for medium-rare, a thermometer should read 135°; medium, 140°; medium-well, 145°), 1-1½ hours. Remove from oven, tent with foil and let stand for 15 minutes before slicing.

3. Meanwhile, in a large saucepan, saute onion in oil until tender. Stir in tomato paste and Worcestershire sauce until blended. Add wines. Bring to a boil; cook until liquid is reduced to about 1½ cups. Serve with roast.

5 OZ. COOKED BEEF: 444 cal., 26g fat (10g sat. fat), 99mg chol., 275mg sod., 12g carb. (9g sugars, 0 fiber), 32g pro.

OLD-WORLD KIELBASA

I've been making this recipe for most of my life. No one can resist this hearty old-fashioned fare.

—Ethel Harrison, North Fort Myers, FL

PREP: 5 MIN. • COOK: 30 MIN. • MAKES: 10 SERVINGS

1 medium onion, sliced
2 Tbsp. butter
8 cups shredded cabbage
1 lb. smoked kielbasa, cut into ½-in. slices
1 can (14½ oz.) stewed tomatoes
½ cup water
4 tsp. caraway seeds
1 tsp. paprika

In a Dutch oven, saute onion in butter. Add remaining ingredients; bring to a boil. Reduce heat; cover and simmer for 30 minutes or until cabbage is tender. Serve with a slotted spoon.

1 CUP: 115 cal., 6g fat (0 sat. fat), 30mg chol., 454mg sod., 8g carb. (0 sugars, 0 fiber), 8g pro. DIABETIC EXCHANGES: 1½ vegetable, 1 meat.

"No wonder she has been making this for so many years. It's wonderful! My family loved it! I also thinly sliced potatoes and added them to the pot to make it a one-dish meal."

—LAURIEHENGELS, TASTEOFHOME.COM

CABBAGE ROLL CASSEROLE

I layer cabbage with tomato sauce and beef to create a hearty casserole that tastes like cabbage rolls—but without all the work.
—*Doreen Martin, Kitimat, BC*

PREP: 20 MIN. • BAKE: 55 MIN. • MAKES: 12 SERVINGS

- 2 **lbs. ground beef**
- 1 **large onion, chopped**
- 3 **garlic cloves, minced**
- 2 **cans (15 oz. each) tomato sauce, divided**
- 1 **tsp. dried thyme**
- ½ **tsp. dill weed**
- ½ **tsp. rubbed sage**
- ¼ **tsp. salt**
- ¼ **tsp. pepper**
- ¼ **tsp. cayenne pepper**
- 2 **cups cooked rice**
- 4 **bacon strips, cooked and crumbled**
- 1 **medium head cabbage (2 lbs.), shredded**
- 1 **cup shredded part-skim mozzarella cheese**
  Coarsely ground pepper, optional

1. Preheat oven to 375°. In a large skillet, cook beef and onion over medium heat, crumbling beef, until meat is no longer pink. Add garlic; cook 1 minute longer. Drain. Stir in 1 can tomato sauce and next 6 ingredients. Bring to a boil. Reduce heat; simmer, covered, 5 minutes. Stir in rice and bacon; remove from heat.

2. Layer a third of the cabbage in a greased 13x9-in. baking dish. Top with half the meat mixture. Repeat layers; top with remaining cabbage. Pour the remaining tomato sauce over top.

3. Cover and bake 45 minutes. Uncover; sprinkle with cheese. Bake until the cheese is melted, about 10 minutes. Let stand for 5 minutes before serving. If desired, sprinkle with coarsely ground pepper.

1 SERVING: 256 cal., 13g fat (5g sat. fat), 56mg chol., 544mg sod., 17g carb. (4g sugars, 3g fiber), 20g pro.

FROM GRANDMA'S KITCHEN: Minimize mess by using 90% lean ground beef or ground sirloin (so you can skip the draining step) and use coleslaw mix (so you don't have to chop cabbage). Try serving with a splash of red wine or cider vinegar.

OLD-COUNTRY SAUERBRATEN

This recipe has been a well-guarded secret in my family for generations but I have decided to share it because it is so yummy. It's sure to be a hit in your family as well.
—Inge Perreault, Oxford, NJ

PREP: 20 MIN. + MARINATING • COOK: 1½ HOURS • MAKES: 10 SERVINGS

2 bay leaves
4 whole cloves
4 cups water
4 cups white vinegar
4 medium onions, sliced
4 garlic cloves, minced
2 tsp. salt
1 tsp. pepper
1 beef sirloin tip roast
   (3 to 4 lbs.)
3 Tbsp. butter
¼ cup sugar
2 Tbsp. molasses
1 to 2 Tbsp. cornstarch
2 Tbsp. cold water
5 to 6 gingersnap cookies,
   crushed
   Hot cooked spaetzle

1. Place the bay leaves and cloves on a double thickness of cheesecloth; bring up corners of cloth and tie with kitchen string to form a bag. In a large saucepan, combine the water, vinegar, onions, garlic, salt and pepper. Add spice bag. Bring to a boil. Remove from the heat; cool completely.

2. Place the roast in a shallow bowl. Add half of the marinade; turn to coat. Cover and refrigerate for 3 days, turning once each day. Cover and refrigerate remaining marinade.

3. Remove meat from marinade; discard the used marinade, onions and spice bag. In a Dutch oven, brown roast in butter on all sides. Sprinkle with sugar. Add reserved marinade. Bring to a boil. Stir in molasses. Reduce heat; cover and simmer until meat is tender, 1¼-1½ hours.

4. Remove roast to a cutting board. Cut into thin slices; set aside. Skim the fat from the cooking juices. In a small bowl, combine the cornstarch and cold water until smooth; gradually stir into juices. Add crushed gingersnaps. Bring to a boil; cook and stir until thickened, about 2 minutes. Return meat to gravy; heat through. Serve with spaetzle.

1 CUP: 290 cal., 10g fat (4g sat. fat), 96mg chol., 656mg sod., 21g carb. (12g sugars, 2g fiber), 28g pro.

FAST BAKED FISH

We always have a good supply of fresh fish where we live, so I make this dish often. It's moist, tender and flavorful. You can use haddock, trout or walleye in this recipe.
—Judie Anglen, Riverton, WY

TAKES: 25 MIN. • MAKES: 4 SERVINGS

1¼ lbs. fish fillets
1 tsp. seasoned salt
   Pepper to taste
   Paprika, optional
3 Tbsp. butter, melted

1. Preheat oven to 400°. Place fish in a greased 11x7-in. baking dish. Sprinkle with seasoned salt, pepper and, if desired, paprika. Drizzle with butter.

2. Cover and bake until fish just begins to flake easily with a fork, 15-20 minutes.

1 FILLET: 270 cal., 17g fat (7g sat. fat), 110mg chol., 540mg sod., 0 carb. (0 sugars, 0 fiber), 28g pro.

HAM & CHEESE PASTA

Whenever we had leftover ham, we could look forward to my mother preparing her yummy, comforting pasta. Horseradish gives it a nice tangy taste. I sped up the preparation by using Velveeta instead of making a cheese sauce from scratch. Now my kids love it, too.
—*Karen Kopp, Indianapolis, IN*

PREP: 15 MIN. • BAKE: 30 MIN. • MAKES: 4 SERVINGS

8 oz. uncooked medium pasta shells
1 lb. Velveeta, cubed
½ cup 2% milk
2 Tbsp. ketchup
1 Tbsp. prepared horseradish
2 cups cubed fully cooked ham
1 pkg. (8 oz.) frozen peas, thawed

1. Preheat oven to 350°. Cook pasta according to package directions. Meanwhile, in a microwave-safe bowl, combine cheese and milk. Cover and microwave on high for 2 minutes; stir. Heat 1-2 minutes longer or until smooth, stirring twice. Stir in ketchup and horseradish until blended.

2. Drain pasta and place in a large bowl. Stir in the ham, peas and cheese sauce.

3. Transfer to a greased 2-qt. baking dish. Cover and bake for 30-35 minutes or until bubbly.

1 CUP: 761 cal., 36g fat (20g sat. fat), 114mg chol., 2425mg sod., 63g carb. (16g sugars, 5g fiber), 47g pro.

HOT DOG ROLL-UPS

Not only do my grandchildren love these cheese-filled hot dogs, they enjoy helping put the meal together, too. It's the perfect solution when you need a last-minute lunch.
—*Lyletta Searle, Morgan, UT*

TAKES: 30 MIN. • MAKES: 8 SERVINGS

8 hot dogs
1 block (4 oz.) cheddar cheese, cut into 8 strips
2 bacon strips, cooked and crumbled
1 tube (8 oz.) refrigerated crescent rolls

1. Preheat oven to 375°. Cut a lengthwise slit in each hot dog; fill with a strip of cheese and about ½ tsp. bacon.

2. Separate crescent dough into 8 triangles. Place a hot dog on the wide end of each triangle; roll toward the point.

3. Place cheese side up on an ungreased baking sheet. Bake until golden brown, about 12 minutes.

1 ROLL-UP: 325 cal., 25g fat (10g sat. fat), 41mg chol., 797mg sod., 12g carb. (3g sugars, 0 fiber), 11g pro.

"This was so much fun [making these] with the grandkids—and delicious too! Definitely a keeper!"
—HTIMM, TASTEOFHOME.COM

NEW ENGLAND LAMB BAKE

This hearty dish is perfect for warming up on a chilly winter evening.
When you smell it baking, you'll be glad you stayed home.
—*Frank Grady, Fort Kent, ME*

PREP: 25 MIN. • BAKE: 1½ HOURS • MAKES: 8 SERVINGS

1 Tbsp. canola oil
2 lbs. boneless leg of lamb, cut into 1-in. cubes
1 large onion, chopped
¼ cup all-purpose flour
3 cups chicken broth
2 large carrots, sliced
2 large leeks (white portion only), cut into ½-in. slices
2 Tbsp. minced fresh parsley, divided
½ tsp. dried rosemary, crushed
½ tsp. salt
¼ tsp. pepper
¼ tsp. dried thyme
3 large potatoes, peeled and sliced
3 Tbsp. butter, melted, divided

1. Preheat oven to 375°. In a Dutch oven, heat oil over medium heat. Add lamb and onion; cook and stir until meat is no longer pink. Stir in flour until blended. Gradually add broth. Bring to a boil; cook until thickened, 1-2 minutes, stirring to loosen browned bits from pan. Add carrots, leeks, 1 Tbsp. parsley, rosemary, salt, pepper and thyme.

2. Spoon into a greased 13x9-in. or 3-qt. baking dish. Cover with potato slices; brush with 2 Tbsp. melted butter. Bake for 1 hour; brush the potatoes with remaining 1 Tbsp. butter.

3. Return to oven; bake until the meat is tender and potatoes are golden, 30 minutes to 1 hour longer. Cool briefly; sprinkle with the remaining 1 Tbsp. parsley.

FREEZE OPTION: Before adding final 1 Tbsp. parsley, cover and freeze the baked, cooled casserole. To use, partially thaw in the refrigerator overnight. Remove from the refrigerator 30 minutes before baking. Reheat, covered, at 350° until a thermometer reads 165°, about 1 hour. Sprinkle with parsley.

1 SERVING: 356 cal., 13g fat (5g sat. fat), 82mg chol., 631mg sod., 34g carb. (4g sugars, 4g fiber), 25g pro. DIABETIC EXCHANGES: 3 starch, 3 lean meat, 1½ fat.

GREAT-GRANDMA'S ITALIAN MEATBALLS

A classic Italian dish isn't complete without homemade meatballs.
This versatile recipe can be used in other dishes starring meatballs, too.
—*Audrey Colantino, Winchester, MA*

PREP: 30 MIN. • BAKE: 20 MIN. • MAKES: 8 SERVINGS

2 tsp. olive oil
1 medium onion, chopped
3 garlic cloves, minced
¾ cup seasoned bread
   crumbs
½ cup grated Parmesan
   cheese
2 large eggs, lightly beaten
1 tsp. each dried basil,
   oregano and parsley
   flakes
¾ tsp. salt
1 lb. lean ground turkey
1 lb. lean ground beef
   (90% lean)
   Optional: Hot cooked
   pasta and pasta sauce

1. Preheat oven to 375°. In a small skillet, heat oil over medium-high heat. Add onion; cook and stir until tender, 3-4 minutes. Add garlic; cook 1 minute longer. Cool slightly.

2. In a large bowl, combine the bread crumbs, cheese, eggs, seasonings and onion mixture. Add turkey and beef; mix lightly but thoroughly. Shape into 1½-in. balls.

3. Place meatballs on a rack coated with cooking spray in a 15x10x1-in. baking pan. Bake until lightly browned and cooked through, 18-22 minutes. If desired, serve with pasta and sauce.

ABOUT 7 MEATBALLS: 271 cal., 13g fat (5g sat. fat), 125mg chol., 569mg sod., 10g carb. (1g sugars, 1g fiber), 27g pro. **DIABETIC EXCHANGES:** 4 lean meat, 1 fat, ½ starch.

OLD-WORLD PIZZA MEAT LOAF

Good food and memories are made in the kitchen. This recipe
came from my grandma and we all love it.
—*Nicholas King, Duluth, MN*

PREP: 20 MIN. • BAKE: 55 MIN. + STANDING • MAKES: 8 SERVINGS

1   large egg, lightly beaten
1½   cups seasoned bread
     crumbs
1   can (4¼ oz.) chopped ripe
     olives, drained
1   can (4 oz.) mushroom
     stems and pieces,
     drained
1   cup shredded part-skim
     mozzarella cheese
1   small green pepper,
     chopped
1   small onion, chopped
2   Tbsp. onion soup mix
1   cup pizza sauce, divided
2   lbs. ground beef
¼   cup grated Parmesan
     cheese

1. Preheat oven to 350°. In a large bowl, combine egg, bread crumbs, olives, mushrooms, mozzarella cheese, pepper, onion, soup mix and ½ cup pizza sauce. Crumble beef over mixture and mix well. Shape into a 10x6-in. rectangle and place in a greased 15x10x1-in. baking pan. Spoon remaining pizza sauce over top.

2. Bake, uncovered, for 45 minutes. Sprinkle with Parmesan cheese. Bake 10-15 minutes longer or until no pink remains and a thermometer reads 160°. Let stand 10 minutes before slicing.

1 PIECE: 417 cal., 22g fat (8g sat. fat), 114mg chol., 1037mg sod., 23g carb. (4g sugars, 3g fiber), 32g pro.

GRANDMA'S
SECRET
Preparing meatballs in bulk
saves on prep time. Make several
batches, bake them and then freeze
until needed. Simply thaw the
frozen meatballs in the
refrigerator overnight and
you'll be ready to go.

GREAT-GRANDMA'S
ITALIAN MEATBALLS

ROASTED CITRUS & HERB TURKEY

Thanksgiving has never been the same since I tried this recipe. I have made it for the past few years, and it never fails to impress both in presentation and taste. This is a true showstopper!

—*Nancy Niemerg, Dieterich, IL*

PREP: 30 MIN. • **BAKE:** 3½ HOURS + STANDING • **MAKES:** 16 SERVINGS (2 CUPS GRAVY)

¼ **cup butter, softened**
2 **Tbsp. Italian seasoning**
1 **turkey (14 to 16 lbs.)**
2 **tsp. salt**
2 **tsp. pepper**
1 **large onion, quartered**
1 **medium orange, quartered**
1 **medium lemon, quartered**
3 **fresh rosemary sprigs**
3 **fresh sage sprigs**
3 **cups chicken broth, divided**
3 **to 4 Tbsp. all-purpose flour**
⅛ **tsp. browning sauce, optional**

1. Preheat oven to 325°. Mix butter and Italian seasoning.

2. Place turkey on a rack in a roasting pan, breast side up; pat dry. With your fingers, carefully loosen skin from turkey breast; rub half of the butter mixture under the skin. Secure skin to underside of breast with toothpicks. Rub cavity with salt and pepper; fill with onion, orange, lemon and herbs. Tuck wings under turkey; tie the drumsticks together.

3. Melt the remaining butter mixture; brush over outside of turkey. Add 2 cups broth to roasting pan.

4. Roast, uncovered, until a thermometer inserted in thickest part of a thigh reads 170°-175°, 3½-4 hours. Baste occasionally with the pan drippings. (Cover loosely with foil if turkey browns too quickly.) Remove turkey from oven; tent with foil. Let stand 20 minutes before carving.

5. Pour pan drippings into a small saucepan; skim fat. Mix flour, remaining broth and, if desired, browning sauce until smooth; whisk into pan. Bring to a boil; cook and stir until thickened, 1-2 minutes. Serve with turkey.

7 OZ. COOKED TURKEY WITH 2 TBSP. GRAVY: 500 cal., 24g fat (8g sat. fat), 223mg chol., 653mg sod., 2g carb. (0 sugars, 0 fiber), 64g pro.

TRADITIONAL LASAGNA

My family tasted this rich lasagna at a friend's home on Christmas Eve, and it became our holiday tradition. My sister's Italian in-laws request it often.
—*Lorri Foockle, Granville, IL*

PREP: 30 MIN. + SIMMERING • **BAKE:** 70 MIN. + STANDING • **MAKES:** 12 SERVINGS

1 lb. ground beef
¾ lb. bulk pork sausage
3 cans (8 oz. each) tomato sauce
2 cans (6 oz. each) tomato paste
2 garlic cloves, minced
2 tsp. sugar
1 tsp. Italian seasoning
½ to 1 tsp. salt
¼ to ½ tsp. pepper
3 large eggs
3 Tbsp. minced fresh parsley
3 cups 4% small-curd cottage cheese
1 cup ricotta cheese
½ cup grated Parmesan cheese
9 lasagna noodles, cooked and drained
6 slices provolone cheese (about 6 oz.)
3 cups shredded part-skim mozzarella cheese, divided

1. In a large skillet over medium heat, cook and crumble the beef and sausage until no longer pink; drain. Add next 7 ingredients. Bring to a boil. Reduce heat; simmer, uncovered, for 1 hour, stirring occasionally. Adjust seasoning with additional salt and pepper, if desired.

2. Meanwhile, in a large bowl, lightly beat eggs. Add parsley; stir in cottage cheese, ricotta and Parmesan cheese.

3. Preheat oven to 375°. Spread 1 cup of the meat sauce in an ungreased 13x9-in. baking dish. Layer with 3 noodles, the provolone cheese, 2 cups cottage cheese mixture, 1 cup mozzarella, 3 noodles, 2 cups meat sauce, the remaining cottage cheese mixture and 1 cup of mozzarella. Top with the remaining noodles, meat sauce and mozzarella (dish will be full).

4. Cover; bake for 50 minutes. Uncover; bake until heated through, about 20 minutes. Let stand 15 minutes before cutting.

1 PIECE: 503 cal., 27g fat (13g sat. fat), 136mg chol., 1208mg sod., 30g carb. (9g sugars, 2g fiber), 36g pro.

FROM GRANDMA'S KITCHEN: If you want to add vegetables to your lasagna, it's best to cook them first. Be sure to strain out any excess liquid from the cooking process. Not doing so might make your dish watery.

BEEF TENDERLOIN IN MUSHROOM SAUCE

My mother-in-law has been using this recipe for more than 30 years. When our kids are away, I make this recipe for just my husband, Derek, and me. I especially look forward to preparing it as part of a special Valentine's Day menu.
—*Denise McNab, Warminster, PA*

TAKES: 25 MIN. • **MAKES:** 2 SERVINGS

4 **Tbsp. butter, divided**
1 **tsp. canola oil**
2 **beef tenderloin steaks**
  (1 in. thick and 4 oz. each)
1 **cup sliced fresh**
  mushrooms
1 **Tbsp. chopped green**
  onion

1 **Tbsp. all-purpose flour**
⅛ **tsp. salt**
  Dash pepper
⅔ **cup chicken or beef broth**
⅛ **tsp. browning sauce,**
  optional

1. In a large skillet, heat 2 Tbsp. butter and oil over medium-high heat; cook steaks to desired doneness (for medium-rare, a thermometer should read 135°; medium, 140°), 5-6 minutes per side. Remove from pan, reserving drippings; keep warm.

2. For the sauce, in same pan, heat drippings and the remaining 2 Tbsp. butter over medium-high heat; saute mushrooms and green onion until tender. Stir in flour, salt and pepper until blended; gradually stir in broth and, if desired, browning sauce. Bring to a boil, stirring constantly; cook and stir until thickened, 1-2 minutes. Serve with steaks.

1 SERVING: 417 cal., 32g fat (17g sat. fat), 112mg chol., 659mg sod., 5g carb. (1g sugars, 1g fiber), 26g pro.

SLOW-COOKED CHICKEN A LA KING

When I know I'll be having a busy day with little time to prepare a meal, I use my slow cooker to make chicken a la king. It smells so good while it's cooking.

—Eleanor Mielke, Snohomish, WA

PREP: 10 MIN. • COOK: 7½ HOURS • MAKES: 6 SERVINGS

1 can (10¾ oz.) reduced-fat reduced-sodium condensed cream of chicken soup, undiluted
3 Tbsp. all-purpose flour
¼ tsp. pepper
Dash cayenne pepper
1 lb. boneless skinless chicken breasts, cubed
1 celery rib, chopped
½ cup chopped green pepper
¼ cup chopped onion
1 pkg. (10 oz.) frozen peas, thawed
2 Tbsp. diced pimientos, drained
Hot cooked rice

1. In a 3-qt. slow cooker, combine the soup, flour, pepper and cayenne pepper until smooth. Stir in chicken, celery, green pepper and onion.

2. Cover and cook on low for 7-8 hours or until the meat is no longer pink. Stir in peas and pimientos. Cook 30 minutes longer or until heated through. Serve with rice.

1 CUP CHICKEN MIXTURE: 174 cal., 3g fat (1g sat. fat), 44mg chol., 268mg sod., 16g carb. (6g sugars, 3g fiber), 19g pro. DIABETIC EXCHANGES: 2 lean meat, 1 starch.

SEASONED RIBEYE ROAST

This is an especially savory way to prepare a boneless beef roast. Gravy made from the drippings is exceptional.

—Evelyn Gebhardt, Kasilof, AK

PREP: 10 MIN. • BAKE: 1½ HOURS + STANDING • MAKES: 8 SERVINGS

1½ tsp. lemon-pepper seasoning
1½ tsp. paprika
¾ tsp. garlic salt
½ tsp. dried rosemary, crushed
¼ tsp. cayenne pepper
1 beef ribeye roast (3 to 4 lbs.)

1. Preheat oven to 350°. Mix the lemon pepper, paprika, garlic salt, rosemary and cayenne pepper. Place roast on a rack in a roasting pan, fat side up; rub with seasoning mixture.

2. Roast, uncovered, until the meat reaches desired doneness (for medium-rare, a thermometer should read 135°; medium, 140°), 1½-2 hours. Remove from oven; tent with foil. Let stand for 10 minutes before slicing.

4 OZ. COOKED BEEF: 372 cal., 27g fat (11g sat. fat), 100mg chol., 321mg sod., 0 carb. (0 sugars, 0 fiber), 30g pro.

HURRY-UP HAM & NOODLES

The rich-tasting dish is ready to serve in almost the time it takes to cook the noodles. I've made it for luncheons and potlucks, but mostly I make it on days when I'm in a hurry to get something on the table.
—*Lucille Howell, Portland, OR*

TAKES: 25 MIN. • MAKES: 4 SERVINGS

5 to 6 cups uncooked wide egg noodles
¼ cup butter, cubed
1 cup heavy whipping cream
1½ cups chopped fully cooked ham
½ cup grated Parmesan cheese
¼ cup thinly sliced green onions
¼ tsp. salt
⅛ tsp. pepper

1. Cook noodles according to the package directions. Meanwhile, in a large skillet, melt butter over medium heat. Gradually whisk in cream. Bring to a boil, stirring constantly; cook and stir until thickened, about 2 minutes longer.

2. Add the ham, cheese, onions, salt and pepper; cook, uncovered, until heated through. Drain noodles; add to ham mixture. Toss to coat; heat through.

1½ CUPS: 619 cal., 43g fat (25g sat. fat), 193mg chol., 1154mg sod., 38g carb. (3g sugars, 1g fiber), 22g pro.

"This dish was absolutely creamy and delicious! Very easy, so perfect for a weeknight meal. The only change I made was adding peas. A definite keeper."
—CYNANDTOM, TASTEOFHOME.COM

ROUND STEAK

There's no need to brown the steak first, so you can get this main course into the oven in short order. The fork-tender results are sure to remind you of Swiss steak Grandma used to make, with lots of sauce left over for dipping.
—*Sue Call, Beech Grove, IN*

PREP: 10 MIN. • BAKE: 1¾ HOURS • MAKES: 8 SERVINGS

2 lbs. boneless beef round steak (½ in. thick)
¼ tsp. pepper
1 medium onion, thinly sliced
1 can (4 oz.) mushroom stems and pieces, drained
1 can (8 oz.) no-salt-added tomato sauce
Hot cooked noodles

Preheat oven to 325°. Trim beef; cut into serving-size pieces. Place in a greased 13x9-in. baking dish. Sprinkle with pepper. Top with the onion, mushrooms and tomato sauce. Cover and bake for 1¾-2 hours or until meat is tender. Serve over noodles.

3 OZ. COOKED BEEF: 158 cal., 4g fat (1g sat. fat), 63mg chol., 78mg sod., 4g carb. (2g sugars, 1g fiber), 26g pro. DIABETIC EXCHANGES: 3 lean meat, 1 vegetable.

PRESSURE-COOKER
MINI TERIYAKI TURKEY
SANDWICHES

**GRANDMA'S
SECRET**
This recipe also works well with
boneless, skinless chicken breasts.
To spice things up, add crushed red
pepper flakes or slices of
fresh jalapeno.

PRESSURE-COOKER
MINI TERIYAKI TURKEY SANDWICHES

Preparing the pulled turkey in a delicious teriyaki sauce for these snack-size sandwiches is a breeze using a pressure cooker. As a finishing touch, serve them on lightly toasted sweet dinner rolls.

—Amanda Hoop, Seaman, OH

PREP: 20 MIN. • COOK: 25 MIN. + RELEASING • MAKES: 20 SERVINGS

2 boneless skinless
  turkey breast halves
  (2 lbs. each)
⅔ cup packed brown sugar
⅔ cup reduced-sodium
  soy sauce
¼ cup cider vinegar
3 garlic cloves, minced
1 Tbsp. minced fresh
  gingerroot
½ tsp. pepper
2 Tbsp. cornstarch
2 Tbsp. cold water
20 Hawaiian sweet rolls
2 Tbsp. butter, melted

1. Place turkey in a 6-qt. electric pressure cooker. In a small bowl, combine the next 6 ingredients; pour over turkey. Lock lid; close pressure-release valve. Adjust to pressure-cook on high for 25 minutes. Allow pressure to naturally release for 10 minutes; quick-release any remaining pressure.

2. Remove turkey from pressure cooker. Select saute setting and adjust for high heat; bring juices to a boil. In a small bowl, mix cornstarch and water until smooth; gradually stir into the cooking juices. Bring to a boil; cook and stir until sauce is thickened, about 2 minutes. When turkey is cool enough to handle, shred with 2 forks; return meat to pressure cooker. Stir to heat through.

3. Preheat oven to 325°. Split rolls; brush cut sides with butter. Place on an ungreased baking sheet, cut side up. Bake until golden brown, 8-10 minutes. Spoon ⅓ cup turkey mixture onto roll bottoms. Replace tops.

1 MINI SANDWICH: 252 cal., 5g fat (2g sat. fat), 70mg chol., 501mg sod., 25g carb. (13g sugars, 1g fiber), 26g pro.

TOMATO-BASIL BAKED FISH

This recipe can be made with different kinds of fish as desired, and I usually have the rest of the ingredients on hand. Baked fish is wonderful, and I fix this healthy dish often.

—Annie Hicks, Zephyrhills, FL

TAKES: 15 MIN. • MAKES: 2 SERVINGS

1 Tbsp. lemon juice
1 tsp. olive oil
8 oz. red snapper, cod
  or haddock fillets
¼ tsp. dried basil, divided
⅛ tsp. salt, divided
⅛ tsp. pepper, divided
2 plum tomatoes, thinly
  sliced
2 tsp. grated Parmesan
  cheese

Preheat oven to 400°. In a shallow bowl, combine lemon juice and oil. Add fish fillets; turn to coat. Place in a greased 9-in. pie plate. Sprinkle with half each of the basil, salt and pepper. Arrange tomatoes over top; sprinkle with cheese and remaining seasonings. Cover and bake until fish flakes easily with a fork, 10-12 minutes.

1 SERVING: 121 cal., 4g fat (1g sat. fat), 24mg chol., 256mg sod., 4g carb. (2g sugars, 1g fiber), 18g pro. DIABETIC EXCHANGES: 3 lean meat, 1 vegetable, ½ fat.

AUTUMN LAMB SKILLET

I have found that even those who do not prefer lamb will enjoy
this recipe. It is especially delicious on a chilly night!
—*Arlene Aughey, Saddle Brook, NJ*

PREP: 25 MIN. • COOK: 35 MIN. • MAKES: 4 SERVINGS

2 Tbsp. olive oil
8 lamb rib or loin chops
   (about 1 in. thick and
   3 oz. each)
1 tsp. salt, divided
½ tsp. pepper, divided
1 large onion, chopped
2 celery ribs, chopped
1 medium green pepper,
   chopped
1 garlic clove, minced
½ tsp. dried basil
1 can (14½ oz.) stewed
   tomatoes
1 cup uncooked long grain
   rice
½ tsp. ground turmeric,
   optional

1. In a large skillet, heat oil over medium heat. Sprinkle lamb chops with ½ tsp. salt and ¼ tsp. pepper. Brown chops in batches; remove and keep warm.

2. To the same skillet, add onion, celery, green pepper, garlic, basil, and remaining ½ tsp. salt and ¼ tsp. pepper. Cook and stir until crisp-tender, 5-7 minutes.

3. Return lamb to skillet; add tomatoes. Cook, covered, until lamb reaches desired doneness (for medium-rare, a thermometer should read 135°; medium, 140°; medium-well, 145°), about 20 minutes longer.

4. Meanwhile, cook rice according to package directions, adding turmeric if desired. Serve with lamb mixture.

1 SERVING: 455 cal., 14g fat (4g sat. fat), 68mg chol., 856mg sod., 54g carb. (8g sugars, 3g fiber), 27g pro.

ALMOND-TOPPED FISH

A co-worker gave me this recipe, but I didn't try it until recently. What a mistake it was to wait!
It's easier than dipping, coating and frying—and the flavor is outstanding.
Once you've tried this tender fish, you'll never go back to fried.
—*Heidi Kirsch, Waterloo, IA*

TAKES: 30 MIN. • MAKES: 4 SERVINGS

1 Tbsp. butter
1 small onion, thinly sliced
4 cod or haddock fillets
   (6 oz. each)
1 tsp. seasoned salt
½ tsp. dill weed
¼ tsp. pepper
¼ cup grated Parmesan
   cheese
¼ cup reduced-fat
   mayonnaise
1 Tbsp. minced fresh
   parsley
1 Tbsp. lemon juice
2 Tbsp. sliced almonds,
   toasted

1. Preheat oven to 400°. Place butter in a 13x9-in. baking dish; heat in the oven until melted. Spread butter over bottom of dish; cover with onion.

2. Arrange fish over onion; sprinkle with salt, dill and pepper. Combine the Parmesan cheese, mayonnaise, parsley and lemon juice; spread over fish.

3. Return baking dish to oven and bake, uncovered, until fish flakes easily with a fork, 18-20 minutes. Sprinkle with almonds.

1 FILLET: 220 cal., 9g fat (2g sat. fat), 74mg chol., 658mg sod., 5g carb. (2g sugars, 1g fiber), 29g pro. DIABETIC EXCHANGES: 4 lean meat, 2 fat.

AUTUMN LAMB
SKILLET

SALMON WITH CREAMY DILL SAUCE

There's nothing like fresh salmon, and my mom bakes it just right so it nearly melts in your mouth. The sour cream sauce is subtly seasoned with dill and horseradish so it doesn't overpower the delicate salmon flavor.

—*Susan Emery, Everett, WA*

TAKES: 30 MIN. • MAKES: 6 SERVINGS

1 salmon fillet (about 2 lbs.)
1 to 1½ tsp. lemon-pepper seasoning
1 tsp. onion salt
1 small onion, sliced and separated into rings
6 lemon slices
¼ cup butter, cubed

DILL SAUCE
⅓ cup sour cream
⅓ cup mayonnaise
1 Tbsp. finely chopped onion
1 tsp. lemon juice
1 tsp. prepared horseradish
¾ tsp. dill weed
¼ tsp. garlic salt
Pepper to taste

1. Preheat oven to 350°. Line a 15x10x1-in. baking pan with heavy-duty foil; grease lightly. Place salmon skin side down on foil. Sprinkle with lemon pepper and onion salt. Top with onion and lemon. Dot with butter. Fold foil around salmon; seal tightly,

2. Bake for 20 minutes. Open foil carefully, allowing steam to escape. Broil 4-6 in. from the heat for 3-5 minutes or until the fish flakes easily with a fork.

3. Meanwhile, combine the sauce ingredients until smooth. Serve with salmon.

4 OZ. COOKED SALMON WITH ABOUT 2 TBSP. SAUCE: 418 cal., 33g fat (11g sat. fat), 100mg chol., 643mg sod., 3g carb. (1g sugars, 0 fiber), 26g pro.

FROM GRANDMA'S KITCHEN: A thrifty alternative to purchased onion salt is to mix up your own. Just combine 1 tsp. onion powder with 3 tsp. of table salt or other fine-grained salt. The ratio works the same for garlic salt, too.

COMFORTING TUNA PATTIES

My grandmother and mother made these tuna patties on Fridays during Lent. I'm not the biggest fan of tuna, but it's perfect in this dish. These patties are even good cold the next day, if there are any leftovers.
—*Ann Marie Eberhart, Gig Harbor, WA*

PREP: 25 MIN. + CHILLING • COOK: 5 MIN./BATCH • MAKES: 6 SERVINGS

2 Tbsp. butter
3 Tbsp. all-purpose flour
1 cup evaporated milk
1 pouch (6.4 oz.) light tuna in water
⅓ cup plus ½ cup dry bread crumbs, divided
1 green onion, finely chopped
2 Tbsp. lemon juice
½ tsp. salt
¼ tsp. pepper
 Oil for frying

1. In a small saucepan, melt butter over medium heat. Stir in flour until smooth; gradually whisk in milk. Bring to a boil, stirring constantly; cook and stir until thickened, 2-3 minutes. Remove from heat. Transfer to a small bowl; cool.

2. Stir in tuna, ⅓ cup bread crumbs, green onion, lemon juice, salt and pepper. Refrigerate, covered, at least 30 minutes.

3. Place the remaining ½ cup bread crumbs in a shallow bowl. Drop ⅓ cup tuna mixture into crumbs. Gently coat and shape into a ½-in.-thick patty. Repeat. In a large skillet, heat oil over medium heat. Add tuna patties in batches; cook until golden brown, 2-3 minutes on each side. Drain on paper towels.

FREEZE OPTION: Freeze cooked, cooled patties in freezer containers, separating layers with waxed paper. To use, reheat on a baking sheet in a preheated 325° oven until heated through.

1 TUNA PATTY: 255 cal., 17g fat (5g sat. fat), 34mg chol., 419mg sod., 15g carb. (5g sugars, 1g fiber), 10g pro.

CHICKEN WITH CHERRY WINE SAUCE

My dad's a chef, and I learned to cook at home at an early age. This saucy chicken was the first dish I made by myself and it's still a favorite.
—*Ben Diaz, Azusa, CA*

TAKES: 30 MIN. • MAKES: 4 SERVINGS

4 boneless skinless chicken breast halves (8 oz. each)
¼ tsp. salt
¼ tsp. pepper
7 Tbsp. butter, divided
⅔ cup dry red wine
1 Tbsp. sugar
½ cup fresh or frozen pitted dark sweet cherries, thawed

1. Preheat oven to 350°. Sprinkle chicken with salt and pepper. In a large cast-iron or other ovenproof skillet, heat 2 Tbsp. butter over medium-high heat. Brown chicken on both sides. Bake until a thermometer reads 165°, 12-15 minutes.

2. Meanwhile, in a small saucepan, combine the wine and sugar. Bring to a boil; cook, uncovered, until liquid is reduced by half, 4-5 minutes. Reduce heat to low; whisk in remaining 5 Tbsp. butter, 1 Tbsp. at a time, until blended. Stir in cherries; serve with the chicken.

1 CHICKEN BREAST HALF WITH 3 TBSP. SAUCE: 480 cal., 25g fat (14g sat. fat), 179mg chol., 418mg sod., 8g carb. (5g sugars, 0 fiber), 46g pro.

SPECIAL
SLOW-COOKED
BEEF

SPECIAL SLOW-COOKED BEEF

This hearty entree is easy to prepare for Sunday dinner. While the beef cooks, the chef has lots of time to attend to the other details. With mashed potatoes on the side, it's comfort food for the cool months.
—*Juli George, Grandville, MI*

PREP: 35 MIN. • COOK: 6 HOURS • MAKES: 8 SERVINGS

1   **boneless beef chuck roast (3 lbs.), cubed**
1   **Tbsp. canola oil**
1   **Tbsp. Italian seasoning**
1   **tsp. salt**
1   **garlic clove, minced**
½   **cup sliced ripe olives, drained**
⅓   **cup oil-packed sun-dried tomatoes, drained and chopped**
1   **cup beef broth**
½   **cup fresh pearl onions, peeled**
1   **Tbsp. cornstarch**
2   **Tbsp. cold water**

1. In a large skillet, brown meat in oil in batches; drain. Transfer to a 5-qt. slow cooker. Sprinkle with Italian seasoning, salt and garlic; top with olives and tomatoes. Add broth and onions. Cook, covered, on low 6-8 hours or until meat is tender.

2. With a slotted spoon, remove beef and onions to a serving platter and keep warm. Pour cooking juices into a small saucepan; skim fat.

3. Combine cornstarch and water until smooth; gradually stir into the cooking juices. Bring to a boil; cook and stir until thickened, about 2 minutes. Spoon over beef mixture.

1 SERVING: 332 cal., 20g fat (7g sat. fat), 111mg chol., 551mg sod., 3g carb. (0 sugars, 1g fiber), 34g pro.

OLD-WORLD PORK CHOPS

Years ago, a relative ran a restaurant in Milwaukee, where several well-known German restaurants still operate. This is one of the recipes she developed. The savory stuffing and juicy pork chops are always a hit.
—*Jeanne Schuyler, Wauwatosa, WI*

PREP: 15 MIN. • BAKE: 45 MIN. • MAKES: 4 SERVINGS

2   **Tbsp. canola oil**
4   **bone-in pork loin chops (8 oz. each)**
    Salt and pepper to taste
3   **cups dry unseasoned bread cubes**
1   **can (14¾ oz.) cream-style corn**
1   **large egg, lightly beaten**
1   **Tbsp. grated onion**
½   **tsp. rubbed sage**
½   **tsp. dried basil**
½   **tsp. salt**
¼   **tsp. pepper**

1. Preheat oven to 350°. In a large skillet, heat oil over medium heat. Sprinkle the pork chops with salt and pepper; brown on both sides.

2. Meanwhile, in a bowl, combine the remaining ingredients. Alternately arrange stuffing and pork chops lengthwise across a greased 3-qt. baking dish. Bake, uncovered, until a thermometer reads 145°, about 45 minutes. Let stand for 5 minutes before serving.

1 SERVING: 623 cal., 28g fat (8g sat. fat), 158mg chol., 995mg sod., 50g carb. (6g sugars, 4g fiber), 45g pro.

BEEF SPIEDINI

An Italian favorite, spiedini are great for holidays and other special occasions. The hearty skewers hold marinated steak pinwheels stuffed with a marinara-and-crumb filling.

—Desty Lorino, Shorewood, WI

PREP: 45 MIN. • **BROIL:** 5 MIN./BATCH • **MAKES:** 40 APPETIZERS

1 beef top sirloin steak (1 in. thick and 1½ lbs.)

MARINADE
- ½ cup olive oil
- 1 Tbsp. lemon juice
- ½ tsp. salt
- ½ tsp. pepper

BREADING
- 1¼ cups seasoned bread crumbs
- ⅓ cup grated Parmesan cheese
- 2 Tbsp. minced fresh parsley
- ⅛ tsp. salt
- ⅛ tsp. garlic powder
  Dash pepper
- ¾ cup marinara sauce

ASSEMBLY
- 1 medium red onion
- 40 fresh sage leaves
- ¼ cup olive oil

1. Thinly slice steak widthwise into 5-in. strips. In a shallow bowl, combine the marinade ingredients. Add beef; turn to coat. Cover and refrigerate for 4 hours or overnight, turning occasionally.

2. Combine bread crumbs, cheese, parsley, salt, garlic powder and pepper. Transfer half the mixture to a shallow bowl; set aside.

3. For filling, add marinara sauce to the remaining crumb mixture and mix well. Spread 1 tsp. filling over each beef strip and roll up into pinwheels. Coat with the reserved crumb mixture.

4. Cut onion into 1-in. pieces and separate into layers. Thread a piece of onion, a sage leaf and a beef pinwheel onto a soaked wooden appetizer skewer; repeat. Drizzle lightly with oil and place on a greased 15x10x1-in. baking pan.

5. Broil 3-4 in. from heat for 5-7 minutes or until beef reaches desired doneness, turning once.

1 APPETIZER: 59 cal., 3g fat (1g sat. fat), 7mg chol., 101mg sod., 3g carb. (1g sugars, 0 fiber), 4g pro.

FROM GRANDMA'S KITCHEN: To make ahead, skewer spiedini as directed, without adding sage and onion. Freeze unbaked spiedini in a single layer on a waxed paper-lined baking sheet. Once frozen, transfer to a freezer container and freeze for up to 1 month. To use frozen spiedini, thread sage and onion as directed. Bake at 375° for 13-15 minutes or until the beef reaches desired doneness, turning once.

GRANDMA'S
CAJUN CHICKEN
& SPAGHETTI

GRANDMA'S CAJUN CHICKEN & SPAGHETTI

I'm originally from Louisiana, where my grandma spoke Cajun French as she taught me how to make her spicy chicken spaghetti on an old wood stove.
—*Brenda Melancon, McComb, MS*

PREP: 15 MIN. • COOK: 1¼ HOURS • MAKES: 10 SERVINGS

1 broiler/fryer chicken (3 to 4 lbs.), cut up
1 to 1½ tsp. cayenne pepper
¾ tsp. salt
3 Tbsp. canola oil
1 pkg. (14 oz.) smoked sausage, sliced
1 large sweet onion, chopped
1 medium green pepper, chopped
1 celery rib, chopped
2 garlic cloves, minced
2 cans (14½ oz. each) diced tomatoes, undrained
1 can (14½ oz.) diced tomatoes with mild green chiles, undrained
1 pkg. (16 oz.) spaghetti

1. Sprinkle chicken with cayenne pepper and salt. In a Dutch oven, heat oil over medium-high heat. Brown the chicken in batches. Remove from pan.

2. Add sausage, onion, green pepper and celery to same pan; cook and stir over medium heat 3 minutes. Add garlic; cook 1 minute longer. Stir in tomatoes. Return chicken to pan; bring to a boil. Reduce heat; simmer, covered, until chicken juices run clear, about 1 hour.

3. Cook the spaghetti according to package directions. Remove chicken from pan. When chicken is cool enough to handle, remove meat from bones; discard skin and bones. Shred the meat with 2 forks; return to pan. Bring to boil. Reduce heat; simmer, uncovered, until slightly thickened, 8-10 minutes. Skim fat. Drain spaghetti; serve with chicken mixture.

¾ CUP CHICKEN MIXTURE WITH ¾ CUP SPAGHETTI: 550 cal., 26g fat (8g sat. fat), 89mg chol., 917mg sod., 45g carb. (8g sugars, 4g fiber), 33g pro.

MAPLE-GLAZED CORNED BEEF

Corned beef gets a touch of sweetness with a maple syrup glaze. This recipe was passed down from my great-grandmother. Even people who don't care for corned beef will ask for seconds.
—*Gayle Macklin, Vail, AZ*

PREP: 25 MINUTES • COOK: 2½ HOURS • MAKES: 12 SERVINGS

2 corned beef briskets with spice packets (3 lbs. each)
1 large sweet onion, sliced
12 garlic cloves, peeled and halved
¼ cup kosher salt
¼ cup whole peppercorns
8 bay leaves
2 Tbsp. dried basil
2 Tbsp. dried oregano
4 qt. water
3 cups beef broth
¼ cup maple syrup
⅓ cup packed brown sugar

1. Place briskets and contents of the spice packets in a stockpot. Add onion, garlic, salt, peppercorns, bay leaves, basil and oregano. Pour in water and beef broth. Bring to a boil. Reduce heat; cover and simmer for 2½-3 hours or until meat is tender.

2. Transfer meat to a broiler pan. Brush with maple syrup; sprinkle with brown sugar. Broil 4-6 in. from the heat for 2-3 minutes or until beef is glazed. Thinly slice across the grain.

4 OZ. COOKED BEEF: 439 cal., 30g fat (10g sat. fat), 156mg chol., 2014mg sod., 11g carb. (10g sugars, 0 fiber), 29g pro.

BLUE CHEESE-MUSHROOM STUFFED TENDERLOIN

Here's my go-to entree for most special events. Filled with a savory stuffing,
the sliced tenderloin looks and tastes like it comes from an upscale restaurant.
—*Joyce Conway, Westerville, OH*

PREP: 25 MIN. • BAKE: 40 MIN. + STANDING • MAKES: 8 SERVINGS

2 Tbsp. butter
½ lb. sliced baby portobello mushrooms
1 Tbsp. Worcestershire sauce
3 Tbsp. horseradish mustard or spicy brown mustard
1 Tbsp. coarsely ground pepper
1 Tbsp. olive oil
1 tsp. salt
1 beef tenderloin roast (4 lbs.)
¾ cup crumbled blue cheese, divided
1½ cups french-fried onions
   Additional french-fried onions, optional

1. Preheat oven to 425°. In a small skillet, heat the butter over medium-high heat. Add mushrooms and Worcestershire sauce; cook and stir until the mushrooms are tender, 6-8 minutes. In a small bowl, mix mustard, pepper, oil and salt.

2. Cut lengthwise through the center of roast to within ½ in. of the bottom. Open roast and cut lengthwise through the center of each half to within ½ in. of bottom. Open roast flat; cover with plastic wrap. Pound with a meat mallet to ¾-in. thickness.

3. Remove plastic. Spread mushrooms down the center of roast to within ½ in. of ends; top with ½ cup cheese and the onions. Starting at a long side, roll up jelly-roll style; tie at 1½-in. intervals with kitchen string. Secure ends with toothpicks.

4. Place on a rack in a shallow roasting pan; spread with mustard mixture. Roast until meat reaches desired doneness (for medium-rare, a thermometer should read 135°; medium, 140°; medium-well, 145°), 40-50 minutes.

5. Remove roast from oven; tent with foil. Let stand 15 minutes before slicing. Remove string and toothpicks. Top individual servings with the remaining ¼ cup cheese. If desired, warm additional onions in microwave and sprinkle over top.

1 SERVING: 499 cal., 28g fat (11g sat. fat), 116mg chol., 636mg sod., 7g carb. (1g sugars, 1g fiber), 52g pro.

BEST EVER MAC & CHEESE

To make this amazing mac, I make a sauce loaded with three different cheeses to toss with the noodles. When baked, it's ooey-gooey and cheesy good. And don't get me started on the crunchy topping!

—*Beth Jacobson, Milwaukee, WI*

PREP: 40 MIN. • BAKE: 10 MIN. • MAKES: 12 SERVINGS

1 pkg. (16 oz.) uncooked elbow macaroni

4 slices hearty white bread (4 oz.), torn into large pieces

6 Tbsp. butter, cubed and divided

½ cup grated Parmesan cheese

1 tsp. salt, divided

1 tsp. pepper, divided

¼ cup finely chopped onion

1 tsp. ground mustard

¼ tsp. cayenne pepper

¼ cup all-purpose flour

3 cups whole milk

2 cups half-and-half cream

1 cup (4 oz.) Velveeta

1 block (8 oz.) sharp cheddar cheese, shredded

1 block (8 oz.) Monterey Jack cheese, shredded

1 tsp. Worcestershire sauce

1. Preheat oven to 400°. In a stockpot or Dutch oven, cook pasta according to package directions for al dente; drain and return to pan. Pulse bread, 2 Tbsp. butter, Parmesan cheese, ½ tsp. salt and ½ tsp. pepper in a food processor until coarsely ground.

2. Meanwhile, in a large skillet over medium heat, melt the remaining 4 Tbsp. butter. Add onions and cook until tender, about 3 minutes. Add ground mustard and cayenne; stir until blended. Stir in flour until smooth, about 3 minutes. Slowly whisk in milk and cream; bring to a boil. Reduce heat to medium-low; simmer, stirring constantly, until thickened, about 5 minutes. Remove from heat; stir in Velveeta. Slowly add the remaining cheeses, a handful at a time, stirring until cheese is melted. Add Worcestershire sauce and the remaining ½ tsp. salt and ½ tsp. pepper. Pour over pasta; toss to coat.

3. Transfer to a greased 13x9-in. baking dish. Sprinkle bread crumbs over top of casserole. Bake until topping is golden brown and sauce is bubbly, 10-12 minutes.

1 CUP: 762 cal., 43g fat (25g sat. fat), 134mg chol., 1138mg sod., 61g carb. (10g sugars, 3g fiber), 32g pro.

FROM GRANDMA'S KITCHEN: Substitute any (or all) of the following for the bread crumb topping: coarsely crushed pork rinds; coarsely crushed potato chips; coarsely crushed Ritz crackers. Whatever topping or combination of toppings you use, it should equal 2 cups.

INDIVIDUAL TURKEY POTPIES

Savory, creamy potpies are a great way to make leftovers new again. These delectable single-serving meals are made with fresh herbs, a silky homemade Dijon sauce and puff pastry.

—*Victoria Bond, Tempe, AZ*

PREP: 50 MIN. • BAKE: 20 MIN. • MAKES: 6 SERVINGS

2½ cups cubed peeled potatoes
1 cup chopped onion
¾ cup sliced fresh carrots
½ cup chopped celery
1 Tbsp. olive oil
2 garlic cloves, minced
2 cups cubed cooked turkey
½ cup fresh peas
½ tsp. minced fresh thyme or ⅛ tsp. dried thyme
½ tsp. minced fresh rosemary or ⅛ tsp. dried rosemary, crushed
¼ tsp. salt
⅛ tsp. pepper

SAUCE
¼ cup butter, cubed
6 Tbsp. all-purpose flour
2 cups 2% milk
1 cup chicken broth
½ cup heavy whipping cream

3 Tbsp. Dijon mustard
1 Tbsp. capers, drained
1 tsp. minced fresh tarragon or ¼ tsp. dried tarragon
1 tsp. minced fresh thyme or ¼ tsp. dried thyme
1 tsp. minced fresh rosemary or ¼ tsp. dried rosemary, crushed
½ tsp. rubbed sage
½ tsp. dried marjoram
¼ tsp. ground nutmeg
⅛ tsp. salt
⅛ tsp. pepper

CRUST
1 sheet frozen puff pastry, thawed
1 large egg
1 Tbsp. water
2 Tbsp. grated Parmesan cheese

1. In a large skillet, saute the potatoes, onion, carrots and celery in oil for 8 minutes. Add garlic; cook 1 minute longer. Stir in the turkey, peas, thyme, rosemary, salt and pepper; heat through.

2. For the sauce, in a large saucepan, melt butter. Stir in flour until smooth; gradually add milk, broth and cream. Bring to a boil; cook and stir for 1-2 minutes or until thickened. Stir in mustard, capers, herbs, nutmeg, salt, pepper and the potato mixture. Divide among 6 greased 10-oz. ramekins.

3. On a lightly floured surface, roll out puff pastry into a 13x9-in. rectangle. Cut into 6 squares. Place 1 pastry over each ramekin; press to seal edges. Beat egg and water; brush over pastry. Sprinkle with cheese.

4. Place ramekins on a baking sheet. Bake, uncovered, at 400° for 20-25 minutes or until golden brown.

1 POTPIE: 620 cal., 34g fat (15g sat. fat), 126mg chol., 864mg sod., 55g carb. (8g sugars, 6g fiber), 25g pro.

GRANDMA'S SECRET

If you like, use a round cookie cutter to cut a hole in the crust to reveal the savory filling. Be sure to use a cutter with a thin edge for the cleanest cut possible, so your puff pastry is sure to rise.

CHICKEN
AMANDINE

CHICKEN AMANDINE

With colorful green beans and pimientos, this attractive casserole is terrific
for the holidays or family dinners. This is true comfort food at its finest.
—*Kat Woolbright, Wichita Falls, TX*

PREP: 35 MIN. • BAKE: 30 MIN. • MAKES: 8 SERVINGS

¼ cup chopped onion
1 Tbsp. butter
1 pkg. (6 oz.) long grain
and wild rice
2¼ cups chicken broth
3 cups cubed cooked
chicken
2 cups frozen french-style
green beans, thawed
1 can (10¾ oz.) condensed
cream of chicken soup,
undiluted
¾ cup sliced almonds,
divided
1 jar (4 oz.) diced
pimientos, drained
1 tsp. pepper
½ tsp. garlic powder
1 bacon strip, cooked
and crumbled

1. In a large saucepan, saute the onion in butter until tender. Add
rice with contents of seasoning packet and chicken broth. Bring
to a boil. Reduce heat; cover and simmer until liquid is absorbed,
about 25 minutes. Uncover; set aside to cool.

2. In a large bowl, combine the chicken, green beans, soup, ½ cup
almonds, pimientos, pepper and garlic powder. Stir in rice.

3. Transfer to a greased 2½-qt. baking dish. Sprinkle with bacon
and the remaining ¼ cup almonds. Cover and bake at 350° until
heated through, 30-35 minutes.

1 CUP: 297 cal., 13g fat (3g sat. fat), 54mg chol., 912mg sod.,
24g carb. (3g sugars, 3g fiber), 22g pro.

GREEK-STYLE LEMON-GARLIC CHICKEN

I love celebrating my Greek heritage with this super simple and scrumptious Sunday dinner. Prep time is
a breeze, and the ingredient list is short for such a flavorful one-dish meal. Each time I make this, it
reminds me of my yaya (grandma), who used to let me squeeze the lemons when she made it.
—*Lisa Renshaw, Kansas City, MO*

PREP: 15 MIN. • BAKE: 1 HOUR • MAKES: 8 SERVINGS

8 medium Yukon Gold
potatoes (about 3 lbs.)
1 cup pitted Greek olives
8 bone-in chicken thighs
(about 3 lbs.)
½ cup olive oil
3 Tbsp. lemon juice
6 garlic cloves, minced
2 tsp. salt
2 tsp. dried oregano
½ tsp. pepper
1½ cups reduced-sodium
chicken broth

1. Preheat oven to 375°. Scrub potatoes; cut each into 8 wedges
and place in a shallow roasting pan. Top with olives and chicken.
In a small bowl, whisk oil, lemon juice, garlic, salt, oregano and
pepper until blended. Drizzle over chicken and potatoes. Pour
chicken broth into pan around the chicken.

2. Bake, uncovered, until a thermometer inserted in chicken
reads 170°-175° and potatoes are tender, 60-70 minutes. Serve
with pan juices.

1 CHICKEN THIGH WITH 8 POTATO WEDGES AND ABOUT ⅓ CUP PAN
JUICES: 602 cal., 33g fat (6g sat. fat), 81mg chol., 1071mg sod., 48g
carb. (4g sugars, 4g fiber), 29g pro.

OLD-FASHIONED
SCALLOPED
PINEAPPLE, PAGE 172

GRANDMA'S FAVORITE

SIDE DISHES

A great side dish does so much more than fill a space
on the dinner plate—it complements the main dish and
elevates the whole meal. If you're struggling to round
out a menu, look no further than Grandma's staples.
Indulge in these longtime staples that turn
any meal into a special occasion.

SPINACH SOUFFLE

You just can't make an easier, more delicious side dish than this. It's great with beef, pork and lamb, and I especially like serving it for festive occasions like New Year's Eve.
—*Bette Duffy, Kenmore, WA*

PREP: 20 MIN. • **BAKE:** 35 MIN. • **MAKES:** 6 SERVINGS

2 **pkg. (10 oz. each) frozen chopped spinach, thawed and squeezed dry**
1 **pkg. (8 oz.) cream cheese, cubed**
1½ **cups shredded Monterey Jack cheese**
4 **large eggs, lightly beaten**
¼ **cup butter, melted**
1 **garlic clove, minced**
½ **tsp. salt**

Preheat oven to 350°. In a large bowl, combine all ingredients. Transfer to a greased 1½-qt. baking dish. Bake until the edges are lightly browned, 35-40 minutes.

½ CUP: 375 cal., 33g fat (20g sat. fat), 228mg chol., 630mg sod., 5g carb. (0 sugars, 3g fiber), 17g pro.

ROASTED CABBAGE & ONIONS

I roast veggies to bring out their sweetness, and it works wonders with onions and cabbage. The piquant vinegar-mustard sauce makes this dish similar to a slaw.
—*Ann Sheehy, Lawrence, MA*

PREP: 10 MIN. • **COOK:** 30 MIN. + STANDING • **MAKES:** 6 SERVINGS

1 **medium head cabbage (about 2 lbs.), coarsely chopped**
2 **large onions, chopped**
¼ **cup olive oil**
¾ **tsp. salt**
¾ **tsp. pepper**
3 **Tbsp. minced fresh chives**
3 **Tbsp. minced fresh tarragon**

DRESSING
2 **Tbsp. white balsamic vinegar or white wine vinegar**
2 **Tbsp. olive oil**
2 **Tbsp. Dijon mustard**
1 **Tbsp. lemon juice**
½ **tsp. salt**
½ **tsp. pepper**

1. Preheat oven to 450°. Place cabbage and onions in a large bowl. Drizzle with oil; sprinkle with salt and pepper and toss to coat. Transfer to a shallow roasting pan, spreading evenly. Roast until vegetables are tender and lightly browned, 30-35 minutes, stirring halfway.

2. Transfer cabbage mixture to a large bowl. Add chives and tarragon; toss to combine. In a small bowl, whisk dressing ingredients until blended. Drizzle over cabbage mixture; toss to coat. Let stand 10 minutes to allow flavors to blend. Serve warm or at room temperature.

¾ CUP: 183 cal., 14g fat (2g sat. fat), 0 chol., 636mg sod., 15g carb. (7g sugars, 4g fiber), 2g pro.

GRANDMA'S SECRET
You can use fresh spinach in place of frozen in this recipe—you just have to cook it first. Figure on 1 lb. of fresh spinach for each 10-oz. box of frozen.

PEARL ONION BROCCOLI BAKE

With its creamy white cheese sauce and buttery crumb topping, this dish is pure comfort food. If you're looking for a mild way to dress up broccoli, this is the recipe.

—*Charles Keating, Manchester, MD*

PREP: 20 MIN. • BAKE: 25 MIN. • MAKES: 12 SERVINGS

2 pkg. (16 oz. each) frozen broccoli florets
1 pkg. (14.4 oz.) pearl onions
½ cup butter, divided
¼ cup all-purpose flour
¾ tsp. salt
⅛ tsp. pepper
2 cups 2% milk
6 oz. cream cheese, cubed
1 cup shredded cheddar cheese
2 cups soft bread crumbs

1. Preheat oven to 350°. Cook broccoli in 1 in. of water until almost tender; drain. Cook the pearl onions in 1 in. of water until almost tender; drain. Transfer both to a greased 13x9-in. baking dish.

2. In a large saucepan, melt ¼ cup butter; whisk in flour, salt and pepper until smooth. Gradually whisk in milk. Bring to a boil; cook and stir until thickened, 1-2 minutes. Reduce heat; stir in cream cheese until blended. Add to vegetables; stir gently to coat. Sprinkle with cheddar cheese.

3. Melt the remaining ¼ cup butter; toss with bread crumbs. Sprinkle over casserole. Bake, uncovered, until topping is golden brown, 25-30 minutes.

NOTE: To make soft bread crumbs, tear bread into pieces and place in a food processor or blender. Cover and pulse until crumbs form. One slice of bread yields ½-¾ cup crumbs.

¾ CUP: 241 cal., 17g fat (10g sat. fat), 47mg chol., 389mg sod., 15g carb. (5g sugars, 3g fiber), 7g pro.

HONEY-LEMON ASPARAGUS

Everyone who tastes my glazed asparagus takes a second helping, so I usually double the recipe. For another option, try using a root vegetable like turnip or parsnip.
—*Lorraine Caland, Shuniah, ON*

TAKES: 15 MIN. • MAKES: 8 SERVINGS

2 lbs. fresh asparagus, trimmed
¼ cup honey
2 Tbsp. butter
2 Tbsp. lemon juice
1 tsp. sea salt
1 tsp. balsamic vinegar
1 tsp. Worcestershire sauce
Additional sea salt, optional

1. In a large saucepan, bring 8 cups water to a boil. Add the asparagus in batches; cook, uncovered, 1-2 minutes or just until crisp-tender. Drain and pat dry.

2. Meanwhile, in a small saucepan, combine the remaining ingredients. Bring to a boil. Reduce heat; simmer, uncovered, 2 minutes or until slightly thickened.

3. Transfer asparagus to a large bowl; drizzle with glaze and toss gently to coat. If desired, sprinkle with additional sea salt.

1 SERVING: 73 cal., 3g fat (2g sat. fat), 8mg chol., 276mg sod., 12g carb. (10g sugars, 1g fiber), 2g pro. DIABETIC EXCHANGES: 1 vegetable, ½ starch, ½ fat.

MOIST POULTRY DRESSING

Tasty mushrooms and onions complement the big herb flavor in this amazing stuffing. This dressing stays so moist because it's made in the slow cooker.
—*Ruth Ann Stelfox, Raymond, AB*

PREP: 20 MIN. • COOK: 4 HOURS • MAKES: 16 SERVINGS

¾ cup butter, cubed
2 jars (4½ oz. each) sliced mushrooms, drained
4 celery ribs, chopped
2 medium onions, chopped
¼ cup minced fresh parsley
1½ lbs. day-old bread, crusts removed and cubed (about 13 cups)
1½ tsp. salt
1½ tsp. rubbed sage
1 tsp. poultry seasoning
1 tsp. dried thyme
½ tsp. pepper
2 large eggs
1 can (14½ oz.) chicken broth or 14½ oz. vegetable broth

1. In a large skillet, melt the butter; add mushrooms, celery, onions and parsley; saute until the vegetables are tender. In a large bowl, toss the bread cubes with salt, sage, poultry seasoning, thyme and pepper. Add the mushroom mixture. Combine eggs and broth; add to the bread mixture and toss.

2. Transfer to 5-qt. slow cooker. Cover and cook on low for 4-5 hours or until a thermometer reads 160°.

¾ CUP: 212 cal., 11g fat (6g sat. fat), 50mg chol., 694mg sod., 24g carb. (3g sugars, 2g fiber), 5g pro.

SOUTHWESTERN RICE

SOUTHWESTERN RICE

I created this colorful side dish after eating something similar at a restaurant.
It complements any Tex-Mex meal wonderfully. Sometimes I add cubes
of grilled chicken breast to the rice to make it a meal in itself.
—*Michelle Dennis, Clarks Hill, IN*

TAKES: 30 MIN. • MAKES: 8 SERVINGS

1 Tbsp. olive oil
1 medium green pepper, diced
1 medium onion, chopped
2 garlic cloves, minced
1 cup uncooked long grain rice
½ tsp. ground cumin
⅛ tsp. ground turmeric
1 can (14½ oz.) reduced-sodium chicken broth
2 cups frozen corn (about 10 oz.), thawed
1 can (15 oz.) black beans, rinsed and drained
1 can (10 oz.) diced tomatoes and green chiles, undrained

1. In a large nonstick skillet, heat oil over medium-high heat; saute pepper and onion 3 minutes. Add garlic; cook and stir for 1 minute.

2. Stir in rice, spices and broth; bring to a boil. Reduce heat; simmer, covered, until rice is tender, about 15 minutes.

3. Stir in the remaining ingredients; cook, covered, until heated through.

¾ CUP: 198 cal., 3g fat (1g sat. fat), 1mg chol., 339mg sod., 37g carb. (0 sugars, 5g fiber), 7g pro.

CREAMY CRANBERRY SALAD

One of my piano students taught me the perfect lesson—how to make a wonderful salad
for the holidays. The keys are cranberries, pineapple, marshmallows and nuts.
—*Alexandra Lypecky, Dearborn, MI*

PREP: 15 MIN. + CHILLING • MAKES: 16 SERVINGS

3 cups fresh or thawed frozen cranberries, chopped
1 can (20 oz.) unsweetened crushed pineapple, drained
2 cups miniature marshmallows
1 medium apple, chopped
⅔ cup sugar
⅛ tsp. salt
2 cups heavy whipping cream
¼ cup chopped walnuts

1. In a large bowl, mix the first 6 ingredients. Refrigerate, covered, overnight.

2. To serve, beat cream until stiff peaks form. Fold whipped cream and walnuts into cranberry mixture.

½ CUP: 200 cal., 12g fat (7g sat. fat), 34mg chol., 32mg sod., 23g carb. (20g sugars, 1g fiber), 1g pro.

FROM GRANDMA'S KITCHEN: To really bring the walnuts to life, toast them for a few minutes in a dry skillet. Stir occasionally and watch closely so they don't burn. Remove from the heat when fragrant.

GRANDMA'S STUFFED YELLOW SQUASH

My grandma, who raised me, was an awesome cook. This is a recipe she fixed every summer when our garden overflowed with yellow squash. My family still enjoys it.
—*Janie McGraw, Sallisaw, OK*

PREP: 25 MIN. • BAKE: 25 MIN. • MAKES: 2 SERVINGS

1 medium yellow summer squash
¼ cup egg substitute
2 Tbsp. finely chopped onion
¼ tsp. salt
⅛ tsp. pepper
2 slices bread, toasted and diced

1. Preheat oven to 375°. Place squash in a large saucepan; cover with water. Bring to a boil; cover and cook for 7-9 minutes or until crisp-tender. Drain.

2. When squash is cool enough to handle, cut in half lengthwise; scoop out and reserve pulp, leaving two ⅜-in. shells. Invert shells on a paper towel.

3. Combine egg substitute, onion, salt and pepper. Stir in toasted bread cubes and squash pulp. Spoon into the squash shells.

4. Place in an 8-in. square baking dish coated with cooking spray. Cover and bake for 20 minutes. Uncover; bake 5-10 minutes longer or until lightly browned.

1 STUFFED SQUASH HALF: 103 cal., 1g fat (0 sat. fat), 0 chol., 490mg sod., 18g carb. (4g sugars, 3g fiber), 6g pro. DIABETIC EXCHANGES: 1 starch, 1 vegetable.

CUCUMBERS WITH DRESSING

It wouldn't be summer if Mom didn't make lots of these creamy cucumbers. Just a few simple ingredients—mayonnaise, sugar, vinegar and salt—are all you need to dress them up.
—*Michelle Beran, Claflin, KS*

PREP: 10 MIN. + CHILLING • MAKES: 6 SERVINGS

1 cup mayonnaise
¼ cup sugar
¼ cup white vinegar
¼ tsp. salt
4 cups thinly sliced cucumbers

In a large bowl, mix the first 4 ingredients; toss with cucumbers. Refrigerate, covered, 2 hours.

¾ CUP: 283 cal., 27g fat (4g sat. fat), 3mg chol., 286mg sod., 11g carb. (10g sugars, 0 fiber), 0 pro.

COUNTRY POTATO PANCAKES

These versatile potato pancakes can be a side dish for just about any dinner or the main course for a light meal. They go particularly well with pork. We have them often at our house.
—*Lydia Robotewskyj, Franklin, WI*

TAKES: 30 MIN. • MAKES: ABOUT 24 PANCAKES

3 **large potatoes (about 2 lbs.), peeled**
2 **large eggs, lightly beaten**
1 **Tbsp. grated onion**
2 **Tbsp. all-purpose flour**
1 **tsp. salt**
½ **tsp. baking powder**
   Vegetable oil for frying

1. Finely grate potatoes. Drain any liquid. Add the eggs, onion, flour, salt and baking powder. In a frying pan, add oil to a depth of ⅛ in.; heat over medium-high heat to 375°.

2. Drop batter by heaping tablespoonfuls in hot oil. Flatten into patties. Fry until golden brown, turning once. Serve immediately.

2 PANCAKES: 257 cal., 8g fat (1g sat. fat), 31mg chol., 242mg sod., 41g carb. (2g sugars, 5g fiber), 6g pro.

BLUE CHEESE & GRAPE COLESLAW

Dishes like coleslaw beg for a fresh approach. I update mine with almonds, grapes, blue cheese and bacon for a grand bowl of color and crunch.
—*Jeannine Bunge, Hartley, IA*

PREP: 20 MIN. + CHILLING • MAKES: 8 SERVINGS

1 **pkg. (14 oz.) coleslaw mix**
¾ **cup sliced almonds, toasted**
¾ **cup quartered green grapes**
¾ **cup quartered seedless red grapes**
½ **cup crumbled blue cheese**
3 **bacon strips, cooked and crumbled**
¼ **tsp. pepper**
¾ **cup coleslaw salad dressing**

Combine the first 7 ingredients. Pour dressing over salad; toss to coat. Refrigerate 1 hour.

NOTE: To toast nuts, bake in a shallow pan in a 350° oven for 5-10 minutes or cook in a skillet over low heat until lightly browned, stirring occasionally.

¾ CUP: 212 cal., 15g fat (3g sat. fat), 17mg chol., 339mg sod., 16g carb. (12g sugars, 3g fiber), 5g pro.

NEW ENGLAND BAKED BEANS

For a potluck or picnic, you can't beat this classic side dish. Molasses and maple syrup give it sweetness—you can use less brown sugar as needed to suit your tastes.
—*Pat Medeiros, Tiverton, RI*

PREP: 1½ HOURS + SOAKING • **BAKE:** 2½ HOURS • **MAKES:** 12 SERVINGS

1 lb. dried great northern beans
½ lb. thick-sliced bacon strips, chopped
2 large onions, chopped
3 garlic cloves, minced
2 cups ketchup
1½ cups packed dark brown sugar
⅓ cup molasses
⅓ cup maple syrup
¼ cup Worcestershire sauce
½ tsp. salt
¼ tsp. coarsely ground pepper

1. Sort beans and rinse with cold water. Place beans in a Dutch oven; add enough water to cover by 2 in. Bring to a boil; boil for 2 minutes. Remove from the heat; cover and let stand for 1 hour or until the beans are softened.

2. Drain and rinse beans, discarding liquid. Return beans to Dutch oven; add 6 cups water. Bring to a boil. Reduce heat; cover and simmer for 1 hour or until beans are almost tender.

3. In a large skillet, cook bacon over medium heat until crisp. Remove to paper towels with a slotted spoon; drain, reserving 2 Tbsp. drippings in the pan. Saute onions in the drippings until tender. Add garlic; cook 1 minute longer. Stir in ketchup, brown sugar, molasses, syrup, Worcestershire sauce, salt and pepper.

4. Drain beans, reserving cooking liquid; place the beans in an ungreased 3-qt. baking dish. Stir in onion mixture and bacon. Cover and bake at 300° for 2½ hours or until beans are tender and reach desired consistency, stirring every 30 minutes. Add reserved cooking liquid as needed.

⅔ CUP: 385 cal., 5g fat (2g sat. fat), 7mg chol., 810mg sod., 77g carb. (50g sugars, 8g fiber), 11g pro.

"Thanks for a great recipe that reminded me of the oven-baked beans my grandmother made decades ago."
—TKUEHL, TASTEOFHOME.COM

CRUMB-TOPPED MACARONI & CHEESE

Everyone loves this grown-up macaroni and cheese. It's also tasty made with sharp cheddar and cream cheese instead of Gruyere and mascarpone. Throw in crispy bacon for a smoky twist.

—*Jennifer Standing, Taos, NM*

PREP: 30 MIN. • BAKE: 15 MIN. • MAKES: 8 SERVINGS

2 cups uncooked elbow macaroni	2 cups shredded Gruyere cheese or Swiss cheese
½ cup butter, divided	1 carton (8 oz.) mascarpone cheese
½ tsp. crushed red pepper flakes	4½ tsp. Dijon mustard
¼ cup all-purpose flour	¼ tsp. salt
1½ cups whole milk	⅛ tsp. pepper
	¾ cup panko bread crumbs
	1 Tbsp. Italian seasoning

1. Preheat oven to 425°. In a 6-qt. stockpot, cook macaroni according to the package directions for al dente; drain and return to pot.

2. Meanwhile, in a medium saucepan, heat ¼ cup butter and pepper flakes over medium heat until the butter is melted. Stir in flour until smooth; gradually whisk in milk. Bring to a boil, stirring constantly; cook and stir until thickened, 1-2 minutes.

3. Stir in Gruyere, mascarpone, mustard, salt and pepper until blended. Add sauce to macaroni, tossing to combine. Transfer to a greased 13x9-in. baking dish.

4. Melt the remaining ¼ cup butter. Add panko and Italian seasoning; toss to coat. Sprinkle over the macaroni. Bake, uncovered, until topping is golden brown, 10-15 minutes.

¾ CUP: 473 cal., 36g fat (21g sat. fat), 102mg chol., 487mg sod., 23g carb. (3g sugars, 1g fiber), 16g pro.

GRANDMA'S SECRET

Don't overcook! This casserole bakes at a high temperature, so it needs only about 10 minutes in the oven to crisp up the crumb topping and finish cooking the macaroni.

BRUSSELS SPROUTS WITH BACON & GARLIC

When we have company, these sprouts are my go-to side dish—they look and
taste fantastic! For fancier occasions, dress them up with pancetta instead of bacon.

—Mandy Rivers, Lexington, SC

TAKES: 30 MIN. • MAKES: 12 SERVINGS

2 lbs. fresh Brussels
   sprouts (about 10 cups)
8 bacon strips, coarsely
   chopped
3 garlic cloves, minced
¾ cup chicken broth
½ tsp. salt
¼ tsp. pepper

1. Trim Brussels sprouts. Cut sprouts lengthwise in half; cut
crosswise into thin slices. In a 6-qt. Dutch oven or stockpot, cook
bacon over medium heat until crisp, stirring occasionally. Add
garlic; cook 30 seconds longer. Remove with a slotted spoon;
drain on paper towels.

2. Add Brussels sprouts to bacon drippings in pot; cook and stir
until sprouts begin to brown lightly, 4-6 minutes. Stir in broth,
salt and pepper; cook, covered, until Brussels sprouts are tender,
4-6 minutes longer. Stir in bacon mixture.

¾ CUP: 109 cal., 8g fat (3g sat. fat), 13mg chol., 300mg sod.,
7g carb. (2g sugars, 3g fiber), 5g pro. DIABETIC EXCHANGES:
1½ fat, 1 vegetable.

WILD RICE & SQUASH PILAF

This pilaf is wonderful served with fish or poultry and especially
compatible with turkey. It's a fantastic side dish for the holidays!

—Erica Ollmann, San Diego, CA

PREP: 15 MIN. • COOK: 20 MIN. • MAKES: 10 SERVINGS

1½ cups sliced fresh
   mushrooms
1½ cups finely chopped
   peeled winter squash
2 medium onions,
   finely chopped
1 small green pepper,
   chopped
2 Tbsp. olive oil
2 to 3 garlic cloves, minced
3 cups cooked wild rice
½ cup chicken broth
   or vegetable broth
1 Tbsp. reduced-sodium
   soy sauce
½ tsp. dried savory
¼ cup sliced almonds,
   toasted

1. In a large saucepan, saute the mushrooms, squash, onions
and green pepper in oil until crisp-tender. Add garlic; saute for
1 minute longer.

2. Stir in the rice, broth, soy sauce and savory. Cover and cook
over medium-low heat for 13-15 minutes or until the squash is
tender. Stir in almonds.

½ CUP: 118 cal., 4g fat (1g sat. fat), 0 chol., 114mg sod., 18g carb.
(3g sugars, 3g fiber), 4g pro. DIABETIC EXCHANGES: 1 starch, 1 fat.

TWO-TONE BAKED
POTATOES

TWO-TONE BAKED POTATOES

One potato...two potato...this recipe is doubly wonderful as far as spud lovers are concerned.
I'm known at home and at work for trying out new recipes. Everyone is glad I took a chance on this one!
—*Sherree Stahn, Central City, NE*

PREP: 30 MIN. • BAKE: 1¼ HOURS • MAKES: 12 SERVINGS

6 **medium russet potatoes
(about 8 oz. each)**
6 **medium sweet potatoes
(about 8 oz. each)**
⅔ **cup sour cream, divided**
⅓ **cup 2% milk**
¾ **cup shredded cheddar
cheese**
4 **Tbsp. minced fresh
chives, divided**
1½ **tsp. salt, divided**

1. Preheat oven to 400°. Scrub russet and sweet potatoes; pierce several times with a fork. Place in foil-lined 15x10x1-in. pans; bake until tender, 60-70 minutes. Reduce oven setting to 350°.

2. When potatoes are cool enough to handle, cut a third off the top of each russet potato (discard top or save for another use). Scoop out pulp, leaving ½-in.-thick shells. In a bowl, mash pulp, adding ⅓ cup sour cream, milk, cheese, 2 Tbsp. chives and ¾ tsp. salt.

3. Cut a thin slice off the top of each sweet potato; discard slice. Scoop out pulp, leaving ½-in.thick shells. Mash pulp with remaining ⅓ cup sour cream, 2 Tbsp. chives and ¾ tsp. salt.

4. Spoon russet potato mixture into half of each russet and sweet potato skin. Spoon sweet potato mixture into the other half. Return to pans. Bake until heated through, 15-20 minutes.

1 STUFFED POTATO: 237 cal., 5g fat (3g sat. fat), 11mg chol., 365mg sod., 42g carb. (11g sugars, 5g fiber), 6g pro.

BRANDY-GLAZED CARROTS

I found this recipe about 10 years ago in an old cookbook I got at a thrift store. The original recipe called for sugar; I changed it to honey. Once glazed, these carrots are not just delicious, they're pretty, too!
—*Tammy Landry, Saucier, MS*

TAKES: 30 MIN. • MAKES: 12 SERVINGS

3 **lbs. fresh baby carrots**
½ **cup butter, cubed**
½ **cup honey**
¼ **cup brandy**
¼ **cup minced fresh parsley**
½ **tsp. salt**
¼ **tsp. pepper**

1. In a large skillet, bring ½ in. of water to a boil. Add carrots. Cover and cook for 5-9 minutes or until crisp-tender. Drain and set aside.

2. In the same skillet, cook butter and honey over medium heat until butter is melted. Remove from heat; stir in brandy. Bring to a boil; cook until liquid is reduced to about ½ cup. Add the carrots, parsley, salt and pepper; heat through.

¾ CUP: 153 cal., 8g fat (5g sat. fat), 20mg chol., 242mg sod., 21g carb. (17g sugars, 2g fiber), 1g pro.

GRANDMOTHER'S CORN PUDDING

My grandmother always served this pudding at family reunions and other big gatherings.
Corn pudding is an especially popular side dish on Maryland's eastern shore.
—*Susan Brown Langenstein, Salisbury, MD*

PREP: 10 MIN. • BAKE: 50 MIN. • MAKES: 9 SERVINGS

4 **large eggs**
1 **cup whole milk**
1 **can (15 oz.) cream-style corn**
½ **cup sugar**
5 **slices day-old bread, crusts removed**
1 **Tbsp. butter, softened**

Preheat oven to 350°. In a bowl, beat eggs and milk. Add corn and sugar; mix well. Cut bread into ½-in. cubes and place in a greased 9-in. square baking dish. Pour egg mixture over bread. Dot with butter. Bake, uncovered, until a knife inserted in the center comes out clean, 50-60 minutes.

1 SERVING: 175 cal., 5g fat (2g sat. fat), 102mg chol., 264mg sod., 28g carb. (14g sugars, 1g fiber), 6g pro.

POTLUCK CANDIED SWEET POTATOES

To make it easier to bring this traditional southern staple to a potluck, I updated it so
it can be cooked in a slow cooker. When it comes to pleasing a crowd,
it's hard to go wrong with candied sweet potatoes.
—*Deirdre Cox, Kansas City, MO*

PREP: 20 MIN. • COOK: 5 HOURS • MAKES: 12 SERVINGS

1 **cup packed brown sugar**
1 **cup sugar**
8 **medium sweet potatoes, peeled and cut into ½-in. slices**
¼ **cup butter, melted**
2 **tsp. vanilla extract**
¼ **tsp. salt**
2 **Tbsp. cornstarch**
2 **Tbsp. cold water**
Minced fresh parsley, optional

1. In a small bowl, combine sugars. In a greased 5-qt. slow cooker, layer a third of the sweet potatoes; sprinkle with a third of the sugar mixture. Repeat layers twice. In a small bowl, combine the butter, vanilla and salt; drizzle over potatoes. Cover and cook on low for 5-6 hours or until sweet potatoes are tender.

2. Using a slotted spoon, transfer potatoes to a serving dish; keep warm. Pour cooking juices into a small saucepan; bring to a boil. In a small bowl, combine cornstarch and water until smooth; stir into pan. Return to a boil, stirring constantly; cook and stir until thickened, 1-2 minutes. Spoon over sweet potatoes. Sprinkle with parsley if desired.

¾ CUP SWEET POTATO WITH ¼ CUP SAUCE: 252 cal., 4g fat (2g sat. fat), 10mg chol., 91mg sod., 54g carb. (42g sugars, 2g fiber), 1g pro.

EASY ORANGE & RED ONION SALAD

Here's a distinctive salad that's easy to prepare when you're short on time. The combination of red onions and oranges may seem unusual, but it's surprisingly delightful.
—*Edie DeSpain, Logan, UT*

TAKES: 20 MIN. • MAKES: 10 SERVINGS

6 **Tbsp. canola oil**
2 **Tbsp. white wine vinegar**
½ **tsp. grated orange zest**
2 **Tbsp. orange juice**
1 **Tbsp. sugar**
⅛ **tsp. ground cloves**
  Dash salt
  Dash pepper
6 **medium navel oranges, peeled and sliced**
1 **medium red onion, thinly sliced and separated into rings**

For dressing, whisk together the first 8 ingredients. Place the oranges and onion in a large bowl; toss gently with dressing. Refrigerate, covered, until serving.

¾ CUP: 127 cal., 9g fat (1g sat. fat), 0 chol., 148mg sod., 13g carb. (9g sugars, 2g fiber), 1g pro. DIABETIC EXCHANGES: ½ fruit, 1½ fat.

CHEESY GRITS

As a comfy side dish, grits have great potential but sometimes need a flavor boost. The addition of tangy cheddar cheese in this version hits just the right note.
—*Paula Hughes, Birmingham, AL*

TAKES: 25 MIN. • MAKES: 8 SERVINGS

2 **cups 2% milk**
1 **cup chicken or vegetable broth**
1 **cup water**
1 **tsp. salt**
1 **cup uncooked old-fashioned grits**
2 **to 3 cups shredded sharp cheddar or Monterey Jack cheese**
  Pepper and additional salt to taste

1. Combine milk, broth and water in a large saucepan; bring to a boil. Add salt. Whisk in grits; reduce heat to low. Cook, stirring frequently, until creamy, 15-20 minutes.

2. Stir in cheese until melted. Season with pepper and additional salt to taste.

½ CUP: 225 cal., 11g fat (6g sat. fat), 34mg chol., 629mg sod., 20g carb. (3g sugars, 1g fiber), 10g pro.

FROM GRANDMA'S KITCHEN: For an additional burst of flavor, try stirring in ¼-½ tsp. crushed red pepper flakes, 1 tsp. chopped fresh rosemary or 1 tsp. crushed garlic.

ARROZ CON GANDULES (RICE WITH PIGEON PEAS)

Feed a crowd with this authentic Puerto Rican rice dish, which was handed down
to me from my mom. It's a staple with the familia at all our gatherings.
—*Evelyn Robles, Oak Creek, WI*

PREP: 15 MIN. • COOK: 30 MIN. • MAKES: 18 SERVINGS

½ cup sofrito
2 Tbsp. canola oil
4 cups uncooked long
  grain rice
1 envelope Goya sazon
  with coriander and
  annatto
7 cups water
1 can (15 oz.) pigeon peas,
  drained
2 cans (5 oz. each) Vienna
  sausage, drained and
  chopped
½ cup tomato sauce
1¼ tsp. salt
1 envelope Goya ham-
  flavored concentrate
½ tsp. chicken bouillon
  granules
¼ tsp. pepper

In a Dutch oven, cook sofrito in oil over medium-low heat, stirring occasionally, about 5 minutes. Add rice and sazon; cook and stir until rice is lightly toasted, 3-4 minutes. Add all remaining ingredients. Bring to a boil. Reduce heat; cover and simmer until rice is tender, 15-20 minutes. Fluff with a fork.

NOTE: Sofrito is a sauce used in many Latin American, Asian and Mediterranean dishes and usually contains peppers. garlic, onion and aromatic spices; it can be found in the international foods section. Look for Goya sazon, a seasoning blend, in the international foods section as well.

¾ CUP: 220 cal., 5g fat (1g sat. fat), 14mg chol., 537mg sod., 38g carb. (1g sugars, 2g fiber), 6g pro.

FROM GRANDMA'S KITCHEN: To ensure your rice is nice and fluffy, once you cover it, keep it covered the entire cooking time and refrain from stirring. When the timer goes off, allow the rice to sit covered for an additional 5-10 minutes off the heat. This allows the starches to cool down slightly and the moisture to distribute evenly among the rice grains. Fluff with a fork for light and airy texture and to prevent clumps.

SUCCOTASH

You can't get more southern than succotash. This recipe comes from my mother, who was a fantastic cook. The dish made her famous—at least with everyone who ever tasted it!

—*Rosa Boone, Mobile, AL*

PREP: 1¾ HOURS + COOLING • COOK: 1 HOUR • MAKES: 16 SERVINGS

1 smoked ham hock
(about 1½ lbs.)
4 cups water
1 can (28 oz.) diced
tomatoes, undrained
1½ cups frozen lima beans,
thawed
1 pkg. (10 oz.) crowder
peas, thawed, or 1 can
(15½ oz.) black-eyed
peas, drained
1 pkg. (10 oz.) frozen corn,
thawed
1 medium green pepper,
chopped
1 medium onion, chopped
⅓ cup ketchup
1½ tsp. salt
1½ tsp. dried basil
1 tsp. rubbed sage
1 tsp. paprika
½ tsp. pepper
1 bay leaf
1 cup sliced fresh or frozen
okra
Snipped fresh dill and
chives, optional

1. In a Dutch oven or large saucepan, simmer ham hock in water until tender, about 1½ hours.

2. Cool; remove meat from the bone and return to pan. (Discard bone and broth or save for another use.) Add tomatoes, beans, peas, corn, green pepper, onion, ketchup and seasonings. Simmer, uncovered, for 45 minutes.

3. Add okra; simmer, uncovered, until tender, 15 minutes. Discard bay leaf before serving. Garnish with dill and chives, if desired.

¾ **CUP:** 79 cal., 0 fat (0 sat. fat), 2mg chol., 442mg sod., 16g carb. (5g sugars, 3g fiber), 4g pro. **DIABETIC EXCHANGES:** 1 starch.

GRANDMA'S SECRET

Succotash is a distinctly American dish. Native Americans made their stew—called misckquatash—from fresh corn in the summer months and dried corn in the winter.

COWBOY CALICO BEANS

This is a tradition at the table when my friends and I go up north for a girls' weekend.
The husbands and kids are left at home, but the slow cooker comes with us!
—*Julie Butsch, Hartland, WI*

PREP: 30 MIN. • COOK: 4 HOURS • MAKES: 8 SERVINGS

1 lb. lean ground beef
(90% lean)
1 large sweet onion,
chopped
½ cup packed brown sugar
¼ cup ketchup
3 Tbsp. cider vinegar
2 Tbsp. yellow mustard
1 can (16 oz.) butter beans,
drained
1 can (16 oz.) kidney beans,
rinsed and drained
1 can (15 oz.) pork and
beans
1 can (15¼ oz.) lima beans,
rinsed and drained

1. In a large skillet, cook beef and onion over medium heat until meat is no longer pink; drain.

2. Transfer to a 3-qt. slow cooker. Combine the brown sugar, ketchup, cider vinegar and mustard; add to the meat mixture. Stir in the beans. Cover and cook on low 4-5 hours or until heated through.

¾ CUP: 326 cal., 5g fat (2g sat. fat), 35mg chol., 808mg sod., 52g carb. (22g sugars, 10g fiber), 22g pro.

QUICK & EASY AU GRATIN POTATOES

At holidays, a dear friend serves these creamy, cheesy potatoes whenever we
gather to celebrate with lifelong friends and our grown children.
—*Carol Blue, Barnesville, PA*

PREP: 10 MIN. • BAKE: 50 MIN. • MAKES: 12 SERVINGS

2 cups sour cream
1 can (10¾ oz.) condensed
cream of chicken soup,
undiluted
½ tsp. salt
¼ tsp. pepper
1 pkg. (30 oz.) frozen
shredded hash brown
potatoes, thawed
2 cups shredded cheddar
cheese
1 small onion, chopped
2 cups crushed cornflakes
¼ cup butter, melted

1. Preheat oven to 350°. In a large bowl, mix sour cream, condensed soup, salt and pepper; stir in potatoes, cheese and onion. Transfer to a greased 13x9-in. baking dish.

2. In a small bowl, mix crushed cornflakes and melted butter; sprinkle over the potato mixture. Bake, uncovered, 50-60 minutes or until golden brown.

¾ CUP: 394 cal., 22g fat (14g sat. fat), 70mg chol., 680mg sod., 36g carb. (5g sugars, 2g fiber), 11g pro.

GRANDMA'S
COLLARD GREENS

GRANDMA'S COLLARD GREENS

My grandmother made the best collard greens in the world; this is her recipe.
Eating them with a slice of freshly baked buttermilk cornbread is pure bliss.
—*Sherri Williams, Crestview, FL*

PREP: 30 MIN. • COOK: 2 HOURS • MAKES: 6 SERVINGS

3 Tbsp. lard or shortening, divided
1 large onion, chopped
6 garlic cloves, minced
1½ lbs. smoked ham hocks
6 cups water
2 tsp. seasoned salt
1 to 3 tsp. crushed red pepper flakes
¼ tsp. sugar
1 large bunch collard greens (about 2 lbs.), coarsely chopped
1½ cups white wine

1. In a 6-qt. stockpot, melt 1 Tbsp. lard over medium heat. Add onion and garlic; cook and stir until tender. Add ham hocks, water, seasoned salt, pepper flakes, and sugar. Bring to a boil. Reduce heat; simmer, uncovered, 55-60 minutes or until meat is tender.

2. Add collard greens, wine, and remaining 2 Tbsp. lard. Return to a boil. Reduce heat; simmer, uncovered, 55-60 minutes or until the greens are very tender. Remove meat from bones; finely chop and return to pan. Discard bones. Serve with a slotted spoon.

1 CUP: 204 cal., 9g fat (3g sat. fat), 19mg chol., 849mg sod., 13g carb. (3g sugars, 7g fiber), 10g pro.

EASY SLOW-COOKER MAC & CHEESE

My sons always cheer, "You're the best mom in the world!" whenever I make this
creamy mac and cheese perfection. You can't beat a response like that!
—*Heidi Fleek, Hamburg, PA*

PREP: 25 MIN. • COOK: 1 HOUR • MAKES: 8 SERVINGS

2 cups uncooked elbow macaroni
1 can (10¾ oz.) condensed cheddar cheese soup, undiluted
1 cup 2% milk
½ cup sour cream
¼ cup butter, cubed
½ tsp. onion powder
¼ tsp. white pepper
⅛ tsp. salt
1 cup shredded cheddar cheese
1 cup shredded fontina cheese
1 cup shredded provolone cheese

1. Cook macaroni according to package directions for al dente. Meanwhile, in a large saucepan, combine soup, milk, sour cream, butter and seasonings; cook and stir over medium-low heat until blended. Stir in cheeses until melted.

2. Drain macaroni; transfer to a greased 3-qt. slow cooker. Stir in the cheese mixture. Cook, covered, on low 1-2 hours or until heated through.

¾ CUP: 346 cal., 23g fat (14g sat. fat), 71mg chol., 712mg sod., 20g carb. (4g sugars, 1g fiber), 15g pro.

OLD-FASHIONED SCALLOPED PINEAPPLE

My deliciously different dressing goes well with turkey or salty ham. Because of its sweetness,
it also makes a good dessert with a little cream poured over the top!
—*Nancy Brown, Dahinda, IL*

PREP: 10 MIN. • BAKE: 30 MIN. + STANDING • MAKES: 6 SERVINGS

3 **large eggs, beaten**
2 **cups sugar**
1 **can (8 oz.) crushed**
 pineapple, undrained
½ **cup butter, melted**
¼ **cup 2% milk**
4 **cups cubed bread**

Preheat oven to 350°. Combine eggs, sugar, pineapple, butter and milk; add bread cubes and toss to coat. Transfer to a greased 8-in. square baking dish. Bake, uncovered, until a thermometer reads 160°, 30-35 minutes. Let stand 10 minutes before serving. Refrigerate leftovers.

⅔ CUP: 529 cal., 19g fat (11g sat. fat), 135mg chol., 277mg sod., 87g carb. (75g sugars, 1g fiber), 6g pro.

TATER-DIPPED VEGGIES

Deep-fried vegetables are terrific, but it's not always convenient to prepare them for company.
Here's a recipe that produces the same deliciously crisp results in the oven.
Serve these with your favorite ranch-style dressing as a dip.
—*Earleen Lillegard, Prescott, AZ*

PREP: 15 MIN. • BAKE: 20 MIN. • MAKES: 6 SERVINGS

1 **cup instant potato flakes**
⅓ **cup grated Parmesan**
 cheese
½ **tsp. celery salt**
¼ **tsp. garlic powder**
¼ **cup butter, melted**
 and cooled
2 **large eggs**
4 **to 5 cups raw bite-sized**
 vegetables (mushrooms,
 peppers, broccoli,
 cauliflower, zucchini and/
 or parboiled carrots)
 Prepared ranch salad
 dressing or dip, optional

1. Preheat oven to 400°. In a small bowl, combine the potato flakes, Parmesan cheese, celery salt, garlic powder and butter. In another bowl, beat eggs. Dip each vegetable piece into the eggs, then into the potato mixture; coat well.

2. Place on an ungreased baking sheet. Bake for 20-25 minutes. Serve with dressing or dip if desired.

1 SERVING: 159 cal., 11g fat (6g sat. fat), 86mg chol., 282mg sod., 11g carb. (1g sugars, 2g fiber), 6g pro.

ORANGE-GLAZED BEETS

Beets were a popular vegetable in our house when I was growing up, and this recipe is a real favorite of ours. It's easy to make, and the orange gives it a delightful citrus flavor.
—*Susan Punzal, Orchard Park, NY*

TAKES: 25 MIN. • **MAKES:** 8 SERVINGS

- ¾ cup orange marmalade
- 6 Tbsp. orange juice
- ⅓ cup butter, cubed
- ¼ tsp. salt
- ¼ tsp. pepper
- 3 cans (14½ oz. each) sliced beets, drained

In a large skillet, combine the first 5 ingredients. Bring to a boil; cook and stir until thickened, 3-4 minutes. Add the beets; cook and stir until most of the liquid is absorbed, 6-8 minutes longer.

½ CUP: 194 cal., 8g fat (5g sat. fat), 20mg chol., 443mg sod., 32g carb. (27g sugars, 3g fiber), 2g pro.

MOM'S SWEET POTATO BAKE

Mom loves sweet potatoes and fixed them often in this creamy, comforting casserole. With its nutty topping, this side dish could almost serve as a dessert. It's a treat!
—*Sandi Pichon, Memphis, TN*

PREP: 10 MIN. • **BAKE:** 45 MIN. • **MAKES:** 8 SERVINGS

- 3 cups cold mashed sweet potatoes (prepared without milk or butter)
- 1 cup sugar
- 3 large eggs, room temperature
- ½ cup 2% milk
- ¼ cup butter, softened
- 1 tsp. salt
- 1 tsp. vanilla extract

TOPPING
- ½ cup packed brown sugar
- ½ cup chopped pecans
- ¼ cup all-purpose flour
- 2 Tbsp. cold butter

1. Preheat oven to 325°. In a large bowl, beat the sweet potatoes, sugar, eggs, milk, butter, salt and vanilla until smooth. Transfer to a greased 2-qt. baking dish.

2. In a small bowl, combine the brown sugar, pecans and flour; cut in butter until crumbly. Sprinkle over sweet potato mixture. Bake, uncovered, until a thermometer reads 160°, 45-50 minutes.

½ CUP: 417 cal., 16g fat (7g sat. fat), 94mg chol., 435mg sod., 65g carb. (47g sugars, 4g fiber), 6g pro.

FROM GRANDMA'S KITCHEN: Store sweet potatoes just like regular potatoes—in a cool, dark place, for up to 2 weeks.

CRANBERRY ROASTED SQUASH

I created this recipe one day when I wanted a warm, fragrant side dish. The aroma of the squash and cranberries cooking in the oven is just as heavenly as the taste itself.
—Jamillah Almutawakil, Superior, CO

PREP: 15 MIN. • BAKE: 45 MIN. • MAKES: 12 SERVINGS

1 medium butternut squash (5 to 6 lbs.), peeled and cut into 1-in. cubes
1 medium acorn squash (about 1½ lbs.), peeled and cut into 1-in. cubes
⅔ cup chopped fresh or frozen cranberries
¼ cup sugar
2 Tbsp. olive oil
1 Tbsp. butter, melted
1 Tbsp. molasses
2 garlic cloves, minced
1½ tsp. rubbed sage
1 tsp. salt
½ tsp. pepper

Preheat oven to 400°. In a large bowl, combine all ingredients; toss well. Transfer to two 15x10x1-in. baking pans. Roast until squash is tender, stirring and rotating pans halfway through cooking, 45-55 minutes.

¾ CUP: 161 cal., 3g fat (1g sat. fat), 3mg chol., 214mg sod., 35g carb. (12g sugars, 8g fiber), 2g pro. DIABETIC EXCHANGES: 2 starch, ½ fat.

NOODLE KUGEL

I make this traditional dish along with other Jewish specialties as my contribution to the annual Hanukkah/Christmas party we have with friends.
—Lauren Kargen, Buffalo, NY

PREP: 20 MIN. • BAKE: 50 MIN. + STANDING • MAKES: 15 SERVINGS

1 pkg. (1 lb.) egg noodles
½ cup butter, melted
8 large eggs, room temperature
2 cups sugar
2 cups sour cream
2 cups 4% cottage cheese

TOPPING
¾ cup cinnamon graham cracker crumbs (about 4 whole crackers)
3 Tbsp. butter, melted

1. Preheat oven to 350°. Cook noodles according to package directions; drain. Toss with butter; set aside. In a large bowl, beat the eggs, sugar, sour cream and cottage cheese until well blended. Stir in noodles.

2. Transfer to a greased 13x9-in. baking dish. Combine the cracker crumbs and butter; sprinkle over top. Bake, uncovered, for 50-55 minutes or until a thermometer reads 160°. Let stand for 10 minutes before cutting. Serve warm or cold.

1 CUP: 432 cal., 19g fat (11g sat. fat), 191mg chol., 261mg sod., 54g carb. (30g sugars, 1g fiber), 12g pro.

CRANBERRY
ROASTED SQUASH

SPINACH SALAD WITH RASPBERRIES & CANDIED WALNUTS

I created this bright spinach salad with raspberries for a big family dinner. The festive colors fit right in on a holiday table. Even those who don't like spinach change their minds at the very first bite.

—Robert Aucelluzzo, Simi Valley, CA

PREP: 15 MIN. • **BAKE:** 25 MIN. + COOLING • **MAKES:** 8 SERVINGS

- 1 large egg white
- ¾ tsp. vanilla extract
- 2 cups walnut halves
- ½ cup sugar
- 1½ tsp. light corn syrup
- 1 tsp. poppy seeds
- ¼ tsp. salt
- ¼ tsp. ground mustard

DRESSING
- ¼ cup canola oil
- 2 Tbsp. cider vinegar
- 1 Tbsp. sugar

SALAD
- 8 oz. fresh baby spinach (about 10 cups)
- 1½ cups fresh raspberries

1. Preheat oven to 300°. In a small bowl, whisk egg white and vanilla until frothy. Stir in walnuts. Sprinkle with sugar; toss to coat evenly. Spread in a single layer in a greased 15x10x1-in. baking pan. Bake 25-30 minutes or until lightly browned, stirring every 10 minutes. Spread on waxed paper to cool completely.

2. In a small bowl, whisk the dressing ingredients until blended. Place spinach in a large bowl. Drizzle with dressing; toss to coat. Sprinkle with raspberries and 1 cup candied walnuts (save the remaining 1 cup walnuts for another use).

1½ CUPS: 171 cal., 13g fat (1g sat. fat), 0 chol., 100mg sod., 12g carb. (9g sugars, 3g fiber), 3g pro. **DIABETIC EXCHANGES:** 1½ fat, 1 starch, 1 vegetable.

SEASONED BROWN RICE PILAF

For those of us who are white rice lovers at heart, this recipe makes brown rice taste terrific! Everyone takes seconds—it's just that good. To convert for vegetarians, just substitute vegetable broth for the beef broth. Leftovers keep well in the fridge and make a great second meal the next day.

—*Amy Berry, Poland, ME*

PREP: 10 MIN. • COOK: 55 MIN. • MAKES: 10 SERVINGS

1 **Tbsp. olive oil**
2 **cups uncooked brown rice**
1 **small onion, finely chopped**
5 **cups reduced-sodium beef broth**
1 **Tbsp. dried parsley flakes**
1 **tsp. garlic powder**
1 **tsp. seasoned salt**
½ **tsp. onion powder**
½ **tsp. ground turmeric**
½ **tsp. pepper**
½ **cup uncooked whole wheat orzo pasta**

1. In a Dutch oven, heat oil over medium heat. Add rice and onion; saute until rice is lightly browned, 8-10 minutes.

2. Add broth; stir in the next 6 ingredients. Bring to a boil. Reduce heat; simmer, covered, for 35 minutes.

3. Add the orzo. Cook, covered, until the orzo is tender, another 10-15 minutes.

⅔ CUP: 190 cal., 3g fat (0 sat. fat), 3mg chol., 380mg sod., 36g carb. (1g sugars, 4g fiber), 5g pro. **DIABETIC EXCHANGES:** 2½ starch, ½ fat.

GRUYERE MASHED POTATOES

The sophisticated taste of Gruyere cheese and chives takes simple mashed potatoes to a whole new level! This dish is elegant and tasty and comes together just as quickly as a more run-of-the-mill mash. Don't have chives? Use extra green onion instead.

—*Preci D'Silva, Dubai, AE*

TAKES: 25 MIN. • MAKES: 8 SERVINGS

2 **lbs. potatoes, peeled and cubed**
½ **cup sour cream**
⅓ **cup 2% milk, warmed**
1 **garlic clove, minced**
¼ **cup butter, cubed**
¼ **cup shredded Gruyere or Swiss cheese**
¼ **cup minced fresh chives**
2 **green onions, chopped**
½ **tsp. garlic salt**
¼ **tsp. pepper**

1. Place potatoes in a 6-qt. stockpot; add water to cover. Bring to a boil. Reduce heat; simmer, uncovered, until potatoes are tender, 10-15 minutes.

2. Drain; return to pot. Mash potatoes, gradually adding sour cream, milk and garlic. Stir in remaining ingredients.

¾ CUP: 169 cal., 10g fat (6g sat. fat), 23mg chol., 206mg sod., 17g carb. (2g sugars, 1g fiber), 3g pro.

GRANDMA'S SECRET

If you want to get a head start, cover the beans with the water and let them soak overnight. Drain them the next day and continue with the recipe as directed.

HEARTY RED BEANS & RICE

I learned about this mouthwatering combination of meats, beans and seasonings
while I was working for the Navy in New Orleans. I take this dish to
many potlucks and never fail to bring home an empty pot!
—*Kathy Jacques, Summerfield, FL*

PREP: 15 MIN. + SOAKING • COOK: 2 HOURS • MAKES: 10 SERVINGS

1 lb. dried kidney beans
2 tsp. garlic salt
1 tsp. Worcestershire
 sauce
¼ tsp. hot pepper sauce
1 qt. water
½ lb. fully cooked ham,
 diced
½ lb. fully cooked smoked
 sausage, diced
1 cup chopped onion
½ cup chopped celery
3 garlic cloves, minced
1 can (8 oz.) tomato sauce
2 bay leaves
¼ cup minced fresh parsley
½ tsp. salt
½ tsp. pepper
 Hot cooked rice

1. Place beans in a Dutch oven; add water to cover by 2 in. Bring to a boil; boil for 2 minutes. Remove from the heat; cover and let stand for 1-4 hours or until softened.

2. Drain beans, discarding liquid. Add garlic salt, Worcestershire sauce, hot pepper sauce and 1 qt. water; bring to a boil. Reduce heat; cover and simmer for 1½ hours.

3. Meanwhile, in a large skillet, saute ham and sausage until lightly browned. Remove with a slotted spoon and transfer to bean mixture, reserving drippings in pan.

4. Saute onion and celery in drippings until tender. Add minced garlic cloves; cook 1 minute longer. Add to the bean mixture. Stir in tomato sauce and bay leaves. Cover and simmer for 30 minutes or until beans are tender.

5. Discard bay leaves. Measure 2 cups of beans; mash and return to the bean mixture. Stir in the parsley, salt and pepper. Serve over rice.

1 CUP: 276 cal., 9g fat (3g sat. fat), 27mg chol., 1149mg sod., 32g carb. (4g sugars, 8g fiber), 18g pro.

HONEY GARLIC GREEN BEANS

Green beans are wonderful, but they can seem ordinary on their own.
Just a couple of extra ingredients give them a sweet and salty attitude.
—*Shannon Dobos, Calgary, AB*

TAKES: 20 MIN. • MAKES: 8 SERVINGS

4 **Tbsp. honey**
2 **Tbsp. reduced-sodium soy sauce**
4 **garlic cloves, minced**
¼ **tsp. salt**
¼ **tsp. crushed red pepper flakes**
2 **lbs. fresh green beans, trimmed**

1. Whisk together the first 5 ingredients; set aside. In a 6-qt. stockpot, bring 10 cups water to a boil. Add beans in batches; cook, uncovered, just until crisp-tender, 2-3 minutes. Remove beans and immediately drop into ice water. Drain and pat dry.

2. Coat stockpot with cooking spray. Add beans; cook, stirring constantly, over high heat until slightly blistered, 2-3 minutes. Add sauce; continue stirring until beans are coated and sauce starts to evaporate slightly, 2-3 minutes. Remove from heat.

¾ CUP: 72 cal., 0 fat (0 sat. fat), 0 chol., 225mg sod., 18g carb. (12g sugars, 4g fiber), 2g pro. **DIABETIC EXCHANGES:** 1 vegetable, ½ starch.

CANDIED ACORN SQUASH SLICES

This simple but oh-so-good recipe came to me from my grandma, who always served it
at Thanksgiving. Now I make it any time of year, whenever I'm feeling nostalgic.
—*Rita Addicks, Weimar, TX*

PREP: 15 MIN. • BAKE: 40 MIN. • MAKES: 6 SERVINGS

2 **medium acorn squash**
⅔ **cup packed brown sugar**
½ **cup butter, softened**

1. Preheat oven to 350°. Cut squash in half lengthwise; remove and discard seeds. Cut each half crosswise into ½-in. slices; discard ends. Arrange squash slices in a shallow baking pan; cover with foil. Bake until just tender, 25-30 minutes.

2. Combine sugar and butter; spread over squash. Bake, uncovered, 15-20 minutes longer, basting occasionally.

1 SQUASH SLICE: 287 cal., 15g fat (9g sat. fat), 41mg chol., 168mg sod., 40g carb. (27g sugars, 2g fiber), 1g pro.

LEMON PEPPER ROASTED BROCCOLI

Fresh green broccoli turns tangy and tasty when roasted with lemon juice and pepper. A sprinkle of almonds adds crunch.

—*Liz Bellville, Tonasket, WA*

TAKES: 25 MIN. • MAKES: 8 SERVINGS

1½ lbs. fresh broccoli florets (about 12 cups)
2 Tbsp. olive oil
½ tsp. lemon juice
¼ tsp. salt
¼ tsp. coarsely ground pepper, divided
¼ cup chopped almonds
2 tsp. grated lemon zest

1. Preheat oven to 450°. Place broccoli in a large bowl. Whisk oil, lemon juice, salt and ⅛ tsp. pepper until blended; drizzle over broccoli and toss to coat. Transfer to a 15x10x1-in. baking pan.

2. Roast for 10-15 minutes or until tender. Transfer to a serving dish. Sprinkle with almonds, lemon zest and the remaining ⅛ tsp. pepper; toss to combine.

1 CUP: 84 cal., 6g fat (1g sat. fat), 0 chol., 103mg sod., 7g carb. (0 sugars, 4g fiber), 4g pro. DIABETIC EXCHANGES: 1 vegetable, 1 fat.

GRANDMA'S CRANBERRY STUFF

What could taste better than turkey and cranberry on Thanksgiving Day? My grandmother's classic recipe makes the best cranberry stuff to share with your family and friends.

—*Catherine Cassidy, Milwaukee, WI*

TAKES: 10 MIN. • MAKES: 3 CUPS

1 medium navel orange
1 pkg. (12 oz.) fresh or frozen cranberries, thawed
1 cup sugar
1 cup chopped walnuts, toasted

Cut unpeeled orange into wedges, removing any seeds, and place in a food processor. Add cranberries and sugar; pulse until chopped. Add walnuts; pulse just until combined.

NOTE: To toast nuts, bake in a shallow pan in a 350° oven for 5-10 minutes or cook in a skillet over low heat until lightly browned, stirring occasionally.

¼ CUP: 148 cal., 6g fat (1g sat. fat), 0 chol., 1mg sod., 23g carb. (19g sugars, 2g fiber), 2g pro.

CREAMY PINEAPPLE FLUFF SALAD

Guests of all ages will gravitate to this traditional fluff salad,
brimming with pineapple, marshmallows and cherry bits.
—*Janice Hensley, Owingsville, KY*

TAKES: 25 MIN. • MAKES: 16 SERVINGS

1 pkg. (8 oz.) cream cheese, softened
1 can (14 oz.) sweetened condensed milk
¼ cup lemon juice
2 cans (20 oz.) pineapple tidbits, drained
1½ cups multicolored miniature marshmallows, divided
1 carton (8 oz.) frozen whipped topping, thawed
½ cup chopped nuts
⅓ cup maraschino cherries, chopped

In a large bowl, beat the cream cheese, milk and lemon juice until smooth. Add pineapple and 1 cup marshmallows; fold in the whipped topping. Sprinkle with the nuts, cherries and remaining ½ cup marshmallows. Refrigerate leftovers.

½ CUP: 161 cal., 10g fat (6g sat. fat), 16mg chol., 50mg sod., 17g carb. (12g sugars, 1g fiber), 2g pro.

ASPARAGUS, SQUASH & RED PEPPER SAUTE

Bright green asparagus, yellow squash and red peppers make a visually appealing trio;
the wine-scented saute makes it taste just as good as it looks.
—*Deirdre Cox, Kansas City, MO*

TAKES: 30 MIN. • MAKES: 4 SERVINGS

2 medium sweet red peppers, julienned
2 medium yellow summer squash, halved and cut into ¼-in. slices
6 oz. fresh asparagus, trimmed and cut into 1½-in. pieces
¼ cup white wine or vegetable broth
4½ tsp. olive oil
¼ tsp. salt
¼ tsp. pepper

In a large cast-iron or other heavy skillet, saute the peppers, squash and asparagus in wine and oil until crisp-tender. Sprinkle with salt and pepper.

¾ CUP: 90 cal., 5g fat (1g sat. fat), 0 chol., 163mg sod., 8g carb. (5g sugars, 3g fiber), 2g pro. DIABETIC EXCHANGES: 1 vegetable, 1 fat.

FROM GRANDMA'S KITCHEN: This very adaptable recipe can transform depending on what's in season. Substitute some zucchini, different colors of peppers, and even some fresh green beans.

CREAMY PINEAPPLE
FLUFF SALAD

CHEESY CHEDDAR BROCCOLI CASSEROLE

People who don't even like broccoli beg me to make this comforting recipe. It's similar to a classic green bean casserole, but the melted cheese puts it over the top.
—*Elaine Hubbard, Pocono Lake, PA*

PREP: 15 MIN. • **BAKE:** 35 MIN. • **MAKES:** 8 SERVINGS

- 1 **can (10¾ oz.) condensed cream of mushroom soup, undiluted**
- 1 **cup sour cream**
- 1½ **cups shredded sharp cheddar cheese, divided**
- 1 **can (6 oz.) french-fried onions, divided**
- 2 **pkg. (16 oz. each) frozen broccoli florets, thawed**

1. Preheat oven to 325°. In a large saucepan over medium heat, combine soup, sour cream, 1 cup cheese and 1¼ cups onions; heat through, stirring until blended, 4-5 minutes. Stir in broccoli. Transfer to a greased 2-qt. baking dish.

2. Bake, uncovered, until bubbly, 25-30 minutes. Sprinkle with the remaining ½ cup cheese and remaining onions. Bake until cheese is melted, 10-15 minutes.

¾ CUP: 359 cal., 26g fat (11g sat. fat), 30mg chol., 641mg sod., 19g carb. (4g sugars, 3g fiber), 8g pro.

FROM GRANDMA'S KITCHEN: As cheese ages, its flavor becomes more pronounced— sharp cheddar cheese has simply been aged longer than regular cheddar. Using sharp cheese can add complexity and rich flavor to any recipe that calls for cheddar.

POMEGRANATE PERSIMMON SALAD

To bring some sunshine to the table, I toss up a bright salad of persimmons and pomegranate seeds, dressed with a puckery vinaigrette.
—*Linda Tambunan, Dublin, CA*

TAKES: 15 MIN. • MAKES: 12 SERVINGS

½ cup olive oil
½ cup maple syrup
¼ cup rice vinegar
2 Tbsp. Dijon mustard
¼ tsp. salt
¼ tsp. pepper

SALAD
3 ripe Fuyu persimmons or 3 plums, sliced
2 pkg. (10 oz. each) baby kale salad blend
1 cup pomegranate seeds

1. Place the first 6 ingredients in a jar with a tight-fitting lid; secure lid and shake well. Refrigerate until serving.

2. To serve, shake vinaigrette again and toss ½ cup with the persimmons. Toss the remaining vinaigrette with the salad blend. Top with persimmons and pomegranate seeds.

1½ CUPS: 175 cal., 9g fat (2g sat. fat), 0 chol., 220mg sod., 23g carb. (17g sugars, 3g fiber), 2g pro. DIABETIC EXCHANGES: 2 vegetable, 2 fat, ½ starch, ½ fruit.

GRANDMA'S POTATO DUMPLINGS

Day-old rolls and leftover spuds are scrumptious the second time around when you turn them into buttery potato dumplings. Don't be surprised if you start making extra mashed potatoes on purpose after you taste this recipe.
—*Wendy Stenman, Germantown, WI*

TAKES: 25 MIN. • MAKES: 4 SERVINGS

2 day-old hard rolls
½ cup water
2 tsp. canola oil
½ cup leftover mashed potatoes
1 large egg, lightly beaten
Dash ground nutmeg
1 to 2 Tbsp. all-purpose flour
¼ cup butter, cubed

1. Tear rolls into ½-in. pieces; place in a 15x10x1-in. baking pan. Drizzle with water and squeeze dry.

2. In a large skillet, heat oil over medium-high heat. Add torn rolls; cook and stir until lightly toasted, 1-2 minutes.

3. In a small bowl, combine mashed potatoes, egg, nutmeg and bread. Add enough flour to achieve a shaping consistency. With floured hands, shape mixture into 3-in. balls.

4. Fill a Dutch oven two-thirds full with water; bring to a boil. Carefully add dumplings. Reduce heat; simmer, uncovered, until a toothpick inserted in center of dumplings comes out clean, 8-10 minutes.

5. Meanwhile, in a small heavy saucepan, melt butter over medium heat. Heat until golden brown, 4-6 minutes. Serve warm dumplings with butter.

1 DUMPLING WITH 1 TBSP. BUTTER: 255 cal., 17g fat (8g sat. fat), 84mg chol., 322mg sod., 22g carb. (1g sugars, 1g fiber), 5g pro.

LAYERED CHRISTMAS GELATIN

My jewel-toned gelatin always makes an appearance during our Christmas feast.
Filled with cranberries and pineapple, this sweet-tart salad could even serve as a light dessert.
—*Diane Schefelker, Ireton, IA*

PREP: 30 MIN. + CHILLING • **MAKES:** 10 SERVINGS

SIDE DISHES

1 pkg. (3 oz.) lime gelatin
1 cup boiling water
⅓ cup unsweetened
   pineapple juice
1 cup crushed pineapple,
   drained

CREAM CHEESE LAYER

1 tsp. unflavored gelatin
2 Tbsp. cold water
1 pkg. (8 oz.) cream cheese,
   softened
⅓ cup 2% milk

BERRY LAYER

2 pkg. (3 oz. each)
   strawberry gelatin
2 cups boiling water
1 can (14 oz.) whole-berry
   cranberry sauce
   Optional: Thawed
   whipped topping,
   lime wedges and
   fresh strawberries

1. Dissolve lime gelatin in boiling water; stir in pineapple juice. Stir in pineapple. Pour into an 11x7-in. dish; refrigerate until set.

2. In a small saucepan, sprinkle unflavored gelatin over cold water; let stand for 1 minute. Heat over low heat, stirring until gelatin is completely dissolved. Transfer to a small bowl. Beat in cream cheese and milk until smooth. Spread over lime layer; refrigerate until set.

3. Dissolve strawberry gelatin in boiling water; stir in cranberry sauce. Cool for 10 minutes. Carefully spoon over cream cheese layer. Refrigerate until set.

4. Cut into squares. If desired, serve with whipped topping, lime wedges and fresh strawberries.

1 PIECE: 267 cal., 8g fat (5g sat. fat), 26mg chol., 139mg sod., 46g carb. (39g sugars, 1g fiber), 5g pro.

FROM GRANDMA'S KITCHEN: Homemade whipped cream topping truly tastes best. Beat 1 cup heavy whipping cream on high until slightly thickened, then add 3 Tbsp. confectioners' sugar and ½ tsp. vanilla extract; beat until soft peaks form.

FAMILY-PLEASING
TURKEY CHILI, PAGE 195

GRANDMA'S FAVORITE

SOUPS & STEWS

An all-time classic like Grandma's chicken and
dumplings or her hearty beef stew delivers comforting
goodness as few foods can. Nothing compares to
homemade soup simmering on the stove (or in the
slow cooker)! These satisfying, heartwarming dishes
always guarantee a smile, so turn the page
and ladle out a bit of love today.

CHUNKY CREAMY CHICKEN SOUP

I am a stay-at-home mom who relies on my slow cooker for fast, nutritious meals with minimal prep time and cleanup. I knew this recipe was a hit when I didn't have any leftovers and my husband asked me to make it again.
—*Nancy Clow, Mallorytown, ON*

PREP: 15 MIN. • COOK: 4½ HOURS • MAKES: 7 SERVINGS

1½ lbs. boneless skinless
  chicken breasts,
  cut into 2-in. strips
2 tsp. canola oil
⅔ cup finely chopped onion
2 medium carrots, chopped
2 celery ribs, chopped
1 cup frozen corn
2 cans (10¾ oz. each)
  condensed cream of
  potato soup, undiluted
1½ cups chicken broth
1 tsp. dill weed
1 cup frozen peas
½ cup half-and-half cream

1. In a large skillet over medium-high heat, brown chicken in oil. Transfer to a 5-qt. slow cooker; add the onion, carrots, celery and corn.

2. In a large bowl, whisk the soup, broth and dill until blended; stir into slow cooker. Cover and cook on low until chicken and vegetables are tender, about 4 hours.

3. Stir in peas and cream. Cover and cook until heated through, about 30 minutes longer.

1 CUP: 229 cal., 7g fat (3g sat. fat), 66mg chol., 629mg sod., 17g carb. (5g sugars, 3g fiber), 24g pro.

HEARTY BUSY-DAY STEW

When I was still living in Missouri, a friend gave me her family cookbooks. I got the idea for this easy stew from one of those books. The taco seasoning adds just the right touch.
—*Kristen Hills, Layton, UT*

PREP: 10 MIN. • COOK: 7½ HOURS • MAKES: 6 SERVINGS

1½ lbs. beef stew meat
1½ lbs. potatoes
  (about 3 medium), peeled
  and cut into 1-in. cubes
1 can (14½ oz.) diced
  tomatoes, undrained
1 can (14½ oz.) beef broth
2½ cups fresh baby carrots
  (about 12 oz.)
1 large tomato, chopped
1 medium onion, chopped
2 Tbsp. taco seasoning
2 garlic cloves, minced
½ tsp. salt
2 Tbsp. cornstarch
2 Tbsp. cold water

1. In a 5- or 6-qt. slow cooker, combine the first 10 ingredients. Cook, covered, on low 7-9 hours or until the beef and vegetables are tender.

2. In a small bowl, mix the cornstarch and water until smooth; gradually stir into stew. Cook, covered, on high 30-45 minutes longer or until stew is slightly thickened.

1¾ CUPS: 303 cal., 8g fat (3g sat. fat), 71mg chol., 986mg sod., 32g carb. (8g sugars, 4g fiber), 25g pro.

CHUNKY CREAMY
CHICKEN SOUP

SLOW-COOKER MEATBALL STEW

This recipe was a lifesaver when I worked full time and needed a dinner for us all to enjoy when we got home. And your young ones can help prepare it! They can chop, peel, mix and pour. It doesn't matter if the veggies are all different sizes—your children will still devour this fun, tasty stew.
—*Kallee Krong-McCreery, Escondido, CA*

PREP: 20 MIN. • COOK: 6 HOURS • MAKES: 8 SERVINGS

4 **peeled medium potatoes, cut into ½-in. cubes**
4 **medium carrots, cut into ½-in. cubes**
2 **celery ribs, cut into ½-in. cubes**
1 **medium onion, diced**
¼ **cup frozen corn**
1 **pkg. (28 to 32 oz.) frozen fully cooked home-style meatballs**
1½ **cups ketchup**
1½ **cups water**
1 **Tbsp. white vinegar**
1 **tsp. dried basil**
  Optional: Biscuits or dinner rolls

In a 5-qt. slow cooker, combine potatoes, carrots, celery, onion, corn and meatballs. In a bowl, mix ketchup, water, vinegar and basil; pour over meatballs. Cook, covered, on low for 6-8 hours, until meatballs are cooked through. If desired, serve with biscuits or dinner rolls.

1 CUP: 449 cal., 26g fat (12g sat. fat), 41mg chol., 1322mg sod., 40g carb. (17g sugars, 4g fiber), 16g pro.

HEIRLOOM TOMATO SOUP

During the late summer months, I make this soup about once a week.
Even my son, who normally does not like tomatoes, enjoys this soup.
—*Kimberly Danek Pinkson, San Anselmo, CA*

PREP: 30 MIN. • COOK: 20 MIN. • MAKES: 20 SERVINGS (5 QT.)

1 **large sweet onion, halved and thinly sliced**
¼ **cup extra virgin olive oil**
6 **garlic cloves, minced**
12 **medium heirloom tomatoes, quartered (about 8 lbs.)**
1 **large carrot, chopped**
1 **cup fresh corn**
¼ **cup loosely packed basil leaves**
2 **tsp. sea salt**
5½ **cups reduced-sodium chicken broth**
⅓ **cup heavy whipping cream**

1. In a stockpot, saute onion in oil until tender. Add garlic; cook 1 minute longer. Add the tomatoes, carrot, corn, basil and salt.

2. Stir in broth. Bring to a boil. Reduce heat; cover and simmer for 15-20 minutes or until tomatoes are softened, stirring occasionally. Cool slightly.

3. In a food processor, process soup in batches until smooth. Return all to pan and heat through. Ladle into bowls; drizzle each individual serving with ¾ tsp. cream.

1 CUP: 73 cal., 4g fat (1g sat. fat), 5mg chol., 356mg sod., 7g carb. (4g sugars, 2g fiber), 2g pro. **DIABETIC EXCHANGES:** 1 vegetable, 1 fat.

SHRIMP GUMBO

A crisp green salad and crusty French bread complete this shrimp gumbo meal. I always have hot sauce available when I serve this and have found that the instant microwave rice packages make the process a little easier.
—*Jo Ann Graham, Ovilla, TX*

PREP: 30 MIN. • **COOK:** 1 HOUR • **MAKES:** 11 SERVINGS

¼ cup all-purpose flour
¼ cup canola oil
3 celery ribs, chopped
1 medium green pepper, chopped
1 medium onion, chopped
4 cups chicken broth
3 garlic cloves, minced
1 tsp. salt
1 tsp. pepper
½ tsp. cayenne pepper
2 lbs. uncooked shrimp (26-30 per pound), peeled and deveined
1 pkg. (16 oz.) frozen sliced okra
4 green onions, sliced
1 medium tomato, chopped
1½ tsp. gumbo file powder
Hot cooked rice

1. In a Dutch oven over medium heat, cook and stir flour and oil until caramel-colored, stirring occasionally, about 12 minutes (do not burn). Add the celery, green pepper and onion; cook and stir until tender, 5-6 minutes. Stir in the broth, garlic, salt, pepper and cayenne; bring to a boil. Reduce heat; cover and simmer for 30 minutes.

2. Stir in the shrimp, okra, green onions and tomato. Return to a boil. Reduce heat; cover and simmer until shrimp turn pink, 10 minutes. Stir in file powder. Serve with rice.

1 CUP: 159 cal., 7g fat (1g sat. fat), 102mg chol., 681mg sod., 9g carb. (3g sugars, 2g fiber), 15g pro. DIABETIC EXCHANGES: 2 lean meat, 1 vegetable, 1 fat.

FROM GRANDMA'S KITCHEN: Gumbo file powder, used to thicken and flavor Creole recipes, is available in spice shops. If it's not available, combine 2 Tbsp. each cornstarch and water until smooth. Gradually stir into gumbo. Bring to a boil; cook and stir for 2 minutes or until thickened.

FAMILY-PLEASING TURKEY CHILI

My children really love this recipe—it's one of their favorite comfort foods.
It's relatively inexpensive, and the leftovers are wonderful!
—*Sheila Christensen, San Marcos, CA*

PREP: 25 MIN. • COOK: 4 HOURS • MAKES: 6 SERVINGS (2¼ QT.)

1 lb. lean ground turkey
1 medium green pepper,
   finely chopped
1 small red onion,
   finely chopped
2 garlic cloves, minced
1 can (28 oz.) diced
   tomatoes, undrained
1 can (16 oz.) kidney beans,
   rinsed and drained
1 can (15 oz.) black beans,
   rinsed and drained
1 can (14½ oz.)
   reduced-sodium
   chicken broth
1¾ cups frozen corn, thawed
1 can (6 oz.) tomato paste
1 Tbsp. chili powder
½ tsp. pepper
¼ tsp. ground cumin
¼ tsp. garlic powder
   Optional: Reduced-fat
   sour cream and
   minced fresh cilantro

1. In a large nonstick skillet, cook the turkey, green pepper and onion over medium heat until meat is no longer pink, breaking it into crumbles. Add garlic; cook 1 minute longer. Drain.

2. Transfer to a 4-qt. slow cooker. Stir in the tomatoes, kidney beans, black beans, broth, corn, tomato paste, chili powder, pepper, cumin and garlic powder. Cover and cook on low until heated through, 4-5 hours. If desired, serve with sour cream and cilantro.

FREEZE OPTION: Freeze cooled chili in freezer containers. To use, partially thaw in refrigerator overnight. Heat through in a saucepan, stirring occasionally; add a little water if necessary.

1½ CUPS: 349 cal., 7g fat (2g sat. fat), 60mg chol., 725mg sod., 47g carb. (11g sugars, 12g fiber), 27g pro. DIABETIC EXCHANGES: 3 lean meat, 2 starch, 2 vegetable.

"This recipe is fantastic! The name of the recipe says it all—definitely a family-pleasing favorite! Sometimes I add 1-3 tablespoons of McCormick's chili powder, depending on how spicy we want it. And I do variations of beans."
—LISA VARGAS, TASTEOFHOME.COM

WEEKDAY BEEF STEW

Beef stew capped with flaky puff pastry adds comfort to the weeknight menu—my family is always glad to see this meal. Make a salad and call your crowd to the table.

—Daniel Anderson, Kenosha, WI

TAKES: 30 MIN. • MAKES: 4 SERVINGS

1   **sheet frozen puff pastry, thawed**

1   **pkg. (15 oz.) refrigerated beef roast au jus**

2   **cans (14½ oz. each) diced tomatoes, undrained**

1   **pkg. (16 oz.) frozen vegetables for stew**

¾   **tsp. pepper**

2   **Tbsp. cornstarch**

1¼ **cups water**

1. Preheat oven to 400°. Unfold puff pastry. Using a 4-in. round cookie cutter, cut out 4 circles. Place 2 in. apart on a greased baking sheet. Bake until golden brown, 14-16 minutes.

2. Meanwhile, shred the beef with 2 forks; transfer to a large saucepan. Add tomatoes, vegetables and pepper; bring to a boil. In a small bowl, mix cornstarch and water until smooth; stir into beef mixture. Return to a boil, stirring constantly; cook and stir until thickened, 1-2 minutes.

3. Ladle stew into 4 bowls; top each individual serving with a pastry round.

1½ CUPS WITH 1 PASTRY ROUND: 604 cal., 25g fat (8g sat. fat), 73mg chol., 960mg sod., 65g carb. (10g sugars, 9g fiber), 32g pro.

SPINACH & WHITE BEAN SOUP

For me, soup is love, comfort, happiness and memories. With all its
veggies and beans, this one appeals to my kitchen-sink style of cooking.
—*Annette Palermo, Beach Haven, NJ*

TAKES: 30 MIN. • MAKES: 6 SERVINGS

2 tsp. olive oil
3 garlic cloves, minced
3 cans (15 oz. each)
  cannellini beans, rinsed
  and drained, divided
¼ tsp. pepper
4 cups vegetable or
  reduced-sodium
  chicken broth
4 cups chopped fresh
  spinach (about 3 oz.)
¼ cup thinly sliced
  fresh basil
  Shredded Parmesan
  cheese, optional

1. In a large saucepan, heat oil over medium heat. Add garlic; cook and stir until tender, 30-45 seconds. Stir in 2 cans of beans, the pepper and the broth.

2. Puree mixture using an immersion blender. Or puree in a blender and return to pan. Stir in the remaining can of beans; bring to a boil. Reduce heat; simmer, covered, 15 minutes, stirring occasionally.

3. Stir in spinach and basil; cook, uncovered, until spinach is wilted, 2-4 minutes. If desired, serve with cheese.

1¼ CUPS: 192 cal., 2g fat (0 sat. fat), 0 chol., 886mg sod., 33g carb. (1g sugars, 9g fiber), 9g pro.

CHEESY CHICKEN CHOWDER

I like to serve this hearty chowder as a meal with garlic bread and a salad.
It's a wonderful dish to prepare for any occasion. The rich, mild flavor and the
tender chicken and vegetables appeal even to children and picky eaters.
—*Hazel Fritchie, Palestine, IL*

PREP: 10 MIN. • COOK: 25 MIN. • MAKES: 8 SERVINGS (2 QT.)

3 cups chicken broth
2 cups diced
  peeled potatoes
1 cup diced carrots
1 cup diced celery
½ cup diced onion
1½ tsp. salt
¼ tsp. pepper
¼ cup butter, cubed
⅓ cup all-purpose flour
2 cups whole milk
2 cups shredded
  cheddar cheese
2 cups diced
  cooked chicken

1. In a 4-qt. saucepan, bring chicken broth to a boil. Reduce heat; add the potatoes, carrots, celery, onion, salt and pepper. Cover and simmer for 12-15 minutes or until the vegetables are tender.

2. Meanwhile, melt butter in a medium saucepan; stir in flour until smooth. Gradually stir in milk. Bring to a boil over medium heat; cook and stir for 2 minutes or until thickened. Reduce heat. Add cheese, stirring until melted; add to broth along with the chicken. Cook and stir until heated through.

1 CUP: 322 cal., 19g fat (12g sat. fat), 85mg chol., 1100mg sod., 18g carb. (6g sugars, 2g fiber), 21g pro.

LOW COUNTRY BOIL

Ideal for camping and relaxing trips to the beach, this crowd-pleasing recipe
makes an appetizing presentation of perfectly seasoned meats, veggies and seafood.
—*Mageswari Elagupillai, Victorville, CA*

PREP: 20 MIN. • COOK: 40 MIN. • MAKES: 4 SERVINGS

2 qt. water
1 bottle (12 oz.) beer
2 Tbsp. seafood seasoning
1½ tsp. salt
4 medium red potatoes,
  cut into wedges
1 medium sweet onion,
  cut into wedges
4 medium ears sweet corn,
  cut in half
⅓ lb. smoked chorizo
  or kielbasa,
  cut into 1-in. slices
3 Tbsp. olive oil
6 large garlic cloves,
  minced
1 Tbsp. ground cumin
1 Tbsp. minced
  fresh cilantro
½ tsp. paprika
½ tsp. pepper
1 lb. uncooked shrimp
  (26-30 per pound),
  deveined
1 lb. uncooked
  snow crab legs
  Optional: Seafood
  cocktail sauce,
  lemon wedges
  and melted butter

1. In a Dutch oven, combine the water, beer, seafood seasoning and salt; add potatoes and onion. Bring to a boil. Reduce heat; simmer, uncovered, for 10 minutes. Add the corn and chorizo; simmer until potatoes and corn are tender, 10-12 minutes longer.

2. Meanwhile, in a small skillet, heat oil. Add the garlic, cumin, cilantro, paprika and pepper. Cook and stir over medium heat for 1 minute.

3. Stir the shrimp, crab legs and garlic mixture into the Dutch oven; cook until shrimp and crab turn pink, 4-6 minutes. Drain; transfer seafood mixture to a large serving bowl. Serve with condiments of your choice.

1 SERVING: 500 cal., 20g fat (5g sat. fat), 212mg chol., 1318mg sod., 41g carb. (6g sugars, 5g fiber), 40g pro.

OLD BAY

SEASONING

CRABS

SHRIMP

CHICKEN

For Seafood,
Poultry, Salads,
Meats

Same great taste
for over 75 years

NET WT 6 OZ

CREAMY CARROT SOUP

Both the bright orange color and the deliciously different flavor of this soup delight guests. A hint of rosemary adds a nice spark to a slightly sweet soup.
—*Grace Yaskovic, Lake Hiawatha, NJ*

PREP: 15 MIN. + COOLING • COOK: 40 MIN. • MAKES: 10 SERVINGS (2½ QT.)

1 cup chopped onion
¼ cup butter, cubed
4½ cups sliced fresh carrots
1 large potato, peeled and cubed
2 cans (14½ oz. each) chicken broth
1 tsp. ground ginger
2 cups heavy whipping cream
1 tsp. dried rosemary, crushed
½ tsp. salt
⅛ tsp. pepper

1. In a Dutch oven, saute onion in butter until tender. Add the carrots, potato, broth and ginger. Cover and cook over medium heat for 30 minutes or until vegetables are tender. Cool for 15 minutes.

2. Transfer soup to a blender in batches; cover and puree. Return all to the pan; stir in the cream, rosemary, salt and pepper. Cook over low heat until heated through.

1 CUP: 267 cal., 22g fat (14g sat. fat), 77mg chol., 367mg sod., 15g carb. (7g sugars, 3g fiber), 3g pro.

SLOW-COOKER PORK POZOLE

I make this heartwarming stew with pork ribs and hominy often. It's a filling recipe of lightly spiced comfort.
—*Genie Gunn, Asheville, NC*

PREP: 10 MIN. • COOK: 3 HOURS • MAKES: 6 SERVINGS

1 can (15½ oz.) hominy, rinsed and drained
1 can (14½ oz.) diced tomatoes, undrained
1 can (14½ oz.) diced tomatoes with mild green chiles, undrained
1 can (10 oz.) green enchilada sauce
2 medium carrots, finely chopped
1 medium onion, finely chopped
3 garlic cloves, minced
2 tsp. ground cumin
¼ tsp. salt
1 lb. boneless country-style pork ribs
Lime wedges
Minced fresh cilantro
Corn tortillas, optional

1. In a 3- or 4-qt. slow cooker, combine the first 9 ingredients; add pork. Cook, covered, on low 3-4 hours or until the pork is tender.

2. Remove pork from slow cooker. Cut into bite-sized pieces; return meat to slow cooker. Serve with lime wedges, cilantro and, if desired, corn tortillas.

1⅓ CUPS: 223 cal., 8g fat (3g sat. fat), 44mg chol., 991mg sod., 22g carb. (7g sugars, 5g fiber), 15g pro.

CHEESEBURGER SOUP

A local restaurant serves a similar soup but wouldn't share its recipe with me. I developed my own, modifying a recipe I already had for potato soup. I was really pleased with the way this all-American dish turned out.

—*Joanie Shawhan, Madison, WI*

PREP: 45 MIN. • **COOK:** 10 MIN. • **MAKES:** 8 SERVINGS (2 QT.)

½ lb. ground beef
4 Tbsp. butter, divided
¾ cup chopped onion
¾ cup shredded carrots
¾ cup diced celery
1 tsp. dried basil
1 tsp. dried parsley flakes
1¾ lbs. (about 4 cups) cubed peeled potatoes

3 cups chicken broth
¼ cup all-purpose flour
2 to 4 cups shredded Velveeta
1½ cups whole milk
¾ tsp. salt
¼ to ½ tsp. pepper
¼ cup sour cream

1. In a large saucepan over medium heat, cook and crumble beef until no longer pink, 6-8 minutes; drain and set aside. In the same saucepan, melt 1 Tbsp. butter over medium heat. Saute onion, carrots, celery, basil and parsley until vegetables are tender, about 10 minutes. Add potatoes, ground beef and broth; bring to a boil. Reduce heat; simmer, covered, until the potatoes are tender, 10-12 minutes.

2. Meanwhile, in a small skillet, melt remaining 3 Tbsp. butter. Add flour; cook and stir until bubbly, 3-5 minutes. Add to soup; bring to a boil. Cook and stir 2 minutes. Reduce heat to low. Stir in cheese, milk, salt and pepper; cook until the cheese melts. Remove from heat; blend in sour cream.

1 CUP: 450 cal., 27g fat (15g sat. fat), 100mg chol., 1421mg sod., 33g carb. (8g sugars, 3g fiber), 19g pro.

FROM GRANDMA'S KITCHEN: To prevent the soup from curdling, be sure to remove it from the heat before adding the sour cream.

RED FLANNEL STEW

RED FLANNEL STEW

When I was a child, every Saturday night was red flannel night. Grandpa and I wore our red flannel long underwear to supper, and Grandma dressed in a long calico dress and sunbonnet. We'd eat this stew spooned over fluffy southern-style biscuits. Grandma learned to make the stew from earlier generations of our family.
—Kathy Padgett, Diamond City, AR

PREP: 25 MIN. • COOK: 1½ HOURS • MAKES: 5 SERVINGS

2 whole fresh beets, washed, trimmed and halved
6 cups water, divided
1 lb. corned beef brisket, trimmed and cut into 1-in. pieces
4 small carrots, sliced
1 large potato, cubed
1 small turnip, peeled and cubed
1 small onion, chopped
1 tsp. each dried parsley flakes, basil and thyme
¼ tsp. salt
⅛ tsp. pepper

1. In a large saucepan, bring beets and 4 cups water to a boil. Reduce heat; simmer, uncovered, until tender, 20-25 minutes. Drain, reserving 2 cups cooking liquid. Peel and dice beets; set aside.

2. In the same pan, combine corned beef, carrots, potato, turnip, onion, seasonings, remaining 2 cups water and the reserved cooking liquid. Bring to a boil. Reduce heat; cover and simmer until meat and vegetables are tender, 1¼-1½ hours. Stir in diced beets; heat through.

FREEZE OPTION: Freeze cooled stew in freezer containers. To use, partially thaw in refrigerator overnight. Heat through in a saucepan, stirring occasionally; add water if necessary.

1⅓ CUPS: 209 cal., 9g fat (3g sat. fat), 31mg chol., 881mg sod., 22g carb. (6g sugars, 3g fiber), 11g pro.

GRANDMA'S HARVEST SOUP

I have fond memories of eating Grandma's soup when I was a child. Now I give my wife a break in the kitchen by making this soup every once in a while. It tastes just like home!
—Ronald Desjardins, St. Andrews West, ON

PREP: 20 MIN. • COOK: 2½ HOURS • MAKES: 18 SERVINGS (4¼ QT.)

3 smoked ham hocks (about 1½ lbs.)
3 qt. water
1 Tbsp. beef bouillon granules
6 medium potatoes, peeled and chopped
6 medium carrots, sliced
2 medium onions, chopped
½ medium head cabbage, chopped
1 small turnip, diced
1½ tsp. salt
¼ tsp. pepper

1. Place ham hocks, water and bouillon in a Dutch oven or soup kettle; bring to a boil. Reduce heat; cover and simmer for 1½ hours. Remove hocks and set them aside to cool.

2. Add potatoes, carrots, onions, cabbage and turnip to broth; cover and simmer for 1 hour or until the vegetables are tender. Using a potato masher, coarsely mash vegetables.

3. Remove meat from bones; cut into bite-sized pieces and add to soup. Stir in salt and pepper; heat through.

1 CUP: 189 cal., 9g fat (3g sat. fat), 41mg chol., 377mg sod., 15g carb. (4g sugars, 2g fiber), 12g pro.

LENTIL, BACON & BEAN SOUP

This quick soup feels extra cozy with lots of lentils and a touch of smoky, bacony goodness. You might want to cook extra since I think it's even better the next day!
—*Janie Zirbser, Mullica Hill, NJ*

PREP: 15 MIN. • **COOK:** 30 MIN. • **MAKES:** 8 SERVINGS (2 QT.)

4 bacon strips, chopped
6 medium carrots, chopped
2 small onions, diced
2 Tbsp. tomato paste
2 garlic cloves, minced
1 tsp. minced fresh thyme
½ tsp. pepper
5 cups chicken stock
1 cup dry white wine or additional chicken stock

2 cans (15 to 16 oz. each) butter beans, rinsed and drained
2 cans (15 oz. each) lentils, rinsed and drained
Fresh thyme sprigs, optional

1. In a Dutch oven, cook the bacon over medium heat until crisp, stirring occasionally. Remove with a slotted spoon; drain on paper towels. Cook and stir carrots and onions in the bacon drippings until crisp-tender, 3-4 minutes. Add tomato paste, garlic, thyme and pepper; cook 1 minute longer.

2. Add stock and wine; increase heat to medium-high. Cook for 2 minutes, stirring to loosen browned bits from pan. Stir in butter beans, lentils and bacon. Bring to a boil. Reduce heat; simmer, covered, 5 minutes.

3. Uncover; continue simmering until vegetables are tender, 15-20 minutes. Garnish with thyme sprigs if desired.

1 CUP: 271 cal., 6g fat (2g sat. fat), 9mg chol., 672mg sod., 41g carb. (7g sugars, 13g fiber), 18g pro. **DIABETIC EXCHANGES:** 3 starch, 1 medium-fat meat.

GRANDMA'S SECRET

You can use shredded chicken or turkey as a leaner alternative to bacon. Top each individual serving with a dollop of sour cream for a cool flavor contrast.

STOVETOP GOULASH

I created this recipe after trying goulash at a local restaurant.
The blend of spices gives it fabulous flavor, and it's so easy to make on a weeknight!
—*Karen Schelert, Portand, OR*

TAKES: 25 MIN. • MAKES: 4 SERVINGS

1 lb. ground beef
1 pkg. (16 oz.) frozen mixed
   vegetables, thawed
2 cans (10¾ oz. each)
   condensed tomato soup,
   undiluted
1 cup water
1 small onion, chopped
2 tsp. Worcestershire
   sauce
1 tsp. garlic salt
1 tsp. chili powder
½ tsp. dried oregano
½ tsp. paprika
⅛ tsp. ground cinnamon
⅛ tsp. pepper
1 pkg. (24 oz.) refrigerated
   mashed potatoes

1. Cook beef in a large skillet over medium heat until no longer pink, 6-8 minutes, breaking it into crumbles; drain. Add mixed vegetables, soup, water, onion, Worcestershire sauce and seasonings; bring to a boil. Reduce heat; simmer, uncovered, 10 minutes or until slightly thickened.

2. Meanwhile, heat potatoes according to package directions. Serve with goulash.

1½ CUPS GOULASH WITH 1 CUP POTATOES: 605 cal., 22g fat (9g sat. fat), 92mg chol., 1425mg sod., 58g carb. (18g sugars, 8g fiber), 28g pro.

ITALIAN WEDDING SOUP

Even in our hot Florida weather, this soup always satisfies! I add cooked
pasta at the end of the simmering time to keep it from getting mushy.
—*Nancy Ducharme, Deltona, FL*

PREP: 20 MIN. • COOK: 15 MIN. • MAKES: 12 SERVINGS (3 QT.)

1 large egg, beaten
¾ cup grated
   Parmesan cheese
½ cup dry bread crumbs
1 small onion, chopped
¾ tsp. salt, divided
1¼ tsp. pepper, divided
1¼ tsp. garlic powder,
   divided
2 lbs. ground beef
2 qt. chicken broth
⅓ cup chopped
   fresh spinach
1 tsp. onion powder
1 tsp. dried parsley flakes
1¼ cups cooked medium
   pasta shells

1. In a large bowl, combine the egg, cheese, bread crumbs, onion, ¼ tsp. salt, ¼ tsp. pepper and ¼ tsp. garlic powder. Crumble beef over mixture and mix well. Shape into 1-in. balls.

2. In a Dutch oven, brown meatballs in small batches; drain. Add broth, spinach, onion powder, parsley and the remaining ½ tsp. salt, 1 tsp. pepper and 1 tsp. garlic powder; bring to a boil. Reduce heat; simmer, uncovered, for 5 minutes. Stir in pasta; heat through.

1 CUP: 226 cal., 12g fat (5g sat. fat), 72mg chol., 942mg sod., 9g carb. (2g sugars, 0 fiber), 20g pro.

GRANDMA'S CHICKEN & DUMPLING SOUP

I've enjoyed making this rich soup for more than 40 years. Every time I serve it, I remember my grandma, who was very special to me and was known for being an amazing cook.

—Paulette Balda, Prophetstown, IL

PREP: 20 MIN. + COOLING • **COOK:** 2¾ HOURS • **MAKES:** 12 SERVINGS (3 QT.)

SOUPS & STEWS

1 broiler/fryer chicken (3½ to 4 lbs.), cut up
2¼ qt. cold water
5 chicken bouillon cubes
6 whole peppercorns
3 whole cloves
1 can (10¾ oz.) condensed cream of chicken soup, undiluted
1 can (10¾ oz.) condensed cream of mushroom soup, undiluted
1½ cups chopped carrots
1 cup fresh or frozen peas
1 cup chopped celery
1 cup chopped peeled potatoes
¼ cup chopped onion
1½ tsp. seasoned salt
¼ tsp. pepper
1 bay leaf

DUMPLINGS
2 cups all-purpose flour
4 tsp. baking powder
1 tsp. salt
¼ tsp. pepper
1 large egg, beaten
2 Tbsp. butter, melted
¾ to 1 cup 2% milk
Snipped fresh parsley, optional

1. Place the chicken, water, bouillon, peppercorns and cloves in a stockpot. Cover and bring to a boil; skim foam. Reduce heat; cover and simmer 45-60 minutes or until chicken is tender. Strain broth; return to stockpot.

2. Remove chicken and set aside until cool enough to handle. Remove meat from bones; discard bones and skin. Cut chicken into chunks. Cool broth and skim off fat.

3. Return chicken to stockpot with soups, vegetables and seasonings; bring to a boil. Reduce heat; cover and simmer for 1 hour. Uncover; increase heat to a gentle boil. Discard bay leaf.

4. For dumplings, combine dry ingredients in a medium bowl. Stir in egg, butter and enough milk to make a moist stiff batter. Drop by teaspoonfuls into soup. Cover and cook without lifting the lid for 18-20 minutes. Sprinkle with parsley if desired.

1 CUP: 333 cal., 14g fat (5g sat. fat), 79mg chol., 1447mg sod., 28g carb. (4g sugars, 3g fiber), 22g pro.

"This soup is delicious. The dumplings are particularly wonderful. I had never made little dumplings like this in chicken soup and I loved them! I think they would be great in a beef soup as well."
—DUBLINLAB, TASTEOFHOME.COM

SUNDAY CHICKEN STEW

We have this dish on Sundays so I too can have a leisurely day off. I prepare the veggies the night before and, in the morning, brown the chicken and assemble everything in the slow cooker before I go to church.
—*Diane Halferty, Corpus Christi, TX*

PREP: 30 MIN. • COOK: 6½ HOURS • MAKES: 6 SERVINGS

½ cup all-purpose flour
1 tsp. salt
½ tsp. white pepper
1 broiler/fryer chicken
   (3 lbs.), cut up and
   skin removed
2 Tbsp. canola oil
3 cups chicken broth
6 large carrots,
   cut into 1-in. pieces
2 celery ribs,
   cut into ½-in. pieces
1 large sweet onion,
   thinly sliced
1 tsp. dried rosemary,
   crushed
1½ cups frozen peas

DUMPLINGS

1 cup all-purpose flour
2 tsp. baking powder
½ tsp. salt
½ tsp. dried rosemary,
   crushed
1 large egg, lightly beaten
½ cup 2% milk

1. In a large shallow dish, combine the flour, salt and pepper; add chicken, a few pieces at a time, and turn to coat. In a large skillet, brown chicken in oil; remove and keep warm. Gradually add broth to the skillet; bring to a boil.

2. In a 5-qt. slow cooker, layer the carrots, celery and onion; sprinkle with rosemary. Add the chicken and hot broth. Cook, covered, on low until the chicken and vegetables are tender and the stew is bubbling, 6-8 hours.

3. Remove chicken; when cool enough to handle, remove meat from the bones and discard bones. Cut meat into bite-sized pieces and return to the slow cooker. Stir in peas.

4. For dumplings, in a small bowl, combine the flour, baking powder, salt and rosemary. Combine the egg and milk; stir into dry ingredients. Drop by heaping teaspoonfuls onto simmering chicken mixture. Cover and cook on high (do not lift cover while simmering) for 25-30 minutes or until a toothpick inserted in a dumpling comes out clean.

1 SERVING: 420 cal., 13g fat (3g sat. fat), 113mg chol., 1403mg sod., 42g carb. (10g sugars, 5g fiber), 33g pro.

STOVETOP SUNDAY CHICKEN STEW: In a Dutch oven, brown the chicken as directed and add the broth to the pan. Add all chicken and rosemary. Cover and simmer for 1 hour. Add the vegetables; cover and simmer 30 minutes longer. Cut chicken and prepare dumplings as directed. Cover and simmer for 20 minutes (do not lift the cover while simmering) or until a toothpick inserted in a dumpling comes out clean.

BEST EVER POTATO SOUP

You'll be surprised at the taste of this rich, cheesy concoction—
it's not a typical potato soup. I came up with the recipe after
enjoying baked potato soup at one of our favorite restaurants.
I added bacon, and we think that makes it even better.
—Coleen Morrissey, Sweet Valley, PA

TAKES: 30 MIN. • **MAKES:** 8 SERVINGS (2 QT.)

6 bacon strips, diced	½ tsp. celery seed
3 cups cubed peeled potatoes	1 can (14½ oz.) chicken broth
1 small carrot, grated	3 Tbsp. all-purpose flour
½ cup chopped onion	3 cups 2% milk
1 Tbsp. dried parsley flakes	8 oz. Velveeta, cubed
½ tsp. salt	2 green onions, thinly sliced, optional
½ tsp. pepper	

1. In a large saucepan, cook bacon over medium heat until crisp, stirring occasionally; drain drippings. Add vegetables, seasonings and broth; bring to a boil. Reduce heat; simmer, covered, until potatoes are tender, 10-15 minutes.

2. Mix flour and milk until smooth; stir into soup. Bring to a boil, stirring constantly; cook and stir until thickened, about 2 minutes. Stir in cheese until melted. If desired, serve with green onions.

1 CUP: 250 cal., 13g fat (7g sat. fat), 35mg chol., 823mg sod., 22g carb. (8g sugars, 2g fiber), 12g pro.

FROM GRANDMA'S KITCHEN: Before you peel potatoes, scrub them with a vegetable brush under cold water. Remove eyes or sprouts. If you have a lot of potatoes, place them in cold water after peeling to prevent discoloring.

STUFFED
PEPPER
SOUP

STUFFED PEPPER SOUP

I was talking about stuffed peppers with the other cooks at the restaurant where I work. We decided to mix similar ingredients for a soup. Customer response was overwhelming!

—*Krista Muddiman, Meadville, PA*

PREP: 15 MIN. • COOK: 45 MIN. • MAKES: 8 SERVINGS (2 QT.)

2 lbs. ground beef
6 cups water
1 can (28 oz.) tomato sauce
1 can (28 oz.) diced tomatoes, undrained
2 cups chopped green peppers
¼ cup packed brown sugar
2 tsp. salt
2 tsp. beef bouillon granules
1 tsp. pepper
2 cups cooked long grain rice
Chopped fresh parsley, optional

1. In a Dutch oven over medium heat, cook and stir beef until no longer pink, 6-8 minutes, breaking it into crumbles; drain. Stir in the next 8 ingredients; bring to a boil. Reduce the heat; simmer, uncovered, until peppers are tender, about 30 minutes.

2. Add cooked rice; simmer, uncovered, 10 minutes longer. If desired, sprinkle with chopped fresh parsley.

1 CUP: 337 cal., 14g fat (5g sat. fat), 70mg chol., 1466mg sod., 30g carb. (13g sugars, 4g fiber), 24g pro.

FROM GRANDMA'S KITCHEN: Dark brown and light brown sugar are generally interchangeable in recipes, but if you prefer a bolder flavor, choose dark brown sugar. It contains more molasses than light or golden brown sugar, so it has a richer, stronger flavor.

OLD-FASHIONED CHUNKY CHICKEN NOODLE SOUP

When winter holds me in its icy grip, I rely on this hearty chicken soup to warm me right down to my toes. It's just like the one Grandma used to make—full of veggies and rich flavor.

—*Sharon Skildum, Maple Grove, MN*

TAKES: 25 MIN. • MAKES: 2 SERVINGS

¼ cup diced carrot
2 Tbsp. diced celery
2 Tbsp. chopped onion
1 tsp. butter
2½ cups reduced-sodium chicken broth
⅔ cup diced cooked chicken
¼ tsp. salt
¼ tsp. dried marjoram
¼ tsp. dried thyme
Dash pepper
½ cup uncooked medium egg noodles
1 tsp. minced fresh parsley

In a large saucepan, saute the carrot, celery and onion in butter until tender. Stir in the broth, chicken and seasonings; bring to a boil. Reduce heat. Add noodles; cook for 10 minutes or until noodles are tender. Sprinkle with parsley.

1¾ CUPS: 167 cal., 6g fat (2g sat. fat), 55mg chol., 511mg sod., 12g carb. (3g sugars, 1g fiber), 16g pro.

CREAMY WHITE CHILI

Years ago, as a time-starved college student, I got this wonderful recipe from my sister-in-law. She had made a big batch and served it to a crowd one night. It was a hit—and easy and quick. In all my years of cooking, I've never had another dish get so many compliments.

—Laura Brewer, Lafayette, IN

PREP: 10 MIN. • **COOK:** 40 MIN. • **MAKES:** 7 SERVINGS

- 1 lb. boneless skinless chicken breasts, cut into ½-in. cubes
- 1 medium onion, chopped
- 1½ tsp. garlic powder
- 1 Tbsp. canola oil
- 2 cans (15½ oz. each) great northern beans, rinsed and drained
- 1 can (14½ oz.) chicken broth
- 2 cans (4 oz. each) chopped green chiles

- 1 tsp. salt
- 1 tsp. ground cumin
- 1 tsp. dried oregano
- ½ tsp. pepper
- ¼ tsp. cayenne pepper
- 1 cup sour cream
- ½ cup heavy whipping cream
  Optional: Tortilla chips, shredded cheddar cheese, sliced seeded jalapeno pepper

1. In a large saucepan, saute the chicken, onion and garlic powder in oil until chicken is no longer pink. Add the beans, broth, chiles and seasonings. Bring to a boil. Reduce heat; simmer, uncovered, for 30 minutes.

2. Remove from the heat; stir in sour cream and heavy cream. If desired, top with tortilla chips, cheese and jalapenos.

1 CUP: 334 cal., 16g fat (8g sat. fat), 81mg chol., 1045mg sod., 24g carb. (3g sugars, 7g fiber), 22g pro.

GRANDMA'S SECRET

You can use half-and-half cream in place of the heavy cream if you want to make a lighter dish. Half-and-half is 10-18% fat, compared to heavy cream's 30-36%.

BARLEY RISOTTO & BEEF STROGANOFF

I was missing my Russian grandma's barley porridge and beef stroganoff, so I combined the two dishes. Cook the barley using the risotto method to keep the grains whole and irresistibly chewy.
—*Tatiana Kireeva, New York, NY*

PREP: 25 MIN. + MARINATING • COOK: 45 MIN. • MAKES: 4 SERVINGS

1 beef top sirloin steak
(1 lb.), cut into 1-in. cubes
3 Tbsp. Cognac or brandy
2 Tbsp. butter, divided
1 Tbsp. all-purpose flour
2 cups chicken stock
1 tsp. Dijon mustard
1 medium beefsteak
tomato
1 tsp. coarsely ground
pepper
¼ tsp. salt
2 Tbsp. sour cream
1 medium onion, sliced

BARLEY RISOTTO
5 cups water
1 Tbsp. butter
1 medium onion,
finely chopped
½ tsp. salt
1 Tbsp. white wine,
optional
1 cup medium pearl barley
2 Tbsp. minced
fresh parsley

1. In a shallow dish, toss beef with Cognac. Refrigerate, covered, 2 hours.

2. In a small saucepan, melt 1 Tbsp. butter over medium heat. Stir in flour until smooth; gradually whisk in the chicken stock and mustard. Bring to a boil, stirring constantly; cook and stir until thickened, 3-5 minutes. Reduce heat; simmer, uncovered, for 5 minutes.

3. Meanwhile, cut tomato into thick strips. In a large skillet over medium-low heat, cook tomato until softened, 3-5 minutes. Stir into mustard sauce; add coarsely ground pepper and salt. Stir in sour cream.

4. In the same skillet, melt 1 Tbsp. butter over medium-high heat. Drain beef, discarding the marinade, and pat beef dry. Add sliced onion and beef to pan; cook and stir until onion is softened and meat is no longer pink, 6-8 minutes. Add the mustard sauce; reduce heat to low and simmer, uncovered, until thickened, about 15 minutes. Keep warm until serving.

5. For risotto, bring water to a boil in a large saucepan. Reduce heat to maintain simmer. In another large saucepan, melt butter over medium heat. Add the chopped onion, salt and, if desired, white wine. Cook and stir until liquid evaporates. Add barley; toast in pan.

6. Stir hot water into barley 1 cup at a time, waiting until liquid has almost absorbed before adding more. Cook until the barley is softened but still slightly chewy, 15-20 minutes; stir in parsley. Serve immediately with beef.

4 OZ. COOKED STEAK WITH 1 CUP RISOTTO: 463 cal., 15g fat (8g sat. fat), 74mg chol., 859mg sod., 48g carb. (4g sugars, 9g fiber), 33g pro.

TURKEY GINGER NOODLE SOUP

I wanted something comforting yet healthy, and ginger is my favorite spice.
This recipe was a must-try for me, and it didn't disappoint.
—*Adina Monson, Nanaimo, BC*

PREP: 20 MIN. • COOK: 4¼ HOURS • MAKES: 8 SERVINGS (3 QT.)

2 medium carrots, sliced
2 cans (8 oz. each) sliced
water chestnuts, drained
3 to 4 Tbsp. minced
fresh gingerroot
2 Tbsp. minced
fresh parsley
2 tsp. chili powder
4 cups chicken stock
1 can (11.8 oz.)
coconut water
3 Tbsp. lemon juice
2 lbs. boneless skinless
turkey breast,
cut into 1-in. cubes
2 tsp. pepper
½ tsp. salt
2 Tbsp. canola oil
1 cup frozen corn
(about 5 oz.), thawed
1 cup frozen peas
(about 4 oz.), thawed
8 oz. rice noodles or
thin spaghetti

1. Place the first 8 ingredients in a 4- or 5-qt. slow cooker.

2. Toss turkey with pepper and salt. In a large skillet, heat oil over medium-high heat; brown turkey in batches. Add to slow cooker.

3. Cook, covered, on low 4-5 hours, until carrots are tender. Stir in corn and peas; heat through.

4. Cook noodles according to package directions; drain. Add to soup just before serving.

1½ CUPS: 351 cal., 6g fat (1g sat. fat), 65mg chol., 672mg sod., 41g carb. (5g sugars, 4g fiber), 33g pro. DIABETIC EXCHANGES: 3 starch, 3 lean meat.

FROM GRANDMA'S KITCHEN: If you know you're not going to eat all of this soup in one sitting, it's best to combine just the noodles and soup you're going to eat. Refrigerate the rest of the noodles and soup in separate containers. Otherwise, the noodles will soak up all the liquid and fall apart.

AFRICAN PEANUT SWEET POTATO STEW

Back when I was in college, my mom made an addicting sweet potato stew. I shared it with my friends, and now all of us serve it to our own kids. They all love it, of course.

—*Alexis Scatchell, Niles, IL*

PREP: 20 MIN. • COOK: 6 HOURS • MAKES: 8 SERVINGS (2½ QT.)

1   **can (28 oz.) diced tomatoes, undrained**
1   **cup fresh cilantro leaves**
½   **cup chunky peanut butter**
3   **garlic cloves, halved**
2   **tsp. ground cumin**
1   **tsp. salt**
½   **tsp. ground cinnamon**
¼   **tsp. smoked paprika**
3   **lbs. sweet potatoes (about 6 medium), peeled and cut into 1-in. pieces**
1   **can (15 oz.) garbanzo beans or chickpeas, rinsed and drained**
1   **cup water**
8   **cups chopped fresh kale**
    Optional: Chopped peanuts and additional cilantro leaves

1. Place the first 8 ingredients in a food processor; process until pureed. Transfer to a 5-qt. slow cooker; stir in sweet potatoes, beans and water.

2. Cook, covered, on low 6-8 hours or until potatoes are tender, adding kale during the last 30 minutes. If desired, top individual servings with chopped peanuts and additional cilantro.

1¼ CUPS: 349 cal., 9g fat (1g sat. fat), 0 chol., 624mg sod., 60g carb. (23g sugars, 11g fiber), 10g pro.

FROM GRANDMA'S KITCHEN: Peanut stew, also called *maafe* or *domodah*, originated in western Africa. An original dish of the Mandinka and Bambara people of Mali, peanut stew shows up in many variations in the cuisines of both western and central Africa. If you want more protein, traditional and authentic additions for this stew include lamb, chicken and beef—and occasionally fish or hard-boiled eggs.

TUSCAN PORTOBELLO STEW

Here's a healthy one-skillet meal that's quick and easy to prepare yet elegant enough for company. I often take this stew to my school's potlucks, where it is devoured by teachers and students alike.

—*Jane Siemon, Viroqua, WI*

PREP: 20 MIN. • COOK: 20 MIN. • MAKES: 4 SERVINGS (1¼ QT.)

2 large portobello mushrooms, coarsely chopped
1 medium onion, chopped
3 garlic cloves, minced
2 Tbsp. olive oil
½ cup white wine or vegetable broth
1 can (28 oz.) diced tomatoes, undrained
2 cups chopped fresh kale

1 bay leaf
1 tsp. dried thyme
½ tsp. dried basil
½ tsp. dried rosemary, crushed
¼ tsp. salt
¼ tsp. pepper
2 cans (15 oz. each) cannellini beans, rinsed and drained

1. In a large skillet, saute the mushrooms, onion and garlic in oil until tender. Add the wine or broth. Bring to a boil; cook until liquid is reduced by half. Stir in tomatoes, kale and seasonings. Bring to a boil. Reduce heat; cover and simmer for 8-10 minutes.

2. Add beans; heat through. Discard bay leaf.

1¼ CUPS: 309 cal., 8g fat (1g sat. fat), 0 chol., 672mg sod., 46g carb. (9g sugars, 13g fiber), 12g pro. DIABETIC EXCHANGES: 2 starch, 2 vegetable, 1½ fat, 1 lean meat.

FROM GRANDMA'S KITCHEN: With their large size and meaty texture, portobello mushrooms are a popular ingredient for vegetarian recipes. Here, the mushrooms are coarsely chopped to give the stew a hearty, rustic appeal.

ROASTED CAULIFLOWER & RED PEPPER SOUP

When cooler weather comes, soup is one of our favorite meals.
I created this as a healthier version of all the cream-based soups out there.
After a bit of trial and error, my husband and I decided this is the keeper.
—*Elizabeth Bramkamp, Gig Harbor, WA*

PREP: 50 MIN. + STANDING • **COOK:** 25 MIN. • **MAKES:** 6 SERVINGS

2   medium sweet
    red peppers, halved
    and seeded
1   large head cauliflower,
    broken into florets
    (about 7 cups)
4   Tbsp. olive oil, divided
1   cup chopped sweet onion
2   garlic cloves, minced
2½ tsp. minced fresh
    rosemary or ¾ tsp.
    dried rosemary, crushed
½   tsp. paprika
¼   cup all-purpose flour
4   cups chicken stock
1   cup 2% milk
½   tsp. salt
¼   tsp. pepper
⅛   to ¼ tsp. cayenne pepper
    Shredded Parmesan
    cheese, optional

1. Preheat broiler. Place peppers on a foil-lined baking sheet, skin side up. Broil 4 in. from heat until skins are blistered, about 5 minutes. Transfer to a bowl; let stand, covered, 20 minutes. Change oven setting to bake; preheat oven to 400°.

2. Toss cauliflower with 2 Tbsp. oil; spread in a 15x10x1-in. pan. Roast until tender, 25-30 minutes, stirring occasionally. Remove skin and seeds from peppers; chop peppers.

3. In a 6-qt. stockpot, heat remaining oil over medium heat. Add onion; cook until golden and softened, 6-8 minutes, stirring occasionally. Add garlic, rosemary and paprika; cook and stir 1 minute. Stir in flour until blended; cook and stir 1 minute. Gradually stir in stock. Bring to a boil, stirring constantly; cook and stir until thickened.

4. Stir in the cauliflower and peppers. Puree the soup using an immersion blender. Or, cool slightly and puree soup in batches in a blender; return to pot. Stir in milk and remaining seasonings; heat through. If desired, serve with cheese.

FREEZE OPTION: Freeze cooled soup in freezer containers. To use, partially thaw in refrigerator overnight. Heat through in a saucepan, stirring occasionally; add a little stock or milk if necessary.

1 CUP: 193 cal., 10g fat (2g sat. fat), 3mg chol., 601mg sod., 19g carb. (8g sugars, 4g fiber), 8g pro. **DIABETIC EXCHANGES:** 2 vegetable, 2 fat, ½ starch.

HEARTY PASTA FAGIOLI

Here's a classic Italian favorite. Spaghetti sauce
and canned broth form the flavorful base.
—*Cindy Garland, Limestone, TN*

PREP: 40 MIN. • **COOK:** 40 MIN. • **MAKES:** 24 SERVINGS (7½ QT.)

- 2 lbs. ground beef
- 6 cans (14½ oz. each) beef broth
- 2 cans (28 oz. each) diced tomatoes, undrained
- 2 jars (26 oz. each) spaghetti sauce
- 3 large onions, chopped
- 8 celery ribs, diced
- 3 medium carrots, sliced
- 1 can (16 oz.) kidney beans, rinsed and drained
- 1 can (15 oz.) cannellini beans, rinsed and drained
- 3 tsp. minced fresh oregano or 1 tsp. dried oregano
- 2½ tsp. pepper
- 1½ tsp. hot pepper sauce
- 8 oz. uncooked medium pasta shells
- 5 tsp. minced fresh parsley

1. In a large stockpot, cook beef over medium heat until no longer pink; drain. Add broth, tomatoes, spaghetti sauce, onions, celery, carrots, beans, oregano, pepper and pepper sauce.

2. Bring to a boil. Reduce heat; simmer, covered, 30 minutes. Add pasta and parsley; simmer, covered, until pasta is tender, 10-14 minutes.

1¼ CUPS: 212 cal., 6g fat (2g sat. fat), 20mg chol., 958mg sod., 25g carb. (8g sugars, 5g fiber), 14g pro.

CHEDDAR PEAR SOUP

Pears and sharp cheddar have always been one of my favorite flavor combos.
This recipe brings the two together in a creamy, delicious soup. I like to serve
it with a warm baguette and fresh fruit for lunch or a light supper.
—*Trisha Kruse, Eagle, ID*

PREP: 15 MIN. • COOK: 35 MIN. • MAKES: 8 SERVINGS (2 QT.)

¼ cup butter, cubed
1 large onion, chopped
2 garlic cloves, minced
⅓ cup all-purpose flour
2 tsp. smoked paprika
5 cups chicken broth
3 medium ripe pears, peeled and chopped
3 cups sharp cheddar cheese, shredded
¼ tsp. freshly ground pepper
Fresh pear slices, optional

1. In a Dutch oven, heat butter over medium-high heat; saute onion and garlic until tender, 7-9 minutes. Stir in flour and paprika until blended; cook and stir 2 minutes. Gradually stir in broth. Add chopped pears; bring to a boil. Reduce heat; simmer, covered, until pears are tender, about 15 minutes, stirring occasionally.

2. Puree soup using an immersion blender, or cool slightly and puree soup in batches in a blender; return to pan. Add cheese and pepper; cook and stir over low heat until cheese is melted, 3-5 minutes. If desired, top with pear slices.

1 CUP: 299 cal., 20g fat (12g sat. fat), 60mg chol., 938mg sod., 18g carb. (8g sugars, 3g fiber), 12g pro.

WILD RICE & MUSHROOM SOUP

Frequently requested at family get-togethers, this rich and hearty soup is ready in a flash.
Cooking for a vegetarian? Swap in vegetable stock for the beef broth.
—*Danielle Noble, Fort Thomas, KY*

PREP: 10 MIN. • COOK: 35 MIN. • MAKES: 8 SERVINGS (2 QT.)

1 lb. baby portobello mushrooms, chopped
2 Tbsp. olive oil
2 pkg. (6 oz. each) long grain and wild rice mix
1 carton (32 oz.) reduced-sodium beef broth
½ cup water
2 cups heavy whipping cream

In a Dutch oven, saute mushrooms in oil until tender. Add the rice, the contents of the seasoning packets, broth and water. Bring to a boil. Reduce heat; cover and simmer for 25 minutes. Add cream and heat through.

1 CUP: 399 cal., 26g fat (14g sat. fat), 84mg chol., 803mg sod., 35g carb. (2g sugars, 1g fiber), 8g pro.

FROM GRANDMA'S KITCHEN: Baby portobello mushrooms are also known as cremini mushrooms. They can be used instead of white mushrooms for a flavor boost.

COMFORTING BARLEY & PUMPKIN BEEF STEW

There's nothing more comforting than a bowl of beef stew—unless, of course, it's a bowl of steaming hot beef stew loaded with lots and lots of barley. This is comfort food at its best—a bowl of stew robust enough to be a meal on its own. Rinsing the barley will help remove any dust, dirt or debris.
—*Colleen Delawder, Herndon, VA*

PREP: 30 MIN. • COOK: 6 HOURS • MAKES: 9 SERVINGS (3½ QT.)

¼ cup all-purpose flour
3 Tbsp. cornstarch
1½ tsp. salt, divided
1½ tsp. pepper, divided
1½ lbs. beef stew meat
3 Tbsp. olive oil
1 large sweet onion, finely chopped
2 cartons (32 oz. each) beef broth
1 can (15 oz.) pumpkin
1 cup medium pearl barley
1 tsp. dried thyme
¼ tsp. garlic powder
¼ tsp. crushed red pepper flakes
Optional: Additional red pepper flakes and minced fresh parsley

1. In a shallow dish, mix flour, cornstarch, 1 tsp. salt and 1 tsp. pepper. Add beef, a few pieces at a time, and toss to coat. In a large skillet, heat oil over medium-high heat; brown meat in batches. Transfer meat to a 5- or 6-qt. slow cooker; leave drippings in the pan.

2. In the same skillet, cook and stir onion in pan drippings until tender, 6-8 minutes; add to slow cooker. Stir in broth, pumpkin, barley, thyme, garlic powder, red pepper flakes, remaining ½ tsp. salt and ½ tsp. pepper. Cook, covered, on low until meat is tender, 6-8 hours. If desired, serve with additional red pepper flakes and parsley.

1½ CUPS: 211 cal., 8g fat (2g sat. fat), 35mg chol., 819mg sod., 20g carb. (3g sugars, 4g fiber), 15g pro. **DIABETIC EXCHANGES:** 2 lean meat, 1 starch, 1 fat.

BUTTERY ONION SOUP

I developed this recipe when I once had an abundance of sweet onions. I like making it for guests, but sometimes I'll halve the recipe and make some just for me!
—*Sharon Berthelote, Sunburst, MT*

PREP: 5 MIN. • COOK: 30 MIN. • MAKES: 6 SERVINGS

2 cups thinly sliced onions
½ cup butter, cubed
¼ cup all-purpose flour
2 cups chicken broth
2 cups 2% milk
1½ to 2 cups shredded part-skim mozzarella cheese
Salt and pepper to taste
Croutons, optional

1. In a large saucepan, cook onions in butter over low heat until tender and transparent, about 20 minutes.

2. Stir in flour. Gradually add broth and milk; cook and stir over medium heat until bubbly. Cook and stir for 1 minute longer; reduce heat to low.

3. Add mozzarella cheese and stir constantly until melted (do not boil). Season to taste with salt and pepper. Serve with croutons if desired.

1 CUP: 294 cal., 23g fat (14g sat. fat), 66mg chol., 600mg sod., 12g carb. (7g sugars, 1g fiber), 11g pro.

COMFORTING BARLEY
& PUMPKIN BEEF STEW

SQUASH & LENTIL LAMB STEW

My family lived in New Zealand many years ago. Every Sunday my mother
made a lamb stew—it was Dad's favorite! I changed the recipe to suit my family's
more modern palates, but it still seems just as exotic and delicious.

—*Nancy Heishman, Las Vegas, NV*

PREP: 30 MIN. • **COOK:** 6 HOURS • **MAKES:** 8 SERVINGS (2½ QT.)

1 can (13.66 oz.)
  coconut milk
½ cup creamy peanut butter
2 Tbsp. red curry paste
1 Tbsp. hoisin sauce
1 tsp. salt
½ tsp. pepper
1 can (14½ oz.)
  chicken broth
3 tsp. olive oil, divided
1 lb. lamb or beef stew
  meat (1½-in. pieces)
2 small onions, chopped
1 Tbsp. minced
  fresh gingerroot
3 garlic cloves, minced
1 cup dried brown lentils,
  rinsed
4 cups cubed peeled
  butternut squash
  (about 1 lb.)
2 cups chopped
  fresh spinach
¼ cup minced fresh cilantro
¼ cup lime juice

1. In a 5- or 6-qt. slow cooker, whisk together first 7 ingredients. In a large skillet, heat 2 tsp. oil over medium heat; brown lamb in batches. Add to slow cooker.

2. In same skillet, saute onions in remaining 1 tsp. oil over medium heat until tender, 4-5 minutes. Add ginger and garlic; cook and stir 1 minute. Add to the slow cooker. Stir in lentils and squash.

3. Cook, covered, on low 6-8 hours, until the meat and lentils are tender. Stir in spinach until wilted. Stir in cilantro and lime juice.

FREEZE OPTION: Freeze cooled stew in freezer containers. To use, partially thaw in refrigerator overnight. Heat through in a saucepan, stirring occasionally; add broth if necessary.

1¼ CUPS: 411 cal., 21g fat (11g sat. fat), 38mg chol., 777mg sod., 34g carb. (7g sugars, 6g fiber), 23g pro.

FROM GRANDMA'S KITCHEN: For the best browning, blot meat dry beforehand. Water on the surface of the meat will transfer to the pan, creating a kind of boiling liquid and preventing the meat from getting a good sear.

POTATO & LEEK SOUP

Full of veggies and smoky bacon, with just a little tanginess from sour cream, this comforting soup tastes just as terrific with sandwiches as it does with crackers.
—*Melanie Wooden, Reno, NV*

PREP: 20 MIN. • COOK: 8 HOURS • MAKES: 8 SERVINGS (2 QT.)

4 cups chicken broth	¼ cup minced fresh parsley
3 medium potatoes, peeled and cubed	½ tsp. salt
1½ cups chopped cabbage	½ tsp. caraway seeds
2 medium carrots, chopped	½ tsp. pepper
1 medium leek (white portion only), chopped	1 bay leaf
1 medium onion, chopped	½ cup sour cream
	1 lb. bacon strips, cooked and crumbled

1. Combine the first 11 ingredients in a 4- or 5-qt. slow cooker. Cover and cook on low until vegetables are tender, 8-10 hours.

2. Before serving, combine sour cream with 1 cup soup; return all to the slow cooker. Stir in bacon and discard bay leaf.

1 CUP: 209 cal., 11g fat (4g sat. fat), 27mg chol., 1023mg sod., 18g carb. (4g sugars, 2g fiber), 10g pro.

ITALIAN CABBAGE SOUP

After doing yardwork on a windy day, we love to come in for a light but hearty soup like this one. It's brimming with veggies and white beans. Pass the crusty bread!
—*Jennifer Stowell, Deep River, IA*

PREP: 15 MIN. • COOK: 6 HOURS • MAKES: 8 SERVINGS (2 QT.)

4 cups chicken stock
1 can (6 oz.) tomato paste
1 small head cabbage (about 1½ lbs.), shredded
4 celery ribs, chopped
2 large carrots, chopped
1 small onion, chopped
1 can (15½ oz.) great northern beans, rinsed and drained
2 garlic cloves, minced
2 fresh thyme sprigs
1 bay leaf
½ tsp. salt
Shredded Parmesan cheese, optional

In a 5- or 6-qt. slow cooker, whisk together stock and tomato paste. Stir in vegetables, beans, garlic and seasonings. Cook, covered, on low until vegetables are tender, 6-8 hours. Remove thyme sprigs and bay leaf. If desired, serve with cheese.

1 CUP: 111 cal., 0 fat (0 sat. fat), 0 chol., 537mg sod., 21g carb. (7g sugars, 6g fiber), 8g pro. DIABETIC EXCHANGES: 1½ starch.

HOMEMADE APPLE CIDER BEEF STEW

It's especially nice to use this recipe in fall, when the weather gets crisp and the local apple orchards start selling fresh apple cider. This entree's subtle sweetness is a welcome change from other savory stews. We enjoy it with biscuits and slices of apple and cheddar cheese.

—*Joyce Glaesemann, Lincoln, NE*

PREP: 30 MIN. • **COOK:** 1¾ HOURS • **MAKES:** 8 SERVINGS

2 lbs. beef stew meat, cut into 1-in. cubes
2 Tbsp. canola oil
3 cups apple cider or juice
1 can (14½ oz.) reduced-sodium beef broth
2 Tbsp. cider vinegar
1½ tsp. salt
¼ to ½ tsp. dried thyme
¼ tsp. pepper
3 medium potatoes, peeled and cubed
4 medium carrots, cut into ¾-in. pieces
3 celery ribs, cut into ¾-in. pieces
2 medium onions, cut into wedges
¼ cup all-purpose flour
¼ cup water
Fresh thyme sprigs, optional

1. In a Dutch oven, brown beef on all sides in oil over medium-high heat; drain. Add the cider, broth, vinegar, salt, thyme and pepper; bring to a boil. Reduce heat; cover and simmer for 1¼ hours.

2. Add the potatoes, carrots, celery and onions; return to a boil. Reduce heat; cover and simmer 30-35 minutes or until the beef and vegetables are tender.

3. Combine flour and water until smooth; stir into the stew. Bring to a boil; cook and stir for 2 minutes or until thickened. If desired, serve with fresh thyme.

1 CUP: 330 cal., 12g fat (3g sat. fat), 72mg chol., 628mg sod., 31g carb. (14g sugars, 2g fiber), 24g pro. **DIABETIC EXCHANGES:** 3 lean meat, 1½ starch, 1 vegetable.

"This is delicious. I like more gravy, so I added an extra cup of cider and an extra can of broth . It has amazing flavor—my family devoured it!"
—CAM625, TASTEOFHOME.COM

CRANBERRY BOG
BARS, PAGE 259

GRANDMA'S FAVORITE

COOKIES, BARS & BROWNIES

Grandma's cookie jar was always full of yummy
home-baked treats, ready for eager little fingers!
Turn to this scrumptious collection of recipes
whenever you need a sweet escape, a bite to share
or a delicious remembrance of simple, happy times.

FROSTED BANANA BARS

These bars are always a hit at potlucks in the small rural farming community where my husband and I live. I also like to provide them for coffee hour after church. They're so moist and delicious that wherever I take them, they don't last long.
—*Karen Dryak, Niobrara, NE*

PREP: 15 MIN. • BAKE: 20 MIN. + COOLING • MAKES: 3 DOZEN

½ cup butter, softened
2 cups sugar
3 large eggs,
   room temperature
1½ cups mashed
   ripe bananas
   (about 3 medium)
1 tsp. vanilla extract
2 cups all-purpose flour
1 tsp. baking soda
   Dash salt

FROSTING
1 pkg. (8 oz.) cream cheese,
   softened
½ cup butter, softened
4 cups confectioners' sugar
2 tsp. vanilla extract

1. Preheat oven to 350°. In a large bowl, cream butter and sugar until light and fluffy, 5-7 minutes. Beat in eggs, bananas and vanilla. Combine flour, baking soda and salt; stir into creamed mixture just until blended.

2. Transfer batter to a greased 15x10x1-in. baking pan. Bake for 20-25 minutes or until a toothpick inserted in the center comes out clean. Cool in pan on a wire rack.

3. For frosting, in a small bowl, beat cream cheese and butter until fluffy. Add confectioners' sugar and vanilla; beat until smooth. Frost bars.

1 BAR: 202 cal., 8g fat (5g sat. fat), 38mg chol., 100mg sod., 32g carb. (25g sugars, 0 fiber), 2g pro.

FROM GRANDMA'S KITCHEN: To ripen bananas quickly, just pop them in a paper bag, fold it over to close and check back in a day. The enclosed environment traps ethylene, the compound responsible for ripening bananas. For even better results, add an apple to the bag.

OLD-FASHIONED
GINGERSNAPS

OLD-FASHIONED GINGERSNAPS

I discovered this recipe years ago, and it's been a favorite among our family and friends ever since. Gingersnaps are timeless—a classic holiday cookie that's welcome year-round.

—*Francis Stoops, Stoneboro, PA*

PREP: 15 MIN. + CHILLING • BAKE: 10 MIN./BATCH + COOLING • MAKES: ABOUT 4 DOZEN

¾ cup butter, softened
1 cup sugar
1 large egg,
   room temperature
¼ cup molasses
2 cups all-purpose flour
2 tsp. baking soda
1 tsp. ground cinnamon
1 tsp. ground cloves
1 tsp. ground ginger
¼ tsp. salt
   Additional sugar

1. Cream butter and sugar until light and fluffy, 5-7 minutes. Beat in egg and molasses. Combine the flour, baking soda, cinnamon, cloves, ginger and salt; gradually add to the creamed mixture. Chill dough until easy to handle.

2. Roll into 1¼-in. balls and dip into sugar. Place 2 in. apart on ungreased baking sheets. Bake at 375° for about 10 minutes or until set and surface cracks. Cool on wire racks.

2 COOKIES: 150 cal., 8g fat (5g sat. fat), 29mg chol., 211mg sod., 19g carb. (10g sugars, 0 fiber), 1g pro.

BLACK WALNUT COOKIES

Black walnuts, which have a more distinctive flavor than traditional English walnuts, have a short shelf life. It's best to store them in the freezer.

—*Doug Black, Conover, NC*

PREP: 20 MIN. + CHILLING • BAKE: 15 MIN./BATCH • MAKES: 10 DOZEN

1 cup butter, softened
2 cups packed brown sugar
2 large eggs,
   room temperature
1 tsp. vanilla extract
3½ cups all-purpose flour
1 tsp. baking soda
¼ tsp. salt
2 cups chopped
   black walnuts
   or walnuts, divided

1. In a large bowl, cream butter and brown sugar until light and fluffy, 5-7 minutes. Beat in eggs and vanilla. Combine the flour, baking soda and salt; gradually add to the creamed mixture. Stir in 1¼ cups walnuts. Finely chop the remaining ¾ cup nuts.

2. Shape dough into two 15-in. rolls. Roll in the finely chopped nuts, pressing gently. Wrap each roll in waxed paper. Refrigerate for 2 hours or until firm.

3. Unwrap dough; cut into ¼-in. slices. Place slices 2 in. apart on greased baking sheets. Bake at 300° for 12 minutes or until lightly browned. Remove from pans to wire racks to cool.

1 COOKIE: 55 cal., 3g fat (1g sat. fat), 7mg chol., 30mg sod., 7g carb. (4g sugars, 0 fiber), 1g pro.

CHERRY COCONUT TREATS

My great-grandmother created this recipe more than 100 years ago, so these tasty bites have appeared at many family parties. If you're preparing these for the holidays, make them festive by using both red and green maraschino cherries.
—Anne Mullen, Windsor, ON

PREP: 15 MIN. • BAKE: 35 MIN. + CHILLING • MAKES: 2 DOZEN

1½ cups all-purpose flour
1 cup graham cracker crumbs
⅔ cup packed brown sugar
1 tsp. baking powder
½ tsp. salt
1 cup butter, melted

FILLING
4 cups unsweetened finely shredded coconut
2 cans (14 oz. each) sweetened condensed milk
2 jars (10 oz. each) maraschino cherries, drained and chopped
2 tsp. vanilla extract
1 tsp. almond extract

1. Preheat oven to 325°. In a small bowl, mix first 5 ingredients; stir in melted butter. Press mixture onto bottom of a greased 13x9-in. baking pan.

2. In another bowl, mix the filling ingredients; pour over crust. Bake until edges are lightly browned, 35-40 minutes. Cool on a wire rack 1 hour. Refrigerate, covered, 4 hours before cutting. Store in an airtight container in the refrigerator.

NOTE: Look for unsweetened coconut in the baking or health food section.

1 BAR: 362 cal., 20g fat (14g sat. fat), 32mg chol., 202mg sod., 45g carb. (35g sugars, 3g fiber), 5g pro.

STRAWBERRY CREAM COOKIES

These delicate cream cheese cookies look lovely on a tea tray or dessert platter. Feel free to experiment with other jam flavors, such as raspberry, blueberry or apricot.
—Glenna Aberle, Sabetha, KS

PREP: 25 MIN. + CHILLING • BAKE: 10 MIN./BATCH • MAKES: 5 DOZEN

1 cup butter, softened
3 oz. cream cheese, softened
1 cup sugar
1 large egg yolk, room temperature
3 tsp. vanilla extract
2½ cups all-purpose flour
Seedless strawberry jam

1. In a large bowl, cream the butter, cream cheese and sugar until light and fluffy, 5-7 minutes. Beat in the egg yolk and vanilla. Add flour and mix well. Cover and refrigerate for 1 hour or until easy to handle.

2. Shape dough into 1-in. balls. Place 2 in. apart on ungreased baking sheets. Using the end of a wooden spoon handle, make a ½-in.-deep indentation in the center of each ball; fill each with about ¼ tsp. jam. Bake at 350° for 10-12 minutes or until set. Remove to wire racks to cool.

2 COOKIES: 139 cal., 7g fat (4g sat. fat), 27mg chol., 71mg sod., 17g carb. (9g sugars, 0 fiber), 1g pro.

FAVORITE FROSTED BROWNIES

I used candy sprinkles to dress up my tried-and-true brownies for Valentine's Day. Everyone always agrees that these are absolutely yummy!

—*Barbara Birk, St. George, UT*

PREP: 15 MIN. • **BAKE:** 25 MIN. + COOLING • **MAKES:** 15 SERVINGS

1	cup butter, softened
2	cups sugar
4	large eggs, room temperature
2	tsp. vanilla extract
1¾	cups all-purpose flour
6	Tbsp. baking cocoa
1	tsp. baking powder
¼	tsp. salt

FROSTING

½	cup butter, softened
¼	cup evaporated milk
1	tsp. vanilla extract
2	Tbsp. baking cocoa
3	cups confectioners' sugar Decorating sprinkles, optional

1. Preheat oven to 350°. In a large bowl, cream the butter and sugar until light and fluffy, 5-7 minutes. Add eggs, 1 at a time, beating well after each addition. Beat in vanilla. Combine flour, cocoa, baking powder and salt; gradually add to the creamed mixture and mix well.

2. Spread into a greased 13x9-in. baking pan. Bake 25-30 minutes or until a toothpick inserted in the center comes out clean. Cool on a wire rack.

3. For frosting, in a bowl, beat the butter, milk and vanilla; add cocoa. Gradually beat in the confectioners' sugar until smooth. Spread over cooled brownies. Decorate with sprinkles if desired.

1 BROWNIE: 445 cal., 20g fat (12g sat. fat), 107mg chol., 273mg sod., 64g carb. (49g sugars, 1g fiber), 4g pro.

"Fantastic brownies! I often add whipped cream instead of milk to the frosting so it is super fluffy. I served these at my niece's wedding reception; everyone loved them."
—JEANEMED, TASTEOFHOME.COM

GRANDMA'S STAR COOKIES

My husband's grandma would make these butter cutouts only with a star cookie cutter. I use various shapes for celebrations throughout the year.
—*Jenny Brown, West Lafayette, IN*

PREP: 1 HOUR + CHILLING • **BAKE:** 10 MIN./BATCH + COOLING • **MAKES:** ABOUT 7 DOZEN

1½ **cups butter, softened**
½ **cup shortening**
1 **cup sugar**
1 **cup packed brown sugar**
2 **large eggs,**
   room temperature
¼ **cup thawed orange juice**
   concentrate
1 **tsp. vanilla extract**
5 **cups all-purpose flour**
1 **tsp. baking soda**
1 **tsp. salt**

FROSTING

3 **cups confectioners' sugar**
¼ **cup butter, melted**
1½ **tsp. thawed orange juice**
   concentrate
1 **tsp. vanilla extract**
3 **to 4 Tbsp. whole milk**
   Optional: Food coloring
   and sprinkles or
   colored sugar

1. In a large bowl, cream the butter, shortening and sugars until light and fluffy, 5-7 minutes. Add eggs, 1 at a time, beating well after each addition. Beat in the orange juice concentrate and vanilla. Combine the flour, baking soda and salt; gradually add to the creamed mixture and mix well. Cover and refrigerate until dough is easy to handle, about 2 hours.

2. On a lightly floured surface, roll out dough to ¼-in. thickness. Cut with a 3-in. star-shaped cookie cutter dipped in flour. Place 1 in. apart on ungreased baking sheets. Bake at 350° until edges are firm, 7-8 minutes. Remove to wire racks to cool.

3. For frosting, combine the confectioners' sugar, butter, orange juice concentrate, vanilla and enough milk to reach spreading consistency. Tint with food coloring if desired. Frost cookies; decorate as desired.

1 COOKIE: 111 cal., 5g fat (3g sat. fat), 15mg chol., 77mg sod., 15g carb. (9g sugars, 0 fiber), 1g pro.

GRANDMA'S SECRET

After rolling out the dough and making cutouts, put the shapes back in the refrigerator to chill for at least another 15 minutes before baking. Chilled dough gives the baked cookies cleaner edges.

CHEWY PECAN PIE BARS

This treat is one of my husband's favorites. I've been making these bars for many years, and we still can't get enough. I never mind making this recipe—it's about as easy as baking can be!
—*Judy Taylor, Shreveport, LA*

PREP: 10 MIN. • **BAKE:** 30 MIN. + COOLING • **MAKES:** 2 DOZEN

¼ **cup butter, melted**
2 **cups packed brown sugar**
⅔ **cup all-purpose flour**
4 **large eggs,**
   room temperature
2 **tsp. vanilla extract**
¼ **tsp. baking soda**
¼ **tsp. salt**
2 **cups chopped pecans**
   Confectioners' sugar,
   optional

Preheat oven to 350°. Pour butter into a 13x9-in. baking pan. In a large bowl, combine the next 6 ingredients; mix well. Stir in pecans. Spread over butter. Bake 30-35 minutes. Remove from oven. If desired, immediately dust with confectioners' sugar. Cool before cutting.

1 BAR: 180 cal., 10g fat (2g sat. fat), 41mg chol., 75mg sod., 22g carb. (18g sugars, 1g fiber), 2g pro.

GRANDMA'S SUGAR COOKIES

We bake these cookies for holidays and other special occasions. The recipe is one of my great-grandmother's that I received years ago from one of my great-aunts.
—*Kristy Deloach, Baton Rouge, LA*

PREP: 15 MIN. + CHILLING • **BAKE:** 10 MIN./BATCH • **MAKES:** 6 DOZEN 2½-IN. COOKIES OR 1½ DOZEN 4¼-IN. COOKIES

2 **cups sugar**
1 **cup butter, softened**
1 **tsp. vanilla extract**
½ **tsp. salt**
2 **large eggs,**
   room temperature,
   lightly beaten
3 **cups all-purpose flour**
2 **tsp. baking powder**
¾ **tsp. baking soda**

ICING
4 **cups confectioners' sugar**
¼ **tsp. almond extract**
½ **to ⅔ cup evaporated milk**
   Assorted food coloring
   Decorations of
   your choice

1. In a large bowl, cream the sugar, butter, vanilla and salt until light and fluffy, 5-7 minutes. Add eggs and mix well. Combine the flour, baking powder and baking soda; add to the creamed mixture. Chill until firm, about 1 hour.

2. On a floured surface, roll dough to ¼-in. thickness. Cut shapes with cookie cutters; place on greased baking sheets. Bake at 375° for 7-12 minutes (depending on size) or until light golden brown. Remove to wire racks to cool completely.

3. For the icing, in a large bowl, combine the confectioners' sugar, extract and enough evaporated milk to achieve desired consistency. Tint with food coloring. Decorate cookies as desired.

1 SMALL COOKIE: 91 cal., 3g fat (2g sat. fat), 13mg chol., 62mg sod., 16g carb. (12g sugars, 0 fiber), 1g pro.

CHEWY
PECAN PIE
BARS

CLASSIC LEMON BARS

These bars are simple enough for a no-fuss dinner yet elegant enough for a special celebration. Regardless of when you serve them, they'll be a hit.
—*Melissa Mosness, Loveland, CO*

PREP: 15 MIN. • **BAKE:** 25 MIN. + COOLING • **MAKES:** 9 SERVINGS

½ **cup butter, softened**
¼ **cup sugar**
1 **cup all-purpose flour**

FILLING
¾ **cup sugar**

2 **large eggs**
3 **Tbsp. lemon juice**
2 **Tbsp. all-purpose flour**
1 **tsp. grated lemon zest**
¼ **tsp. baking powder**
Confectioners' sugar

1. Preheat oven to 350°. In a small bowl, cream the butter and sugar until light and fluffy, 5-7 minutes; gradually beat in flour until blended.

2. Press into an ungreased 8-in. square baking dish. Bake for 15-20 minutes or until edges are lightly browned.

3. For filling, in a small bowl, beat the sugar, eggs, lemon juice, flour, lemon zest and baking powder until frothy. Pour over crust.

4. Bake 10-15 minutes longer or until set and lightly browned. Cool on a wire rack. Sprinkle with confectioners' sugar. Cut into squares.

1 BAR: 250 cal., 11g fat (7g sat. fat), 74mg chol., 99mg sod., 35g carb. (23g sugars, 0 fiber), 3g pro.

"This is a wonderful recipe. Real butter in the crust and fresh lemon juice make a huge difference. I prefer to make a glaze with about a cup of powdered sugar and some more fresh lemon juice—bars glazed store better than those sprinkled with powdered sugar. I like to double the recipe for a 9x13-in. pan, baking for 20-25 minutes until set."
—MONTNAN, TASTEOFHOME.COM

BAKI'S OLD-WORLD COOKIES

My uncles have always called these "cupcake cookies" because of the unique,
pretty way they're baked. My maternal grandmother mixed many batches.
—*Marilyn Louise Riggenbach, Ravenna, OH*

PREP: 25 MIN. + CHILLING • BAKE: 20 MIN./BATCH • MAKES: 3 DOZEN

1 cup butter, softened
1 cup sugar
2 large eggs,
   room temperature
1 cup ground walnuts
1½ cups all-purpose flour
1½ tsp. ground cinnamon
1 tsp. ground cloves
2 tsp. vanilla extract
   Confectioners' sugar

1. Preheat oven to 350°. Cream butter and sugar until light and fluffy, 5-7 minutes. Add eggs, 1 at a time, beating well after each addition. Add nuts. In another bowl, sift together flour, cinnamon and cloves; add with vanilla to creamed mixture. Refrigerate, covered, for 1 hour.

2. Fill 36 generously greased muffin cups or individual 3-in. tins one-third to half full. Press dough around sides, leaving a depression in the center. (If dough is too soft, add flour.)

3. Bake until light brown, about 18 minutes. Cool 2 minutes; tap tins to remove cookies. Dust with confectioners' sugar.

1 COOKIE: 105 cal., 7g fat (3g sat. fat), 24mg chol., 45mg sod., 10g carb. (6g sugars, 0 fiber), 1g pro.

CHOCOLATY DOUBLE CRUNCHERS

I first tried these fun, crispy cookies at a family picnic when I was a child. Packed with oats, cornflakes
and coconut, they quickly became a regular at our house. Years later, I still make them for my own family.
—*Cheryl Johnson, Upper Marlboro, MD*

PREP: 20 MIN. • BAKE: 10 MIN./BATCH + COOLING • MAKES: 2 DOZEN

½ cup butter, softened
½ cup sugar
½ cup packed brown sugar
1 large egg,
   room temperature
½ tsp. vanilla extract
1 cup all-purpose flour
½ tsp. baking soda
¼ tsp. salt
1 cup quick-cooking oats
1 cup crushed cornflakes
½ cup sweetened
   shredded coconut

FILLING
6 oz. cream cheese,
   softened
1½ cups confectioners' sugar
2 cups semisweet
   chocolate chips, melted

1. Preheat oven to 350°. In a large bowl, cream butter and sugars until light and fluffy, 5-7 minutes. Beat in egg and vanilla. Combine the flour, baking soda and salt; gradually add to the creamed mixture and mix well. Stir in the oats, cornflakes and coconut.

2. Shape dough into 1-in. balls and place 2 in. apart on greased baking sheets. Flatten with a glass dipped lightly in flour. Bake for 8-10 minutes or until lightly browned. Remove to wire racks to cool.

3. For filling, beat cream cheese and confectioners' sugar until smooth. Beat in chocolate. Spread about 1 Tbsp. on half the cookies, and top each with another cookie. Store in refrigerator.

1 COOKIE: 234 cal., 10g fat (6g sat. fat), 23mg chol., 138mg sod., 35g carb. (25g sugars, 1g fiber), 3g pro.

CHOCOLATE SNOWBALLS

This is my favorite Christmas cookie recipe. The cookies remind me of the
snowballs I packed as a child during many cold Wisconsin winters.
—*Dee Derezinski, Waukesha, WI*

PREP: 30 MIN. • **BAKE:** 15 MIN./BATCH + COOLING • **MAKES:** ABOUT 4 DOZEN

¾ **cup butter, softened**
½ **cup sugar**
½ **tsp. salt**
1 **large egg,**
   room temperature
2 **tsp. vanilla extract**
2 **cups all-purpose flour**
1 **cup chopped pecans**
   or walnuts
1 **cup (6 oz.)**
   chocolate chips
   Confectioners' sugar

1. Preheat oven to 350°. In a large bowl, cream butter, sugar
and salt until light and fluffy, 5-7 minutes. Beat in egg and vanilla.
Gradually beat in flour. Stir in pecans and chocolate chips.

2. Shape dough into 1-in. balls; place 2 in. apart on ungreased
baking sheets. Bake until set and bottoms are lightly browned,
15-20 minutes. Cool on pans 2 minutes. Roll warm cookies in
confectioners' sugar. Cool completely on wire racks. If desired,
reroll cookies in confectioners' sugar.

1 COOKIE: 92 cal., 6g fat (3g sat. fat), 12mg chol., 49mg sod.,
10g carb. (5g sugars, 1g fiber), 1g pro.

SPRITZ COOKIES

It was a tradition to make these cookies with my grandmother every Christmas.
Now our two daughters help me make them for the holidays.
—*Sharon Claussen, Wheat Ridge, CO*

PREP: 25 MIN. • **BAKE:** 15 MIN./BATCH • **MAKES:** 11 DOZEN

2 **cups butter, softened**
1 **cup sugar**
2 **large eggs,**
   room temperature
2 **tsp. vanilla extract**
4 **cups all-purpose flour**
1 **tsp. baking powder**
½ **cup confectioners' sugar**
1 **to 2 Tbsp. water**
   Colored sugar

1. Preheat oven to 325°. In a large bowl, cream butter and sugar
until light and fluffy, 5-7 minutes. Add eggs, 1 at a time, beating
well after each addition. Beat in vanilla. Combine flour and baking
powder; add to creamed mixture and mix well.

2. Using a cookie press fitted with the disk of your choice, press
dough 2 in. apart onto ungreased baking sheets. Bake until set,
11-12 minutes (do not brown). Remove to wire racks to cool.

3. Place confectioners' sugar in a small bowl; stir in enough
water to reach desired consistency. Working with 1 cookie
at a time, brush glaze on the surface and sprinkle with sugar.
Let stand until set.

1 COOKIE: 49 cal., 3g fat (2g sat. fat), 10mg chol., 28mg sod.,
5g carb. (3g sugars, 0 fiber), 1g pro.

CHOCOLATE
SNOWBALLS

GRANDMA'S SECRET

To make peeling easy, lower peaches into boiling water for about 30 seconds, then move them to an ice water bath to stop them from cooking. Let them cool there, and the skins will come off easily.

PEACH CRUMBLE BARS

PEACH CRUMBLE BARS

My favorite way to enjoy these bars is to eat one while sitting on the porch with an iced tea in hand. Make them for any occasion; they will be gobbled up quickly.
—Ally Billhorn, Wilton, IA

PREP: 20 MIN. • BAKE: 50 MIN. + COOLING • MAKES: 9 SERVINGS

½ cup butter, softened
¾ cup packed brown sugar
Dash salt
1⅓ cups all-purpose flour

FILLING
2 Tbsp. all-purpose flour
1 Tbsp. brown sugar
1 tsp. ground cinnamon
4½ cups fresh or frozen sliced peeled peaches (about 20 oz.), thawed and drained
½ cup chopped pecans, toasted

1. Preheat oven to 350°. Beat butter, brown sugar and salt until blended; beat in flour until crumbly. Reserve 1 cup mixture for topping. Press remaining mixture onto bottom of a greased 8-in. square baking pan. Bake until lightly browned, 12-15 minutes. Cool on a wire rack.

2. For filling, mix flour, brown sugar and cinnamon; toss with peaches. Spread over crust; sprinkle with pecans. Top with reserved topping.

3. Bake until topping is golden brown, 35-40 minutes. Cool on a wire rack. Cut into bars.

NOTE: To toast nuts, bake in a shallow pan in a 350° oven for 5-10 minutes or cook in a skillet over low heat until lightly browned, stirring occasionally.

1 BAR: 332 cal., 15g fat (7g sat. fat), 27mg chol., 250mg sod., 48g carb. (29g sugars, 3g fiber), 4g pro.

NO-BAKE CORNFLAKE COOKIES

I grew up on a farm where we hand-milked cows and had plenty of milk and cream to use for cooking, so sometimes we'd substitute light cream for the evaporated milk in this recipe. We'd rarely let these cookies cool before sampling them, and a batch never lasted a day!
—Denise Marnell, Hereford, TX

TAKES: 25 MIN. • MAKES: ABOUT 4 DOZEN

4 cups cornflakes
1½ cups sweetened shredded coconut
¾ cup chopped pecans
1½ cups sugar
½ cup light corn syrup
½ cup evaporated milk
¼ cup butter
Dash salt

Combine cornflakes, coconut and pecans; set aside. In a small heavy saucepan, combine remaining ingredients. Cook, stirring constantly, over medium heat until a candy thermometer reads 240° (soft-ball stage). Add syrup mixture to the dry ingredients; stir well. Drop by tablespoonfuls onto waxed paper. Let stand until set.

1 COOKIE: 81 cal., 3g fat (2g sat. fat), 3mg chol., 68mg sod., 13g carb. (11g sugars, 0 fiber), 1g pro.

MINTY CHOCOLATE CREAM CHEESE BARS

When I was growing up, I always looked forward to my grandma's gooey rich
cream cheese bars. This version includes mint, which is one of my favorite flavor add-ins.
—Jill Lutz, Woodbury, MN

PREP: 15 MIN. • BAKE: 30 MIN. + COOLING • MAKES: 2 DOZEN

1 pkg. chocolate cake mix
(regular size)
½ cup butter, softened
1 tsp. almond extract
1 tsp. vanilla extract
4 large eggs, room
temperature, divided use
1 pkg. (10 oz.) Andes
creme de menthe
baking chips, divided
8 oz. cream cheese,
softened
1⅔ cups confectioners' sugar

1. Preheat oven to 350°. In a large bowl, beat cake mix, butter, extracts and 2 eggs until blended. Spread into a greased 13x9-in. baking pan. Sprinkle with ¾ cup baking chips.

2. In a small bowl, beat cream cheese and confectioners' sugar until smooth. Add remaining 2 eggs; beat on low speed just until blended. Pour over chocolate layer, spreading evenly; sprinkle with remaining baking chips.

3. Bake 30-35 minutes or until edges begin to brown. Cool in pan on a wire rack. Cut into bars. Refrigerate leftovers.

1 BAR: 260 cal., 14g fat (9g sat. fat), 56mg chol., 219mg sod., 33g carb. (25g sugars, 1g fiber), 3g pro.

CRANBERRY PECAN TASSIES

A traditional pecan tassie is a small tart with nuts, and this festive version adds cranberries.
—Peggy West, Georgetown, DE

PREP: 25 MIN. + CHILLING • BAKE: 20 MIN. • MAKES: 2 DOZEN

½ cup butter, softened
3 oz. cream cheese,
softened
1 cup all-purpose flour
1 large egg
⅔ cup packed brown sugar
1 Tbsp. butter, melted
1 tsp. grated orange zest
½ cup chopped pecans
½ cup fresh or frozen
cranberries, thawed

1. In a small bowl, beat butter and cream cheese until smooth; gradually beat in flour. Refrigerate, covered, 30 minutes or until firm enough to shape.

2. Preheat oven to 325°. Shape dough into 1-in. balls; place in greased mini-muffin cups. Press evenly onto bottoms and up sides of cups.

3. In a small bowl, beat egg, brown sugar, melted butter and orange zest until blended. Stir in pecans. Spoon 1½ tsp. filling into each cup; top with cranberries.

4. Bake 20-25 minutes or until crust is golden and filling is set. Cool in pans 2 minutes. Remove to wire racks to cool.

FREEZE OPTION: Freeze cookies, layered between waxed paper, in freezer containers. To use, thaw before serving.

1 TASSIE: 113 cal., 7g fat (4g sat. fat), 23mg chol., 50mg sod., 11g carb. (6g sugars, 0 fiber), 1g pro.

LEMON BUTTER COOKIES

These tender cutout cookies have a slight lemon flavor that makes them stand out from the rest. They're very easy to roll out compared to other sugar cookies I've worked with.
—*Judy McCreight, Springfield, IL*

PREP: 20 MIN. + CHILLING • **BAKE:** 10 MIN./BATCH • **MAKES:** ABOUT 13 DOZEN

1	cup butter, softened	2	tsp. lemon extract
2	cups sugar	4½	cups all-purpose flour
2	large eggs, room temperature, lightly beaten	2	tsp. baking powder
		½	tsp. salt
		¼	tsp. baking soda
¼	cup whole milk		Colored sugar, optional

1. In a large bowl, cream butter and sugar until light and fluffy, 5-7 minutes. Beat in the eggs, milk and extract. Combine the dry ingredients; gradually add to the creamed mixture and mix well. Cover and chill for 2 hours.

2. Preheat oven to 350°. Roll out dough on a lightly floured surface to ⅛-in. thickness. Cut with a 2-in. cookie cutter dipped in flour. Place cutouts 2 in. apart on ungreased baking sheets. Sprinkle with colored sugar if desired.

3. Bake until the edges just begin to brown, 8-9 minutes. Remove to wire racks to cool.

2 COOKIES: 70 cal., 3g fat (2g sat. fat), 12mg chol., 55mg sod., 11g carb. (5g sugars, 0 fiber), 1g pro.

"I love these cookies. These days I'm all about lemon. They had the perfect amount of lemon flavor and held their shape well during baking."
—CINDIAK, TASTEOFHOME.COM

CHOCOLATE BUTTERMILK SQUARES

Every time I take these squares to a potluck, my pan comes back clean. At home, they vanish as fast as I make them.
—*Clarice Baker, Stromsburg, NE*

PREP: 20 MIN. • BAKE: 20 MIN. • MAKES: 15 SERVINGS

1 cup butter, cubed
¼ cup baking cocoa
1 cup water
2 cups all-purpose flour
2 cups sugar
1 tsp. baking soda
½ tsp. salt
½ cup buttermilk
2 large eggs, room temperature, beaten
1 tsp. vanilla extract
3 to 4 drops red food coloring, optional

FROSTING

½ cup butter, cubed
¼ cup baking cocoa
¼ cup buttermilk
3¾ cups confectioners' sugar
1 tsp. vanilla extract
Dash salt
¾ cup chopped almonds, optional

1. In a large saucepan, bring butter, cocoa and water just to a boil. Cool.

2. Meanwhile, preheat oven to 350°. In a large bowl, combine the flour, sugar, baking soda and salt. Add cocoa mixture and buttermilk; mix well. Beat in the eggs, vanilla and, if desired, food coloring. Pour into a greased and floured 15x10x1-in. baking pan.

3. Bake until set, 20 minutes. For frosting, melt butter with cocoa and buttermilk. Stir in the confectioners' sugar, vanilla and salt. Spread over warm cake. Garnish with nuts if desired.

NOTE: To substitute for 1 cup of buttermilk, use 1 Tbsp. white vinegar or lemon juice plus enough milk to measure 1 cup. Stir, then let stand 5 minutes. Or, use 1 cup plain yogurt or 1¾ tsp. cream of tartar plus 1 cup milk.

1 SQUARE: 466 cal., 19g fat (12g sat. fat), 78mg chol., 380mg sod., 72g carb. (55g sugars, 1g fiber), 4g pro.

FROM GRANDMA'S KITCHEN: For different flavors, try substituting almond, rum or mint extract for the vanilla. Mint packs a punch—reduce it from 1 tsp. to ¼ tsp. in both the batter and the frosting. Brickle bits or other crushed candy bars are also delicious sprinkled over these gooey bars.

CARAMEL HEAVENLIES

Before I cut these bars into triangles, I usually trim the edges so all the cookies look the same. My husband and daughter love that part since they get to eat the scraps!
—*Dawn Burns, Lake St. Louis, MO*

PREP: 20 MIN. • **BAKE:** 15 MIN. + COOLING • **MAKES:** ABOUT 3 DOZEN

12 whole graham crackers
2 cups miniature
  marshmallows
¾ cup butter, cubed
¾ cup packed brown sugar
1 tsp. ground cinnamon
1 tsp. vanilla extract
1 cup sliced almonds
1 cup sweetened
  shredded coconut

1. Preheat oven to 350°. Line a 15x10x1-in. baking pan with foil, letting foil extend over sides by 1 in.; lightly coat foil with cooking spray. Arrange graham crackers in the prepared pan; sprinkle with marshmallows.

2. In a small saucepan, combine the butter, brown sugar and cinnamon; cook and stir over medium heat until the butter is melted and sugar is dissolved. Remove from heat; stir in vanilla.

3. Spoon butter mixture over marshmallows. Sprinkle with almonds and coconut. Bake until browned, 14-16 minutes. Cool completely in pan on a wire rack.

4. Using foil, lift cookies out of pan. Cut into triangles; discard foil.

2 TRIANGLES: 110 cal., 7g fat (3g sat. fat), 10mg chol., 68mg sod., 13g carb. (8g sugars, 1g fiber), 1g pro.

GRANDMA'S OATMEAL RAISIN COOKIES

I look forward to cooking, baking and entertaining during the holidays. These cookies are a mainstay at my gatherings.
—*Susanne Spicker, North Ogden, UT*

PREP: 25 MIN. • **BAKE:** 10 MIN./BATCH • **MAKES:** 4 DOZEN

2 cups raisins, chopped
2 cups boiling water
¾ cup butter-flavored
  shortening
1 cup sugar
3 large eggs,
  room temperature
2½ cups all-purpose flour
2 cups old-fashioned oats
1¼ tsp. baking soda
½ tsp. salt
2 cups chopped walnuts

1. Preheat oven to 325°. Place raisins in a small bowl. Cover with boiling water; let stand for 5 minutes. Drain and set aside.

2. In a large bowl, cream shortening and sugar until light and fluffy, 5-7 minutes. Beat in eggs. Combine the flour, oats, baking soda and salt; gradually add to creamed mixture and mix well. Stir in walnuts and raisins.

3. Drop by rounded tablespoonfuls 2 in. apart onto greased baking sheets. Flatten with a glass. Bake for 8-10 minutes or until the bottoms are browned. Remove to wire racks.

1 COOKIE: 134 cal., 7g fat (1g sat. fat), 13mg chol., 63mg sod., 17g carb. (8g sugars, 1g fiber), 2g pro.

CARAMEL HEAVENLIES

CHOCOLATE MAPLE BARS

My family runs a maple syrup operation, and I'm always looking for new ways to incorporate maple syrup into my cooking and baking. These bars are delicious!
—*Cathy Schumacher, Alto, MI*

PREP: 20 MIN. • BAKE: 25 MIN. + COOLING • MAKES: 3 DOZEN

½ cup shortening
¾ cup maple syrup
½ cup sugar
3 large eggs, room temperature
3 Tbsp. 2% milk
1 tsp. vanilla extract
1¼ cups all-purpose flour
¼ tsp. baking powder
¼ tsp. salt
1½ oz. unsweetened chocolate, melted

½ cup chopped pecans
½ cup sweetened shredded coconut

FROSTING

¼ cup butter, softened
1 cup confectioners' sugar
½ cup baking cocoa
½ cup maple syrup
1 cup miniature marshmallows

1. Preheat oven to 350°. In a large bowl, cream the shortening, syrup and sugar until light and fluffy, 5-7 minutes. Beat in the eggs, milk and vanilla. Combine the flour, baking powder and salt; add to the creamed mixture and mix well. Remove half the batter to another bowl.

2. Combine the melted chocolate and pecans; stir into 1 bowl of batter. Spread into a greased 13x9-in. baking pan. Add coconut to the remaining batter. Spread carefully over chocolate batter.

3. Bake until a toothpick inserted in the center comes out clean, about 25 minutes. Cool completely on a wire rack.

4. In a small bowl, beat butter until smooth. Gradually add the confectioners' sugar and cocoa. Gradually add syrup, beating until smooth. Fold in marshmallows. Frost bars.

1 BAR: 143 cal., 7g fat (3g sat. fat), 21mg chol., 43mg sod., 20g carb. (14g sugars, 1g fiber), 2g pro.

OREGON'S HAZELNUT CHOCOLATE CHIP COOKIE

These nutty cookies are popular with the ladies at my craft club. I grew up during the Depression, and my mother taught me to use what was available—like the plentiful nuts here in Oregon.
—*Selmer Looney, Eugene, OR*

PREP: 15 MIN. • BAKE: 10 MIN./BATCH • MAKES: 3 DOZEN

1 cup butter, softened
½ cup sugar
1 cup packed brown sugar
2 large eggs, room temperature
1 tsp. vanilla extract
2⅓ cups all-purpose flour
1 tsp. baking soda
½ tsp. salt
1 cup semisweet chocolate chips
¾ cup chopped hazelnuts

1. Preheat oven to 350°. In a large bowl, cream the butter and sugars on medium speed for 3-5 minutes. Add eggs, 1 at a time, beating well after each addition. Add vanilla. Combine flour, baking soda and salt; gradually add to batter. Fold in chocolate chips and nuts.

2. Drop by heaping tablespoonfuls 3 in. apart onto lightly greased baking sheets. Flatten lightly with a fork. Bake for 10-12 minutes or until light brown. Remove to a wire rack to cool.

1 COOKIE: 299 cal., 17g fat (8g sat. fat), 51mg chol., 251mg sod., 37g carb. (23g sugars, 1g fiber), 4g pro.

HOLIDAY GUMDROP COOKIES

These cookies were my mother's special treat. They are perfect for keeping children busy—they can cut up the gumdrops and eat all the black ones so they don't turn the dough gray.
—*Letah Chilston, Riverton, WY*

PREP: 15 MIN. + CHILLING • BAKE: 10 MIN./BATCH • MAKES: ABOUT 7 DOZEN

1½ cups spice gumdrops
¾ cup coarsely chopped walnuts
½ cup golden raisins
1¾ cups all-purpose flour, divided
½ cup shortening
1 cup packed brown sugar
1 large egg, room temperature
¼ cup buttermilk
½ tsp. baking soda
½ tsp. salt

1. Cut gumdrops into small pieces; place in a bowl. Add walnuts, raisins and ¼ cup flour; toss to coat.

2. In a large bowl, beat the shortening and brown sugar until blended. Beat in egg, then buttermilk. In another bowl, whisk the remaining 1½ cups flour, the baking soda and salt; gradually beat into shortening mixture. Stir in gumdrop mixture. Refrigerate, covered, for 1 hour.

3. Preheat oven to 400°. Drop dough by rounded teaspoonfuls 2 in. apart onto ungreased baking sheets. Bake 8-10 minutes or until golden brown. Cool on pans for 2 minutes, then remove to wire racks to cool.

1 COOKIE: 53 cal., 2g fat (0 sat. fat), 2mg chol., 26mg sod., 9g carb. (5g sugars, 0 fiber), 1g pro.

CHOCOLATE-COVERED CHERRY THUMBPRINTS

When I dig out my best cookie recipes, I'm reminded of baking with my children when they were little. These thumbprints with cherries elicit such sweet memories.
—*Deborah Puette, Lilburn, GA*

PREP: 30 MIN. + CHILLING • **BAKE:** 10 MIN. + COOLING • **MAKES:** 2 DOZEN

¼ cup butter, softened
¼ cup shortening
¼ cup packed brown sugar
¼ tsp. salt
1 large egg, separated, room temperature
½ tsp. vanilla extract
1 cup all-purpose flour
1 cup finely chopped salted roasted almonds

FILLING
⅓ cup confectioners' sugar
1 Tbsp. maraschino cherry juice
2 tsp. butter, softened
1 tsp. 2% milk

TOPPINGS
24 maraschino cherries
4 oz. milk chocolate candy coating, melted

1. Preheat oven to 350°. In a large bowl, cream butter, shortening, brown sugar and salt until light and fluffy, 5-7 minutes. Beat in egg yolk and vanilla. Gradually beat flour into the creamed mixture. Refrigerate, covered, until easy to handle, 30 minutes.

2. Preheat oven to 350°. Shape dough into 1¼-in. balls. In a shallow bowl, whisk egg white until foamy. Place almonds in a separate shallow bowl. Dip balls in egg white; roll in almonds.

3. Place balls 2 in. apart on ungreased baking sheets. Press a deep indentation in center of each with your thumb. Bake until edges are light brown, 10-12 minutes. Remove from pans to wire racks.

4. In a small bowl, beat confectioners' sugar, cherry juice, butter and milk until smooth. Fill each cookie with ¼ tsp. filling. Top with 1 cherry and drizzle with candy coating. Let stand until set.

1 COOKIE: 145 cal., 9g fat (3g sat. fat), 14mg chol., 75mg sod., 15g carb. (10g sugars, 1g fiber), 2g pro.

LEMON COCONUT BITES

The tangy lemon flavor of this no-fuss dessert is especially delicious on a warm day. It gives me delightful flashbacks of selling lemonade on the sidewalk as a little girl.
—*Donna Biddle, Elmira, NY*

PREP: 25 MIN. • **BAKE:** 20 MIN. + COOLING • **MAKES:** 4 DOZEN

1½ cups all-purpose flour
½ cup confectioners' sugar
¾ cup cold butter, cubed
4 large eggs, room temperature
1½ cups sugar
½ cup lemon juice
1 tsp. baking powder
¾ cup sweetened shredded coconut

1. Preheat oven to 350°. In a small bowl, combine flour and confectioners' sugar; cut in the butter until crumbly. Press into a lightly greased 13x9-in. baking pan. Bake for 15 minutes.

2. Meanwhile, in another small bowl, beat the eggs, sugar, lemon juice and baking powder until combined. Pour over crust; sprinkle with coconut.

3. Bake until golden brown, 20-25 minutes. Cool on a wire rack. Cut into bars.

1 BAR: 82 cal., 4g fat (2g sat. fat), 25mg chol., 46mg sod., 11g carb. (8g sugars, 0 fiber), 1g pro.

CHOCOLATE-COVERED
CHERRY THUMBPRINTS

GRANDMA BRUBAKER'S
ORANGE COOKIES

GRANDMA BRUBAKER'S ORANGE COOKIES

At least two generations of my family have enjoyed the recipe for
these delicate, orange-flavored, cakelike cookies.
—*Sheri DeBolt, Huntington, IN*

PREP: 20 MIN. • BAKE: 10 MIN./BATCH + COOLING • MAKES: ABOUT 6 DOZEN

1 cup shortening
2 cups sugar
2 large eggs, separated,
    room temperature
1 cup buttermilk
5 cups all-purpose flour
2 tsp. baking powder
2 tsp. baking soda
    Pinch salt
    Juice and grated zest of
    2 medium navel oranges

ICING

2 cups confectioners' sugar
¼ cup orange juice
1 Tbsp. butter
1 Tbsp. grated orange zest

1. Preheat oven to 325°. In a bowl, cream shortening and sugar until light and fluffy, 5-7 minutes. Beat in egg yolks and buttermilk. Sift together flour, baking powder, baking soda and salt; add to the creamed mixture alternately with orange juice and zest. Add egg whites and beat until smooth.

2. Drop by rounded teaspoonfuls onto greased cookie sheets. Bake until set, about 10 minutes, then remove to wire racks to cool completely.

3. For icing, combine all ingredients and beat until smooth. Frost cooled cookies.

1 COOKIE: 97 cal., 3g fat (1g sat. fat), 6mg chol., 58mg sod., 16g carb. (9g sugars, 0 fiber), 1g pro.

DATE OATMEAL BARS

In no time at all, you'll be able share these treats with your family.
They'll be surprised at how light and tasty the snacks are.
—*Helen Cluts, Eden Prairie, MN*

PREP: 20 MIN. • BAKE: 20 MIN. + COOLING • MAKES: 16 SERVINGS

1 cup chopped dates
½ cup water
¼ cup sugar
1½ cups quick-cooking oats
1 cup all-purpose flour
1 cup packed brown sugar
½ tsp. baking soda
¼ tsp. salt
⅓ cup butter, melted
1 large egg white,
    room temperature

1. Preheat oven to 350°. Place dates, water and sugar in a small saucepan; bring to a boil, stirring constantly. Reduce heat; simmer, uncovered, until thickened, about 5 minutes, stirring constantly.

2. In a large bowl, mix oats, flour, brown sugar, baking soda and salt; stir in the melted butter and egg white. Press half the mixture into an 8-in. square baking pan coated with cooking spray. Spread carefully with the date mixture; top with the remaining oat mixture.

3. Bake until lightly browned, 20-25 minutes. Cool in pan on a wire rack. Cut into bars.

1 BAR: 182 cal., 4g fat (3g sat. fat), 10mg chol., 114mg sod., 35g carb. (23g sugars, 2g fiber), 2g pro. DIABETIC EXCHANGES: 1½ starch, 1 fat, ½ fruit.

GLAZED APPLE-MAPLE BLONDIES

My 6-year-old son and I conjured up this recipe to use the last of the apples we picked from the local apple orchard. Each bar goes beautifully with a dollop of sweetened whipped cream.
—*Heather Bates, Athens, ME*

PREP: 25 MIN. • BAKE: 25 MIN. + COOLING • MAKES: 2 DOZEN

1⅓ cups packed brown sugar
½ cup butter, melted
and cooled
½ cup maple syrup
2 tsp. vanilla extract
2 large eggs,
room temperature
2 cups all-purpose flour
¾ tsp. salt
¼ tsp. baking soda
3 cups chopped peeled
apples (about 3 medium)

GLAZE
¼ cup butter, cubed
½ cup maple syrup
¼ cup packed brown sugar

1. Preheat oven to 350°. Line a 13x9-in. baking pan with parchment, letting ends extend up sides.

2. In a large bowl, beat brown sugar, melted butter, syrup and vanilla until blended. Beat in eggs, 1 at a time, beating well after each addition. In another bowl, whisk flour, salt and baking soda; gradually beat into the brown sugar mixture. Stir in apples (the batter will be thick).

3. Transfer batter to prepared pan. Bake until top is golden brown and a toothpick inserted in center comes out with moist crumbs, 25-30 minutes.

4. Meanwhile, in a small saucepan, melt butter over medium-low heat; stir in syrup and brown sugar. Bring to a boil over medium heat; cook and stir until slightly thickened, 2-3 minutes. Remove from heat; cool slightly.

5. Pour glaze over warm blondies. Cool completely in pan on a wire rack. Cut into bars.

1 BLONDIE: 192 cal., 6g fat (4g sat. fat), 31mg chol., 149mg sod., 33g carb. (25g sugars, 0 fiber), 2g pro.

PECAN PUFFS

I just had to share my mom's recipe for these drop cookies.
The light-as-a-cloud taste is simply heavenly.
—*Leslie Link-Terry, Greendale, WI*

PREP: 15 MIN. • BAKE: 50 MIN. • MAKES: 3 DOZEN

3 large egg whites,
room temperature
Pinch salt
1 cup packed brown sugar
½ tsp. vanilla extract
1 cup chopped pecans

Preheat oven to 225°. In a bowl, beat egg whites and salt until soft peaks form. Gradually add the brown sugar, beating until stiff peaks form, 5-8 minutes. Fold in vanilla and pecans. Drop by well-rounded teaspoonfuls onto greased baking sheets. Bake 50-55 minutes or until firm to the touch. Store in an airtight container.

2 PUFFS: 95 cal., 5g fat (0 sat. fat), 0 chol., 22mg sod., 13g carb. (12g sugars, 1g fiber), 1g pro.

CRANBERRY BOG BARS

Sweet and chewy, these fun bars combine the flavors
of oats, cranberries, brown sugar and pecans. I like to sprinkle
the squares with confectioners' sugar before serving.
—*Sally Wakefield, Gans, PA*

PREP: 25 MIN. • **BAKE:** 25 MIN. • **MAKES:** 2 DOZEN

1¼ cups butter, softened,
   divided
1½ cups packed
   brown sugar, divided
3½ cups old-fashioned oats,
   divided

1 cup all-purpose flour
1 can (14 oz.) whole-berry
   cranberry sauce
½ cup finely chopped
   pecans

1. In a large bowl, cream 1 cup butter and 1 cup brown sugar until light and fluffy, 5-7 minutes. Combine 2½ cups oats and the flour. Gradually add to the creamed mixture until crumbly. Press into a greased 13x9-in. baking pan. Spread with cranberry sauce.

2. In a microwave-safe bowl, melt remaining ¼ cup butter; stir in the pecans and the remaining ½ cup brown sugar and 1 cup oats. Sprinkle over cranberry sauce. Bake at 375° until lightly browned, 25-30 minutes. Cool on a wire rack. Cut into bars.

1 BAR: 239 cal., 12g fat (6g sat. fat), 25mg chol., 88mg sod., 32g carb. (18g sugars, 2g fiber), 2g pro.

GROSSMUTTER'S PEPPERNUTS

Before Christmas, my grandmother would bake peppernuts and store them
until the big day. When we'd come home from school, the whole house would
smell like anise and we knew the holiday season was about to begin.
—*Marilyn Kutzli, Clinton, IA*

PREP: 40 MIN. + CHILLING • **BAKE:** 10 MIN./BATCH + COOLING • **MAKES:** ABOUT 30 DOZEN

3 large eggs,
   room temperature
2 cups sugar
2¾ cups all-purpose flour
1 tsp. anise extract or
   crushed aniseed

1. Beat eggs and sugar at medium speed for 15 minutes. Reduce speed; gradually add flour and anise. Beat until well combined. On a lightly floured surface, shape dough into ½-in.-thick ropes. Refrigerate, covered, for 1 hour.

2. Preheat oven to 350°. Cut ropes into ½-in. pieces; place on greased baking sheets. Bake until set, 6-8 minutes. Cool completely on baking sheets on wire racks. Cookies will harden upon standing. Store in airtight containers.

6 COOKIES: 51 cal., 0 fat (0 sat. fat), 9mg chol., 4mg sod., 11g carb. (7g sugars, 0 fiber), 1g pro. **DIABETIC EXCHANGES:** 1 starch.

BANANA SPLIT BROWNIES

How's this for a dish? All the joy of a banana split without the mess!
Everything in this recipe fits into one pan of delectable brownie bars.
—*Constance Sheckler, Chestertown, MD*

PREP: 45 MIN. • BAKE: 40 MIN. + COOLING • MAKES: 2 DOZEN

- 8 oz. unsweetened
  chocolate, chopped
- ¾ cup butter, cubed
- 3 large eggs,
  room temperature
- 2 cups sugar
- 1 tsp. vanilla extract
- 1 cup plus 2 Tbsp.
  all-purpose flour
- 1 cup maraschino cherries,
  chopped

TOPPING

- 1 pkg. (8 oz.) cream cheese,
  softened
- ½ cup mashed ripe banana
  (about 1 medium)
- ⅓ cup strawberry
  preserves
- 1 large egg,
  room temperature,
  lightly beaten
- ¼ cup chopped
  salted peanuts
  Optional: Sliced bananas
  and additional chopped
  maraschino cherries

1. Preheat oven to 350°. In a microwave, melt chocolate and butter; stir until smooth.

2. In a large bowl, beat eggs and sugar on high speed 10 minutes. Stir in vanilla and chocolate mixture. Gradually stir in flour. Fold in cherries. Spread into a greased 13x9-in. baking pan.

3. For topping, in a small bowl, beat cream cheese until smooth. Beat in mashed banana and preserves. Add egg; beat on low speed just until blended. Spread over brownie batter; sprinkle with peanuts.

4. Bake until topping is set and a toothpick inserted in brownie portion comes out mostly clean, 40-45 minutes. Cool completely on a wire rack.

5. Cut into bars. If desired, serve bars garnished with banana slices and additional cherries. Store in an airtight container in the refrigerator.

1 BROWNIE: 262 cal., 16g fat (9g sat. fat), 57mg chol., 101mg sod., 31g carb. (23g sugars, 2g fiber), 4g pro.

OMA'S APFELKUCHEN
(GRANDMA'S APPLE CAKE),
PAGE 273

GRANDMA'S FAVORITE

CAKES & PIES

Sitting down to a slice of one of Grandma's
famous from-scratch desserts is like getting
a big warm hug just when you need it most.
Relish every last bite of these heavenly treats
that always make even the most trying
day a bit brighter.

STRAWBERRY POKE CAKE

Strawberry shortcake takes on a wonderful new twist with this
super-simple recipe. Strawberries liven up each pretty slice.
—*Mary Jo Griggs, West Bend, WI*

PREP: 25 MIN. • BAKE: 25 MIN. + CHILLING • MAKES: 12 SERVINGS

1 pkg. white cake mix
(regular size)
1¼ cups water
2 large eggs,
room temperature
¼ cup canola oil
2 pkg. (10 oz. each) frozen
sweetened sliced
strawberries, thawed
2 pkg. (3 oz. each)
strawberry gelatin
1 carton (12 oz.) frozen
whipped topping, thawed,
divided
Fresh strawberries,
optional

GRANDMA'S SECRET

When you're pouring the sauce
into the holes, tap the pan on
the countertop a few times to
get rid of any air bubbles and
make sure the sauce fills
the holes completely.

1. Preheat oven to 350°. In a large bowl, combine the cake mix, water, eggs and oil; beat on low speed for 30 seconds. Increase speed to medium and beat for 2 minutes longer.

2. Pour batter into 2 greased and floured 9-in. round baking pans. Bake until a toothpick inserted in the center comes out clean, 25-35 minutes. Cool in pans for 10 minutes; remove to wire racks to cool completely.

3. Drain juice from strawberries into a 2-cup measuring cup; refrigerate berries. Add water to juice to measure 2 cups; pour into a small saucepan. Bring to a boil; stir in the gelatin until dissolved. Chill for 30 minutes.

4. Using a serrated knife, level tops of cakes if necessary. Return layers, top side up, to 2 clean 9-in. round baking pans. Pierce cakes with a meat fork or wooden skewer at ½-in. intervals. Gently spoon juice mixture over each cake layer. Chill for 2-3 hours.

5. Dip bottom of 1 pan into warm water for 10 seconds. Invert onto a serving platter. Top with chilled strawberries and 1 cup whipped topping. Place second cake layer over topping.

6. Frost cake with remaining whipped topping. Chill for at least 1 hour. Serve with fresh berries if desired. Refrigerate leftovers.

1 PIECE: 376 cal., 14g fat (7g sat. fat), 35mg chol., 301mg sod., 56g carb. (37g sugars, 1g fiber), 4g pro.

SOUTHERN SWEET POTATO TART

We love sweet potatoes, so I try to incorporate them in as many dishes as I can—
even dessert! My secret ingredient is the bourbon—that's what makes it so delicious.
—*Marie Bruno, Watkinsville, GA*

PREP: 1 HOUR • BAKE: 25 MIN. + COOLING • MAKES: 8 SERVINGS

1 lb. sweet potatoes
(about 2 small)
Dough for single-crust
pie
¼ cup butter, softened
½ cup packed dark brown
sugar
2 Tbsp. all-purpose flour
1 tsp. pumpkin pie spice
¼ tsp. salt
1 large egg, room
temperature
¼ cup heavy whipping
cream
1 Tbsp. bourbon or 1 Tbsp.
whipping cream plus
½ tsp. vanilla extract

TOPPING
2 Tbsp. butter, softened
2 Tbsp. dark brown sugar
2 Tbsp. dark corn syrup
½ cup chopped pecans

1. Preheat oven to 400°. Place potatoes on a foil-lined baking sheet. Bake until tender, 40-50 minutes.

2. On a lightly floured surface, roll dough to a ⅛-in.-thick circle; transfer to a 9-in. tart pan with removable bottom. Press onto bottom and sides of pan; trim edges to edge of pan. Refrigerate while preparing filling.

3. Remove potatoes from oven; increase oven setting to 425°. When potatoes are cool enough to handle, remove skin and place pulp in a large bowl; beat until smooth.

4. Measure out 1 cup of mashed potato into another bowl; add butter, brown sugar, flour, pie spice and salt; beat until blended. Beat in egg, cream and bourbon. Pour into crust. Bake on a lower oven rack 15 minutes.

5. Meanwhile, for topping, mix butter, brown sugar and corn syrup until blended. Stir in pecans.

6. Remove pie; reduce oven setting to 350°. Spoon topping evenly over pie. Bake until a knife inserted in the center comes out clean, 8-10 minutes.

7. Cool on a wire rack. Serve within 2 hours or refrigerate, covered, and serve cold.

DOUGH FOR SINGLE-CRUST PIE (9 IN.): Combine 1¼ cups all-purpose flour and ¼ tsp. salt; cut in ½ cup cold butter until crumbly. Gradually add 3-5 Tbsp. ice water, tossing with a fork until dough holds together when pressed. Wrap and refrigerate 1 hour.

1 PIECE: 477 cal., 29g fat (15g sat. fat), 85mg chol., 326mg sod., 52g carb. (27g sugars, 3g fiber), 5g pro.

FRESH PLUM KUCHEN

In summer when plums are in season, this tender fruit-topped cake
is delectable! For variety, you can use fresh pears or apples instead.
—*Anna Daley, Montague, PE*

PREP: 20 MIN. • BAKE: 40 MIN. + COOLING • MAKES: 12 SERVINGS

¼ cup butter, softened
¾ cup sugar
2 large eggs, room temperature
1 cup all-purpose flour
1 tsp. baking powder
¼ cup 2% milk
1 tsp. grated lemon zest
2 cups sliced fresh plums (about 4 medium)
½ cup packed brown sugar
1 tsp. ground cinnamon

1. Preheat oven to 350°. In a small bowl, cream butter and sugar until light and fluffy, 5-7 minutes. Beat in eggs. Combine flour and baking powder; add to the creamed mixture alternately with milk, beating well after each addition. Add lemon zest. Pour into a greased 10-in. springform pan. Arrange plums on top; gently press into batter. Sprinkle with brown sugar and cinnamon.

2. Place pan on a baking sheet. Bake for 40-50 minutes or until top is golden and a toothpick inserted in the center comes out clean. Cool for 10 minutes. Run a knife around edge of pan; remove sides. Cool on a wire rack.

1 PIECE: 185 cal., 5g fat (3g sat. fat), 46mg chol., 89mg sod., 33g carb. (24g sugars, 1g fiber), 3g pro.

GRANDMA'S BLACKBERRY CAKE

A lightly seasoned spice cake lets the wonderful flavor of fresh blackberries shine through.
—*Diana Martin, Moundsville, WV*

PREP: 15 MIN. • BAKE: 45 MIN. • MAKES: 9 SERVINGS

1 cup fresh blackberries
2 cups all-purpose flour, divided
½ cup butter, softened
1 cup sugar
2 large eggs, room temperature
1 tsp. baking soda
1 tsp. ground cinnamon
1 tsp. ground nutmeg
½ tsp. salt
¼ tsp. ground cloves
¼ tsp. ground allspice
¾ cup buttermilk
Optional: Whipped cream and confectioners' sugar

1. Preheat oven to 350°. Toss blackberries with ¼ cup flour; set aside. In a large bowl, cream butter and sugar until light and fluffy, 5-7 minutes. Beat in eggs. Combine baking soda, cinnamon, nutmeg, salt, cloves, allspice and the remaining 1¾ cups flour; add to the creamed mixture alternately with buttermilk, beating well after each addition. Fold in blackberries.

2. Pour batter into a greased and floured 9-in. square baking pan. Bake until a toothpick inserted in center comes out clean, 45-50 minutes. Cool on a wire rack.

3. If desired, serve with whipped cream and top with confectioners' sugar and additional fresh blackberries.

1 PIECE: 312 cal., 12g fat (7g sat. fat), 75mg chol., 410mg sod., 47g carb. (24g sugars, 2g fiber), 5g pro.

CHOCOLATE CHESS PIE

This is one of my mother's go-to recipes. It's a yummy personal spin on classic chocolate chess pie.
—*Ann Dickens, Nixa, MO*

PREP: 30 MIN. • **COOK:** 40 MIN. + CHILLING • **MAKES:** 8 SERVINGS

1¼ cups all-purpose flour
¼ tsp. salt
¼ cup cold butter, cubed
¼ cup shortening
3 to 4 Tbsp. ice water

FILLING
2 large eggs, room temperature
1 cup packed brown sugar
½ cup sugar
1½ oz. unsweetened chocolate, melted and cooled
2 Tbsp. 2% milk
1 Tbsp. all-purpose flour
1 tsp. vanilla extract
½ cup butter, melted

1. Combine flour and salt; cut in butter and shortening until crumbly. Gradually add ice water, tossing with a fork until the dough holds together when pressed. Shape dough into a disk. Wrap and refrigerate 1 hour or overnight.

2. On a floured surface, roll out dough to fit a 9-in. pie plate. Trim and flute edge. Refrigerate 30 minutes. Preheat oven to 425°. Line unpricked crust with a double thickness of foil. Fill with pie weights. Bake on a lower oven rack until light golden brown, 15-20 minutes. Remove the foil and weights; bake until golden brown, 3-6 minutes. Cool on a wire rack. Reduce oven setting to 325°.

3. In a large bowl, whisk eggs, sugars, melted chocolate, milk, flour and vanilla. Gradually whisk in butter. Pour into crust. Cover edge with foil to prevent overbrowning.

4. Bake at 325° until a knife inserted in the center comes out clean, 35-40 minutes. Remove the foil. Cool pie on a wire rack. Refrigerate, covered, for 3 hours or until chilled.

1 PIECE: 436 cal., 22g fat (13g sat. fat), 93mg chol., 240mg sod., 57g carb. (40g sugars, 1g fiber), 5g pro.

ORANGE CHOCOLATE
RICOTTA PIE

ORANGE CHOCOLATE RICOTTA PIE

This traditional Italian dessert is usually served during the holidays and
for special occasions. The orange and chocolate flavors make a classic pairing.
—*Trisha Kruse, Eagle, ID*

PREP: 20 MIN. • **BAKE:** 40 MIN. + COOLING • **MAKES:** 8 SERVINGS

2 **cartons (15 oz. each) whole-milk ricotta cheese**
2 **large eggs, lightly beaten**
½ **cup dark chocolate chips**
⅓ **cup sugar**
1 **Tbsp. grated orange zest**
2 **Tbsp. orange liqueur, optional**
  Dough for double-crust pie

1. Preheat oven to 425°. Combine the ricotta cheese, eggs, dark chocolate chips, sugar, orange zest and, if desired, orange liqueur.

2. On a floured surface, roll out half the dough to fit a 9-in. pie plate; transfer to pie plate. Fill with ricotta mixture.

3. Roll out the remaining dough into an 11-in. circle; cut into 1-in.-wide strips. Lay half of the strips across the pie, about 1 in. apart. Fold back every other strip halfway. Lay another strip across center of pie at a right angle. Unfold strips over center strip. Fold back the alternate strips; place a second strip across the pie. Continue to add strips until pie is covered with lattice. Trim, seal and flute edges.

4. Bake until crust is golden brown, 40-45 minutes. Refrigerate any leftovers.

DOUGH FOR DOUBLE-CRUST PIE: Combine 2-½ cups all-purpose flour and ½ tsp. salt; cut in 1 cup cold butter until crumbly. Gradually add ⅓ to ⅔ cup ice water, tossing with a fork until dough holds together when pressed. Divide dough in half. Shape each into a disk; wrap and refrigerate 1 hour.

1 PIECE: 525 cal., 31g fat (16g sat. fat), 106mg chol., 346mg sod., 49g carb. (23g sugars, 0 fiber), 17g pro.

RHUBARB & STRAWBERRY COFFEE CAKE

Vanilla cake with cream cheese filling and strawberry rhubarb sauce makes a grand finale for a Mother's Day brunch. I made this to honor our moms and grandmothers.

—Danielle Lee, West Palm Beach, FL

PREP: 50 MIN. • BAKE: 50 MIN. + COOLING • MAKES: 12 SERVINGS

1½ tsp. cornstarch
3 Tbsp. sugar
¾ cup chopped fresh strawberries
¾ cup chopped fresh or frozen rhubarb
1 Tbsp. water

FILLING

1 pkg. (8 oz.) cream cheese, softened
¼ cup sugar
1 large egg, lightly beaten

CAKE

2 cups all-purpose flour
¾ cup sugar
½ cup cold butter, cubed
½ tsp. baking powder
½ tsp. baking soda
¼ tsp. salt
1 large egg, room temperature, lightly beaten
¾ cup fat-free sour cream
1 tsp. vanilla extract

1. Preheat oven to 350°. Line bottom of a greased 9-in. springform pan with parchment; grease parchment. In a small saucepan, mix cornstarch and sugar; stir in strawberries, rhubarb and water. Bring to a boil. Reduce heat and simmer, uncovered, until thickened, 6-8 minutes, stirring occasionally.

2. For filling, in a small bowl, beat cream cheese and sugar until smooth. Beat in egg.

3. For the cake, in a large bowl, combine flour and sugar; cut in butter until crumbly. Reserve ¾ cup for topping. Stir baking powder, baking soda and salt into the remaining flour mixture. In a small bowl, whisk egg, sour cream and vanilla until blended; gently stir into the flour mixture (do not overmix).

4. Spread batter onto bottom and ½ in. up sides of prepared pan. Spread filling over crust, leaving a ½-in. border around edge of pan. Spoon strawberry mixture over top; sprinkle with reserved crumb mixture.

5. Bake until edges are golden brown, 50-60 minutes. Cool on a wire rack for 20 minutes. Loosen sides from pan with a knife. Cool completely. Remove rim from pan. Refrigerate leftovers.

FREEZE OPTION: Securely wrap cooled cake in plastic wrap and foil, then freeze. To use, thaw in refrigerator.

NOTE: If using frozen rhubarb, measure rhubarb while it is still frozen, then thaw completely. Drain in a colander, but do not press the liquid out.

1 PIECE: 320 cal., 15g fat (9g sat. fat), 75mg chol., 274mg sod., 41g carb. (22g sugars, 1g fiber), 6g pro.

OMA'S APFELKUCHEN (GRANDMA'S APPLE CAKE)

For more than 150 years, members of my husband's German family have shared this scrumptious apple cake recipe. Try it with any apples you have on hand—I like to use Granny Smith.
—*Amy Kirchen, Loveland, OH*

PREP: 20 MIN. • **BAKE:** 45 MIN. + COOLING • **MAKES:** 10 SERVINGS

2 medium tart apples, peeled, cored and halved
1 cup plus 2 Tbsp. unsalted butter, softened
1¼ cups sugar
5 large egg yolks, room temperature

2 cups all-purpose flour
2 Tbsp. cornstarch
2 tsp. cream of tartar
1 tsp. baking powder
½ tsp. salt
¼ cup 2% milk
Confectioners' sugar

1. Preheat oven to 350°. Starting ½ in. from 1 end, cut apple halves lengthwise into ¼-in. slices, leaving them attached at the top so they fan out slightly. Set aside.

2. Cream butter and sugar until light and fluffy, 5-7 minutes. Add the egg yolks, 1 at a time, beating well after each addition. In another bowl, sift flour, cornstarch, cream of tartar, baking powder and salt twice. Gradually beat into the creamed mixture. Add milk; mix well (batter will be thick).

3. Spread batter into a greased 9-in. springform pan wrapped in a sheet of heavy-duty foil. Gently press apples, round side up, into batter. Bake until a toothpick inserted in the center comes out with moist crumbs, 45-55 minutes. Cool on a wire rack for 10 minutes. Loosen sides from pan with a knife; remove foil. Cool 1 hour longer. Remove rim from pan. Dust with confectioners' sugar.

1 PIECE: 422 cal., 23g fat (14g sat. fat), 148mg chol., 177mg sod., 50g carb. (28g sugars, 1g fiber), 4g pro.

"Rich to say the least but absolutely delicious. I remember my grandmother making a similar cake years ago. It was always a treat since it did use a lot of butter. Be prepared— this isn't like the light, fluffy cakes you normally eat. This one is a rich, dense, decadent and delicious dessert. It's a home run for me."
—LINDAS_WI, TASTEOFHOME.COM

MOM'S CITRUS BUTTERMILK CAKE

Everyone raves over this lovely lemon cake. It's divine with
fresh raspberries and a scoop of vanilla ice cream.
—*Joan Hallford, North Richland Hills, TX*

PREP: 25 MIN. • BAKE: 45 MIN. + COOLING • MAKES: 12 SERVINGS

1 cup shortening
2 cups sugar
4 large eggs, room
   temperature
2 tsp. lemon extract
3 cups all-purpose flour
1 tsp. baking powder
½ tsp. baking soda
½ tsp. salt
1 cup buttermilk

GLAZE
1½ cups confectioners' sugar
1 Tbsp. grated orange zest
5 Tbsp. orange juice
1 Tbsp. grated lemon zest
5 Tbsp. lemon juice
¼ tsp. salt

1. Preheat oven to 350°. Grease and flour a 10-in. fluted tube pan.

2. Cream shortening and sugar until light and fluffy, 5-7 minutes.
Add eggs, 1 at a time, beating well after each addition. Beat in the
extract. In another bowl, whisk together flour, baking powder,
baking soda and salt; add to the creamed mixture alternately with
buttermilk, beating after each addition.

3. Transfer batter to prepared pan. Bake until a toothpick inserted
in center comes out clean, 45-50 minutes.

4. Poke holes in warm cake using a fork or wooden skewer. Mix
glaze ingredients; spoon slowly over cake. Let cool 15 minutes
before removing from pan to a wire rack to cool completely.

NOTE: To remove cakes easily, use solid shortening to grease plain
and fluted tube pans.

1 PIECE: 488 cal., 18g fat (5g sat. fat), 63mg chol., 304mg sod.,
75g carb. (50g sugars, 1g fiber), 6g pro.

GRANDMA'S
SECRET

If you don't have buttermilk, stir
1 Tbsp. white vinegar or lemon
juice into enough milk to measure
1 cup and let stand for 5 minutes.
You can also use 1 cup plain
yogurt, or 1 cup of milk with
1¾ tsp. cream of tartar.

SPICED DEVIL'S FOOD CAKE

One of my mom's friends gave her this recipe when I was a child, and it has been a family favorite ever since. When your chocolate sweet tooth acts up, this really hits the spot!
—*Linda Yeamans, Ashland, OR*

PREP: 25 MIN. • BAKE: 30 MIN. + COOLING • MAKES: 12 SERVINGS

1 cup butter, softened
1½ cups sugar
3 large eggs, room temperature
1 tsp. vanilla extract
2 cups all-purpose flour
¼ cup baking cocoa
1 tsp. baking powder
1 tsp. baking soda
1 tsp. ground cinnamon
½ to 1 tsp. ground nutmeg
¼ to ½ tsp. ground cloves
1 cup buttermilk

MOCHA ICING
3¾ cups confectioners' sugar
¼ cup baking cocoa
6 Tbsp. strong brewed coffee
6 Tbsp. butter, melted
1 tsp. vanilla extract
Toasted whole or chopped almonds, optional

1. Preheat oven to 350°. Cream butter and sugar until light and fluffy, 5-7 minutes. Add eggs, 1 at a time, beating well after each addition. Add vanilla.

2. Sift together all dry ingredients; add to the creamed mixture alternately with buttermilk. Pour into 2 greased and floured 9-in. round baking pans.

3. Bake until a toothpick inserted in center comes out clean, 30-35 minutes. Cool on wire racks for 10 minutes before removing from pans to cool completely.

4. In a small bowl, combine all icing ingredients except nuts. Spread frosting between layers and over the top and sides of cake. If desired, top with almonds.

1 PIECE: 543 cal., 23g fat (14g sat. fat), 110mg chol., 389mg sod., 82g carb. (61g sugars, 1g fiber), 5g pro.

MAMA ARNOLD'S HONEY PIE

This sweet, custardy pie could not be simpler to make, but will have your guests asking for more. The boiled honey gives it a caramel-like flavor that's divine.
—*Ruth Arnold, Pearsall, TX*

PREP: 15 MIN. • BAKE: 25 MIN. • MAKES: 8 SERVINGS

1 cup honey
3 large eggs, lightly beaten
3 Tbsp. butter
1 tsp. vanilla extract
1 cup chopped pecans
Dash nutmeg
1 pie shell (9 in.), unbaked

Preheat oven to 325°. In a large saucepan, bring honey to a boil. Remove from the heat. Stir a small amount of hot honey into the eggs; return all to the pan, stirring constantly. Bring to a gentle boil; gently stir in the butter, vanilla, pecans and nutmeg. Pour into crust and bake for 25 minutes or until filling is set.

1 PIECE: 418 cal., 24g fat (7g sat. fat), 96mg chol., 169mg sod., 50g carb. (35g sugars, 2g fiber), 5g pro.

RHUBARB UPSIDE-DOWN CAKE

I've baked this cake every spring for many years. At potlucks it gets eaten up quickly, even by folks who don't normally go for rhubarb. Use your own fresh rhubarb, hit up a farmers market or find a neighbor who will trade stalks for the recipe!

—*Helen Breman, Mattydale, NY*

PREP: 20 MIN. • **BAKE:** 35 MIN. • **MAKES:** 10 SERVINGS

3 cups sliced fresh or frozen rhubarb
1 cup sugar
2 Tbsp. all-purpose flour
¼ tsp. ground nutmeg
¼ cup butter, melted

BATTER
¼ cup butter, melted
¾ cup sugar

1 large egg, room temperature
1½ cups all-purpose flour
2 tsp. baking powder
½ tsp. ground nutmeg
¼ tsp. salt
⅔ cup 2% milk
Sweetened whipped cream, optional

1. Preheat oven to 350°. Place rhubarb in a greased 10-in. cast-iron or other heavy ovenproof skillet. Combine sugar, flour and nutmeg; sprinkle over rhubarb. Drizzle with butter; set aside.

2. For the batter, beat the butter and sugar until blended. Beat in the egg. Combine the flour, baking powder, nutmeg and salt. Gradually add to the egg mixture alternately with milk, beating well after each addition.

3. Spread batter over rhubarb mixture. Bake until a toothpick inserted in the center comes out clean, about 35 minutes. Loosen edges immediately and invert onto a serving dish. Serve warm. If desired, serve with whipped cream.

1 PIECE: 316 cal., 10g fat (6g sat. fat), 48mg chol., 248mg sod., 53g carb. (36g sugars, 1g fiber), 4g pro.

"This cake is so delicious! And relatively easy to make— mine came out looking just like the picture. My rhubarb was more green than red, but still worked just fine. I also used a circular cake pan instead of the skillet, which also worked really well. If you're a fan of rhubarb, this recipe is a keeper!"

—NOLANSCABIN, TASTEOFHOME.COM

BLACK FOREST CHOCOLATE TORTE

If you're thinking about pulling out all the stops for a dessert, look no further. This cherry-crowned beauty stacked with layers of chocolate cake and cream filling will have everyone talking.
—*Doris Grotz, York, NE*

PREP: 1 HOUR • **BAKE:** 15 MIN. + COOLING • **MAKES:** 16 SERVINGS

⅔ cup butter, softened
1¾ cups sugar
4 large eggs, room temperature
1¼ cups water
4 oz. unsweetened chocolate, chopped
1 tsp. vanilla extract
1¾ cups all-purpose flour
1 tsp. baking powder
¼ tsp. baking soda

CHOCOLATE FILLING
6 oz. German sweet chocolate, chopped
¾ cup butter, cubed
½ cup sliced almonds, toasted

WHIPPED CREAM
2 cups heavy whipping cream
1 Tbsp. sugar
1½ tsp. vanilla extract

TOPPING
1½ cups sliced almonds, toasted
1 cup cherry pie filling

1. Preheat oven to 350°. Line bottoms of 4 greased 9-in. round baking pans with parchment; grease parchment.

2. Cream butter and sugar until light and fluffy, 5-7 minutes. Add eggs, 1 at a time, beating well after each addition. Beat in water just until blended.

3. In a microwave, melt unsweetened chocolate; stir until smooth. Stir in vanilla extract. In a small bowl, whisk together flour, baking powder and baking soda; add to the creamed mixture alternately with the chocolate mixture, beating after each addition. Divide batter among prepared pans.

4. Bake until a toothpick inserted in center comes out clean, 15-20 minutes. Cool 10 minutes before removing from pans to wire racks; remove paper. Cool completely.

5. For the chocolate filling, melt chocolate in a microwave; stir until smooth. Stir in butter until blended. Stir in almonds.

6. For whipped cream, in a small bowl, beat cream until it begins to thicken. Add sugar and vanilla; beat until soft peaks form.

7. To assemble, place 1 cake layer on a serving plate; spread with ⅓ cup chocolate filling and 1 cup whipped cream. Repeat layers twice. Top with the the remaining cake layer and chocolate filling.

8. Spread the remaining whipped cream over sides of cake. Press almonds onto sides. Spoon pie filling over top of cake. Refrigerate until serving.

NOTE: To toast nuts, bake in a shallow pan in a 350° oven for 5-10 minutes or cook in a skillet over low heat until lightly browned, stirring occasionally.

1 PIECE: 596 cal., 41g fat (22g sat. fat), 124mg chol., 210mg sod., 46g carb. (26g sugars, 3g fiber), 8g pro.

LEMON CREAM CUPCAKES

Delicate cupcakes like these are sure to
disappear at your next potluck or bake sale.
—*Ruth Ann Stelfox, Raymond, AB*

PREP: 20 MIN. • **BAKE:** 25 MIN. + COOLING • **MAKES:** ABOUT 2½ DOZEN

1 cup butter, softened
2 cups sugar
3 large eggs,
   room temperature
2 tsp. grated lemon zest
1 tsp. vanilla extract
3½ cups all-purpose flour
1 tsp. baking soda
½ tsp. baking powder
½ tsp. salt
2 cups sour cream

FROSTING
3 Tbsp. butter, softened
2¼ cups confectioners' sugar
2 Tbsp. lemon juice
¾ tsp. vanilla extract
¼ tsp. grated lemon zest
1 to 2 Tbsp. 2% milk
   Additional lemon zest,
   optional

1. Preheat oven to 350°. In a large bowl, cream butter and sugar until light and fluffy, 5-7 minutes. Add eggs, 1 at a time, beating well after each addition. Beat in lemon zest and vanilla. Combine the flour, baking soda, baking powder and salt; add to creamed mixture alternately with sour cream, beating well after each addition (the batter will be thick).

2. Fill greased or paper-lined muffin cups with ¼ cup of batter. Bake for 25-30 minutes or until a toothpick inserted in the center comes out clean. Cool in pans for 10 minutes before removing to wire racks to cool completely.

3. For frosting, cream butter and confectioners' sugar in a small bowl until light and fluffy, 5-7 minutes. Add the lemon juice, vanilla, lemon zest and milk; beat until smooth. Frost cupcakes. If desired, sprinkle with additional lemon zest.

1 CUPCAKE: 244 cal., 11g fat (6g sat. fat), 48mg chol., 178mg sod., 34g carb. (22g sugars, 0 fiber), 3g pro.

RUSTIC CRANBERRY TARTS

For gatherings with family and friends, we love a dessert with a splash of red. These beautiful tarts are filled with cranberry and citrus-packed flavor and are easy to make and serve.
—*Holly Bauer, West Bend, WI*

PREP: 15 MIN. • **BAKE:** 20 MIN./BATCH • **MAKES:** 2 TARTS (6 SERVINGS EACH)

1 cup orange marmalade
¼ cup sugar
¼ cup all-purpose flour
4 cups fresh or frozen cranberries, thawed
2 sheets refrigerated pie crust
1 large egg white, lightly beaten
1 Tbsp. coarse sugar

1. Preheat oven to 425°. In a large bowl, mix marmalade, sugar and flour; stir in cranberries.

2. Unroll 1 pie crust onto a parchment-lined baking sheet. Spoon half of the cranberry mixture over crust to within 2 in. of edge. Fold edge of crust over filling, pleating as you go and leaving a 5-in. opening in the center. Brush the folded crust with egg white; sprinkle with half of the coarse sugar. Repeat with the remaining ingredients.

3. Bake 18-22 minutes or until crust is golden and filling is bubbly. Transfer tarts to wire racks to cool.

1 PIECE: 260 cal., 9g fat (4g sat. fat), 6mg chol., 144mg sod., 45g carb. (24g sugars, 2g fiber), 2g pro.

BREAD PUDDING PIE

This distinctive dessert is a bread pudding-pie combo. It was created by my paternal grandmother's family. They had a farm and made their own bread, which made this a low-cost dessert.
—*Kelly Barnes, Lexington, IN*

PREP: 15 MIN. • **BAKE:** 55 MIN. + CHILLING • **MAKES:** 8 SERVINGS

Dough for single-crust pie (9 in.)
1 cup cubed bread
2 large eggs, room temperature
2 cups 2% milk
¾ cup sugar
½ tsp. vanilla extract
¼ tsp. ground nutmeg
2 tsp. butter

1. Preheat oven to 425°. On a lightly floured surface, roll dough to a ⅛-in.-thick circle; transfer to a 9-in. pie plate. Trim crust to ½ in. beyond rim of plate; flute edge. Arrange bread in bottom of pie crust. In a large bowl, whisk eggs, milk, sugar and vanilla; pour over bread. Sprinkle with nutmeg and dot with butter. Bake 10 minutes.

2. Reduce oven setting to 350°; continue to bake until a knife inserted in the center comes out clean, 45-50 minutes longer. Cover edge loosely with foil during the last 15 minutes if needed to prevent overbrowning. Remove foil. Cool on a wire rack 1 hour. Refrigerate for at least 3 hours before serving.

DOUGH FOR SINGLE-CRUST PIE (9 IN.): Combine 1¼ cups all-purpose flour and ¼ tsp. salt; cut in ½ cup cold butter until crumbly. Gradually add 3-5 Tbsp. ice water, tossing with a fork until dough holds together when pressed. Cover and refrigerate 1 hour.

1 PIECE: 314 cal., 15g fat (9g sat. fat), 84mg chol., 230mg sod., 39g carb. (22g sugars, 1g fiber), 6g pro.

MOM-MOM BESSIE'S
COCONUT MOLASSES PIE

MOM-MOM BESSIE'S COCONUT MOLASSES PIE

I'm the keeper of my husband's grandmother's handwritten recipe book.
Mom-Mom Bessie was one of the best cooks I knew, and we think of her every time we
make this pie. The flavor combination of coconut and molasses is a family favorite.
—Susan Bickta, Kutztown, PA

PREP: 10 MIN. • BAKE: 45 MIN. + COOLING • MAKES: 8 SERVINGS

1 cup packed light brown
  sugar
1 cup sour cream
½ cup dark corn syrup
½ cup dark molasses
2 large eggs, room
  temperature, lightly
  beaten
¼ cup 2% milk
2 Tbsp. all-purpose flour
¼ tsp. baking soda
1½ cups sweetened
  shredded coconut
1 frozen deep-dish pie
  crust (9 in.)
  Whipped cream, optional

Preheat oven to 350°. In a large bowl, combine first 8 ingredients. Stir in coconut. Pour filling into crust; cover edge loosely with foil. Bake until center is set, 45-55 minutes. Remove foil; cool on a wire rack. If desired, serve with whipped cream.

1 PIECE: 486 cal., 19g fat (10g sat. fat), 54mg chol., 243mg sod., 80g carb. (66g sugars, 1g fiber), 5g pro.

FROM GRANDMA'S KITCHEN: This pie has a strong molasses flavor. If you like a little less intensity, substitute ½ cup additional dark corn syrup in place of the molasses.

STRAWBERRY SCHAUM TORTE

This crisp schaum torte features an easy-to-make strawberry gelatin filling.
—Geraldine Sauke, Alberta Lea, MN

PREP: 25 MIN. • BAKE: 45 MIN. + COOLING • MAKES: 12 SERVINGS

6 large egg whites, room
  temperature
2 tsp. water
2 tsp. white vinegar
2 tsp. vanilla extract
1 tsp. baking powder
¼ tsp. salt
2 cups sugar

FILLING
1 pkg. (3 oz.) strawberry
  gelatin
½ cup boiling water
1 cup fresh or frozen sliced
  strawberries
1 tsp. lemon juice
  Dash salt
1½ cups whipped cream

1. Preheat oven to 300°. Place egg whites in a large bowl; add water, vinegar, vanilla, baking powder and salt. Beat on medium speed until soft peaks form. Gradually beat in sugar, 2 Tbsp. at a time, on high until stiff glossy peaks form and sugar is dissolved.

2. Spread evenly into a greased 13x9-in. baking pan. Bake for 45 minutes. Turn off oven and do not open door; let crust dry in oven overnight.

3. For filling, in a bowl, dissolve gelatin in boiling water. Stir in the strawberries, lemon juice and salt (mixture will thicken quickly). Fold in cream. Spread over crust. Store in the refrigerator.

1 PIECE: 222 cal., 5g fat (3g sat. fat), 17mg chol., 150mg sod., 41g carb. (41g sugars, 0 fiber), 3g pro.

MOCHA HAZELNUT TORTE

I make this pretty cake on birthdays and other special occasions because it looks and tastes so amazing. The combination of mild hazelnut and coffee flavors is impossible to resist.

—*Christina Pope, Speedway, IN*

PREP: 35 MIN. • **BAKE:** 25 MIN. + COOLING • **MAKES:** 16 SERVINGS

¾ **cup butter, softened**
1¼ **cups packed brown sugar**
1 **cup sugar**
3 **large eggs, room temperature**
3 **oz. unsweetened chocolate, melted and cooled slightly**
2 **tsp. vanilla extract**
2¼ **cups all-purpose flour**
1 **Tbsp. instant espresso powder**
1 **tsp. baking soda**
½ **tsp. baking powder**
¼ **tsp. salt**
1½ **cups 2% milk**

FROSTING
1 **cup butter, softened**
1 **cup Nutella**
4 **cups confectioners' sugar**
1 **tsp. vanilla extract**
3 **to 4 Tbsp. 2% milk**
½ **cup chopped hazelnuts, toasted**

1. Preheat oven to 350°. Line bottoms of 2 greased 9-in. round baking pans with parchment; grease parchment.

2. In a large bowl, cream butter and sugars until light and fluffy, 5-7 minutes. Add eggs, 1 at a time, beating well after each addition. Beat in melted chocolate and vanilla. In another bowl, whisk together flour, espresso powder, baking soda, baking powder and salt; add to the creamed mixture alternately with milk, beating well after each addition.

3. Transfer batter to prepared pans. Bake 25-30 minutes or until a toothpick inserted in center comes out clean. Cool in pans 10 minutes before removing to wire racks; remove parchment. Cool completely.

4. For frosting, in a large bowl, beat butter and Nutella until blended. Gradually beat in confectioners' sugar, vanilla and enough milk to reach desired consistency.

5. Place 1 cake layer on a serving plate; spread with 1 cup frosting. Sprinkle with ¼ cup hazelnuts. Top with remaining cake layer. Frost top and sides with remaining frosting. Sprinkle with remaining ¼ cup hazelnuts.

NOTE: To toast nuts, bake in a shallow pan in a 350° oven for 5-10 minutes or cook in a skillet over low heat until lightly browned, stirring occasionally.

1 PIECE: 639 cal., 32g fat (16g sat. fat), 94mg chol., 311mg sod., 88g carb. (69g sugars, 2g fiber), 6g pro.

RAISIN PECAN PIE

I remember my Grandmother Voltie and Great-Aunt Ophelia making this southern-style pie for Thanksgivings. It was always one of the many cakes and pies lined up for dessert.
—*Angie Price, Bradford, TN*

PREP: 20 MIN. + CHILLING • BAKE: 35 MIN. + COOLING • MAKES: 8 SERVINGS

Dough for single-crust pie (9 in.)
½ cup boiling water
½ cup golden raisins
3 large eggs, room temperature
1½ cups sugar
½ cup butter, melted
2 tsp. cider vinegar
1 tsp. vanilla extract
½ tsp. ground cinnamon
½ tsp. ground cloves
¼ tsp. ground nutmeg
½ cup chopped pecans

1. On a lightly floured surface, roll dough to a ⅛-in.-thick circle; transfer to a 9-in. pie plate. Trim crust to ½ in. beyond rim of plate; flute edge. Refrigerate 30 minutes.

2. Preheat oven to 350°. Pour boiling water over raisins in a small bowl; let stand 5 minutes. Drain. In a large bowl, beat eggs, sugar, melted butter, vinegar, vanilla and spices until blended. Stir in pecans and drained raisins. Pour filling into crust.

3. Bake on a lower oven rack until filling is set, 35-40 minutes. Cool on a wire rack. Refrigerate leftovers.

DOUGH FOR SINGLE-CRUST PIE (9 IN.): Combine 1¼ cups all-purpose flour and ¼ tsp. salt; cut in ½ cup cold butter until crumbly. Gradually add 3-5 Tbsp. ice water, tossing with a fork until dough holds together when pressed. Cover and refrigerate 1 hour.

1 PIECE: 524 cal., 30g fat (16g sat. fat), 130mg chol., 275mg sod., 61g carb. (44g sugars, 2g fiber), 6g pro.

GRANDMA'S TANDY KAKE

My grandmother made this for all our family gatherings. Everyone loves it, and now I make it for every party we attend or host.
—*John Morgan III, Lebanon, PA*

PREP: 20 MIN. • BAKE: 20 MIN. + CHILLING • MAKES: 24 SERVINGS

4 large eggs, room temperature
2 cups sugar
1 cup 2% milk
1 tsp. vanilla extract
2 cups all-purpose flour
1 tsp. baking powder
¼ tsp. salt
1¾ cups creamy peanut butter
5 milk chocolate candy bars (1.55 oz. each), chopped
2 Tbsp. butter

1. Preheat oven to 350°. In a large bowl, beat eggs and sugar until thick and lemon-colored. Beat in milk and vanilla. In another bowl, combine flour, baking powder and salt; gradually add to the egg mixture and mix well.

2. Spread batter into a greased 15x10x1-in. baking pan. Bake for 20-25 minutes or until lightly browned. Cool 15 minutes on a wire rack. Spread peanut butter over top; let cool completely.

3. In a double boiler or metal bowl over simmering water, melt chocolate and butter; stir until smooth. Gently spread over peanut butter. Refrigerate 30 minutes or until firm.

1 PIECE: 290 cal., 14g fat (5g sat. fat), 36mg chol., 156mg sod., 35g carb. (24g sugars, 2g fiber), 7g pro.

DEEP-DISH APPLE PIE

This classic recipe is a winner! The crust is so flaky and the filling is sure to please everyone. You can top it with whatever you like—vanilla ice cream, whipped cream or a drizzle of caramel syrup.
—*Salem Cross Inn, West Brookfield, MA*

PREP: 50 MIN. • BAKE: 40 MIN. + COOLING • MAKES: 15 SERVINGS

2 cups all-purpose flour
½ cup shortening
1 large egg
¼ cup cold water
2 Tbsp. white vinegar

FILLING
10 cups sliced peeled tart apples (about 8 medium)

1 tsp. lemon juice
¼ cup sugar
¼ cup packed brown sugar
3 Tbsp. all-purpose flour
1 tsp. ground cinnamon
½ tsp. ground nutmeg
1 Tbsp. butter
1 large egg
1 Tbsp. 2% milk

1. Place flour in a large bowl; cut in shortening until crumbly. In a small bowl, whisk egg, water and vinegar; gradually add to the crumb mixture, tossing with a fork until dough holds together when pressed. Shape into a rectangle. Wrap and refrigerate 30 minutes or overnight.

2. Preheat oven to 375°. For filling, in a large bowl, toss apples with lemon juice. In a small bowl, combine the sugars, flour, cinnamon and nutmeg; add to the apple mixture and toss to coat. Transfer to a 13x9-in. baking dish; dot with butter.

3. On a lightly floured surface, roll out dough to fit top of pie. Place dough over filling. Trim and flute edges. In a small bowl, whisk egg with milk; brush over the crust. Cut slits in top. Bake 40-50 minutes or until crust is golden brown and apples are tender. Cool on a wire rack.

1 PIECE: 208 cal., 8g fat (2g sat. fat), 30mg chol., 18mg sod., 31g carb. (15g sugars, 2g fiber), 3g pro.

"This pie was delicious! I was going to use a store-bought crust but then decided to try this one—I'm so glad I did. It's tender and flaky and oh, so good. This would be perfect for Thanksgiving or any time you want to serve a lot of people."
—KARISUE305, TASTEOFHOME.COM

GRANDMA'S SECRET
If your cake layers crack, it's usually because they've been baked at too high a temperature and are quickly baking from the outside in. Check your oven temperature with an oven thermometer.

MARVELOUS MARBLE CAKE

Nothing's better than pound cake and chocolate. This is the best marble cake I've ever had.
—*Ellen Riley, Murfreesboro, TN*

PREP: 45 MIN. • BAKE: 20 MIN. + COOLING • MAKES: 16 SERVINGS

- 4 oz. bittersweet chocolate, chopped
- 3 Tbsp. plus 1¼ cups butter, softened, divided
- 2 cups sugar
- 5 large eggs, room temperature
- 3 tsp. vanilla extract
- 2¼ cups all-purpose flour
- 2 tsp. baking powder
- ½ tsp. salt
- ½ cup sour cream
- ½ cup miniature semisweet chocolate chips, optional

FROSTING

- ¾ cup butter, softened
- 6¾ cups confectioners' sugar
- 2 tsp. vanilla extract
- ½ to ⅔ cup 2% milk
- 2 Tbsp. miniature semisweet chocolate chips

1. In top of a double boiler or a metal bowl over barely simmering water, melt chocolate and 3 Tbsp. butter; stir until smooth. Cool to room temperature.

2. Preheat oven to 375°. Line the bottoms of 3 greased 8-in. round baking pans with parchment; grease parchment.

3. In a large bowl, cream the remaining 1¼ cups butter and the sugar until light and fluffy, 5-7 minutes. Add eggs, 1 at a time, beating well after each addition. Beat in vanilla. Whisk flour, baking powder and salt; add to the creamed mixture alternately with sour cream, beating well after each addition.

4. Remove 2 cups batter to a small bowl; stir in cooled chocolate mixture and, if desired, chocolate chips, until blended. Drop plain and chocolate batters by tablespoonfuls into the prepared pans, dividing batters evenly among pans. To make batter level in pans, tap them several times on countertop.

5. Bake until a toothpick inserted in center comes out clean, 20-25 minutes. Cool in pans 10 minutes before removing to wire racks; remove parchment. Cool completely.

6. For frosting, in a large bowl, beat butter until smooth. Gradually beat in confectioners' sugar, vanilla and enough milk to reach desired consistency.

7. If cake layers have rounded tops, trim with a serrated knife to level. Place 1 cake layer on a serving plate; spread with ½ cup frosting. Repeat layers. Top with remaining cake layer. Frost top and sides of cake.

8. In a microwave, melt chocolate chips; stir until smooth. Cool slightly. Drop cooled chocolate by ½ teaspoonfuls over frosting. Using a large offset spatula, smear chocolate to create a marble design in frosting.

1 PIECE: 683 cal., 33g fat (20g sat. fat), 138mg chol., 330mg sod., 97g carb. (79g sugars, 1g fiber), 5g pro.

MAPLE WALNUT CAKE

This cake reminds me of my beloved grandpa, who made delicious maple syrup when I was a child.
It honors his memory, and has proven to be a favorite with family and friends.
—*Lori Fee, Middlesex, NY*

PREP: 45 MIN. • **BAKE:** 15 MIN. + COOLING • **MAKES:** 16 SERVINGS

½ cup unsalted butter, softened
1½ cups packed light brown sugar
3 large eggs, room temperature
1 tsp. maple flavoring or maple syrup
2 cups all-purpose flour
1 tsp. baking powder
1 tsp. baking soda
¼ tsp. salt
1 cup buttermilk

CANDIED WALNUTS
1 Tbsp. unsalted butter
1½ cups coarsely chopped walnuts
1 Tbsp. maple syrup
¼ tsp. salt

FROSTING
2 cups unsalted butter, softened
1 tsp. maple flavoring or maple syrup
¼ tsp. salt
5 cups confectioners' sugar
¼ to ½ cup half-and-half cream
3 Tbsp. maple syrup, divided

1. Preheat oven to 350°. Line the bottoms of 3 greased 9-in. round baking pans with parchment; grease the parchment; set aside.

2. In a large bowl, cream butter and brown sugar until light and fluffy, 5-7 minutes. Add eggs, 1 at a time, beating well after each addition. Beat in maple flavoring. In another bowl, whisk together flour, baking powder, baking soda and salt; add to the creamed mixture alternately with buttermilk, beating after each addition.

3. Transfer batter to prepared pans. Bake until a toothpick inserted in the center comes out clean, 11-13 minutes. Cool in pans 10 minutes before removing to wire racks; remove paper. Cool completely.

4. For candied walnuts, in a large skillet, melt butter over medium heat; add walnuts and saute until toasted, about 5 minutes. Stir in maple syrup and salt; cook and stir 1 minute. Spread onto foil; let cool completely.

5. For frosting, beat butter until creamy. Beat in maple flavoring and salt. Gradually beat in the confectioners' sugar and enough cream to reach desired consistency.

6. Place 1 cake layer on a serving plate; spread with 1 cup frosting. Sprinkle with ½ cup candied walnuts and drizzle with 1 Tbsp. maple syrup. Repeat layers.

7. Top with the remaining layer. Frost top and sides of cake. Top with remaining ½ cup walnuts and 1 Tbsp. syrup.

1 PIECE: 653 cal., 38g fat (20g sat. fat), 116mg chol., 275mg sod., 75g carb. (61g sugars, 1g fiber), 5g pro.

BLUEBERRY DREAM PIE

This gorgeous pie can be decorated to fit any season. I make leaves for fall, hearts for Valentine's and flowers for spring. Have fun with it!
—*Kerry Nakayama, New York, NY*

PREP: 40 MIN. • **BAKE:** 35 MIN. + COOLING • **MAKES:** 8 SERVINGS

Dough for double-crust pie (9 in.)

CHEESE FILLING

- 4 oz. reduced-fat cream cheese
- ½ cup confectioners' sugar
- 1 Tbsp. lemon juice
- 1 large egg yolk, room temperature

BLUEBERRY FILLING

- ½ cup plus 1 Tbsp. sugar, divided
- 2 Tbsp. all-purpose flour
- 1 Tbsp. cornstarch
- ¼ cup cold water
- 6 cups fresh or frozen blueberries, divided
- 2 Tbsp. lemon juice
- 1 Tbsp. minced fresh mint or 1 tsp. dried mint
- 1 large egg white, beaten

1. Preheat oven to 450°. On a floured surface, roll each disk of dough to fit a 9-in. deep-dish ovenproof skillet. Line skillet with the bottom crust. Trim crust to ½ in. beyond edge of skillet; flute edges. Line unpricked crust with a double thickness of heavy-duty foil. Bake at 450° for 8 minutes. Remove foil; bake 5 minutes longer. Cool on a wire rack. Reduce heat to 375°.

2. In a small bowl, beat cream cheese, confectioners' sugar and lemon juice until light and fluffy. Beat in egg yolk until blended. Spread into crust.

3. In a large saucepan, combine ½ cup sugar, the flour and cornstarch; stir in water until smooth. Stir in 2 cups berries. Bring to a boil; cook and stir until thickened, 1-2 minutes. Cool slightly. Gently stir in the lemon juice, mint and the remaining 2 cups berries. Pour over cheese filling.

4. Cut decorative cutouts from remaining crust; arrange over the filling, leaving center uncovered. Brush crust with egg white; sprinkle with remaining 1 Tbsp. sugar.

5. Bake at 375° until golden brown and the filling is bubbly, 35-40 minutes. If necessary, cover edges with foil during the last 15 minutes to prevent overbrowning. Cool on a wire rack.

DOUGH FOR DOUBLE-CRUST PIE: Combine 2½ cups all-purpose flour and ½ tsp. salt; cut in 1 cup cold butter until crumbly. Gradually add ⅓ to ⅔ cup ice water, tossing with a fork until dough holds together when pressed. Divide dough in half. Shape each into a disk; wrap and refrigerate 1 hour.

1 PIECE: 442 cal., 18g fat (8g sat. fat), 46mg chol., 269mg sod., 67g carb. (35g sugars, 3g fiber), 5g pro.

RICH RUM CAKE

We like a touch of rum for the holidays, and this orangy rum cake
is decadent all on its own or with big scoops of whipped cream.
—*Nancy Heishman, Las Vegas, NV*

PREP: 35 MIN. • BAKE: 25 MIN. + COOLING • MAKES: 12 SERVINGS

2½ cups confectioners' sugar
¾ cup orange juice
¼ cup butter, cubed
¾ cup rum
1 cup all-purpose flour
1 tsp. baking powder
½ tsp. ground cinnamon
¼ tsp. salt
¼ tsp. ground nutmeg
4 large eggs, separated,
    room temperature
½ cup packed brown sugar,
    divided
1 tsp. vanilla extract
¾ cup butter, melted
    Optional: Whipped cream
    and finely chopped
    glazed pecans

GRANDMA'S SECRET

Overbeaten egg whites will
look grainy, with liquid pooling in
the bottom of the bowl. If you
do overbeat your whites, you
may be able to recover them
by mixing in one more room-
temperature egg white.

1. In a saucepan, combine confectioners' sugar, juice and
cubed butter; cook and stir over medium-low heat until the
sugar is dissolved. Remove from heat; stir in rum. Reserve
¾ cup sauce for serving.

2. Preheat oven to 375°. Grease and flour a 10-in. tube pan. Sift
flour, baking powder, cinnamon, salt and nutmeg together twice;
set aside.

3. In a bowl, beat egg whites on medium until soft peaks form.
Gradually add ¼ cup brown sugar, 1 Tbsp. at a time, beating on
high after each addition until sugar is dissolved. Continue beating
until stiff peaks form.

4. In another bowl, beat the egg yolks until slightly thickened.
Gradually add remaining ¼ cup brown sugar and the vanilla,
beating on high speed until thick. Fold a fourth of the egg whites
into the batter. Alternately fold in the flour mixture and the
remaining whites. Fold in the melted butter.

5. Transfer batter to prepared pan. Bake on lowest oven rack for
25-30 minutes or until the top springs back when lightly touched.
Immediately poke holes in cake with a fork; slowly pour the sauce
over the cake, allowing it to absorb into cake. Cool completely in
pan on a wire rack.

6. Invert onto a serving plate. Serve with the reserved ¾ cup
sauce and, if desired, whipped cream and glazed pecans.

NOTE: To remove cakes easily, use solid shortening to grease
plain and fluted tube pans.

1 PIECE: 371 cal., 17g fat (10g sat. fat), 103mg chol., 233mg sod.,
44g carb. (35g sugars, 0 fiber), 3g pro.

MAMA'S COCONUT PIE

My mama showed me how to make this buttermilk coconut pie about 40 years ago, and her mama showed her how to make it. I was 6 when Mawmaw passed away, but I can still remember her cooking in the kitchen in her beautiful cotton dresses dusted with flour. I am honored to teach my daughter how to make this pie.

—*Lisa Allen, Joppa, AL*

PREP: 20 MIN. • BAKE: 50 MIN. • MAKES: 8 SERVINGS

Dough for single-crust pie (9 in.)
1 **cup sugar**
3 **large eggs, room temperature**
½ **cup buttermilk**
½ **cup unsalted butter, melted and cooled**
2 **Tbsp. all-purpose flour**
1½ **tsp. vanilla extract**
Dash salt
1½ **cups sweetened shredded coconut**

1. Preheat oven to 325°. On a lightly floured surface, roll dough to a ⅛-in.-thick circle; transfer to a 9-in. pie plate. Trim to ½ in. beyond rim of plate; flute edge. Place pie plate on a rimmed baking sheet.

2. In a large bowl, beat sugar, eggs, buttermilk, melted butter, flour, vanilla and salt until blended. Stir in coconut. Pour into the crust. Bake until top is light golden brown and center is almost set, 50-60 minutes. Cool on a wire rack; serve or refrigerate within 2 hours.

DOUGH FOR SINGLE-CRUST PIE (9 IN.): Combine 1¼ cups all-purpose flour and ¼ tsp. salt; cut in ½ cup cold butter until crumbly. Gradually add 3-5 Tbsp. ice water, tossing with a fork until dough holds together when pressed. Shape into a disk; wrap and refrigerate 1 hour.

1 PIECE: 550 cal., 35g fat (23g sat. fat), 142mg chol., 318mg sod., 54g carb. (34g sugars, 1g fiber), 6g pro.

COCOA COLA CAKE

I love this tender cake because I usually have the ingredients on hand and it mixes up in a jiffy. The rich fudge frosting is easy to prepare, and the chopped pecans add nice crunch.
—*Ellen Champagne, New Orleans, LA*

PREP: 15 MIN. + STANDING • **BAKE:** 35 MIN. + COOLING • **MAKES:** 15 SERVINGS

1 pkg. white cake mix (regular size)
1 cup cola
2 large eggs, room temperature
½ cup buttermilk
½ cup butter, melted
¼ cup baking cocoa
1 tsp. vanilla extract
1½ cups miniature marshmallows

FUDGE FROSTING
¼ cup baking cocoa
½ cup butter, cubed
⅓ cup cola
4 cups confectioners' sugar
1 cup chopped pecans, toasted

1. Preheat oven to 350°. Combine first 7 ingredients; beat on low speed for 30 seconds. Beat on medium for 2 minutes. Fold in marshmallows.

2. Pour batter into a greased 13x9-in. baking pan. Bake for 35-40 minutes or until a toothpick inserted in the center comes out clean. Cool on a wire rack for 15 minutes.

3. Meanwhile, for frosting, combine cocoa and butter in a small saucepan. Cook over low heat until the butter is melted. Stir in cola until blended. Bring to a boil, stirring constantly. Remove from the heat; stir in confectioners' sugar until smooth. Fold in toasted pecans.

4. Spread frosting over cake. Let cake stand for 20 minutes before cutting.

1 PIECE: 479 cal., 22g fat (9g sat. fat), 61mg chol., 363mg sod., 69g carb. (50g sugars, 2g fiber), 4g pro.

STRAWBERRY BAVARIAN TORTE

This beautiful make-ahead dessert is deliciously light...the perfect ending to any meal.
—*Christine Azzarello, Elmhurst, IL*

PREP: 15 MIN. + CHILLING • **MAKES:** 12 SERVINGS

1 pkg. (6 oz.) strawberry gelatin
1 cup boiling water
2 qt. fresh strawberries, sliced
½ pint heavy whipping cream, whipped
1 sponge cake, cut into cubes
Additional whipped cream
Whole strawberries for garnish

1. In a bowl, dissolve gelatin in water. Add berries; allow to thicken partially. Fold in whipped cream. Fold in cake cubes; stir until well coated. Spread into a greased springform pan; cover and chill overnight.

2. Remove from pan and place on a torte plate. Frost with whipped cream and garnish with berries.

1 PIECE: 258 cal., 9g fat (5g sat. fat), 66mg chol., 133mg sod., 43g carb. (34g sugars, 2g fiber), 4g pro.

COOKIE SWIRL
COBBLER, PAGE 327

GRANDMA'S FAVORITE

DESSERTS

From cobblers, crumbles and buckles to custards,
puddings and candies, old-fashioned desserts always
get thumbs-up approval. Whether a gorgeous layered
trifle, a decadent cheesecake, a delicate flaky strudel
or something you never knew you could do with Jell-O,
Grandma sure knew how to turn out just the thing
to end every meal on the sweetest note.

RED VELVET CHEESECAKE

This cheesecake will become a fixture on your holiday menu. The red velvet filling is spiked with cocoa, baked in a chocolate cookie crust and topped with fluffy cream cheese frosting.
—*Karen Dively, Chapin, SC*

PREP: 30 MIN. • **BAKE:** 1 HOUR + CHILLING • **MAKES:** 16 SERVINGS

17 chocolate cream
    Oreo cookies, crushed
¼ cup butter, melted
1 Tbsp. sugar

FILLING
3 pkg. (8 oz. each)
   cream cheese, softened
1½ cups sugar
1 cup sour cream
½ cup buttermilk
3 Tbsp. baking cocoa
2 tsp. vanilla extract
4 large eggs,
   room temperature,
   lightly beaten
1 bottle (1 oz.) red
   food coloring

FROSTING
3 oz. cream cheese,
   softened
¼ cup butter, softened
2 cups confectioners' sugar
1 tsp. vanilla extract

1. Preheat oven to 325°. Place a greased 9-in. springform pan on a double thickness of heavy-duty foil (about 18 in. square). Securely wrap foil around pan.

2. In a small bowl, combine the cookie crumbs, butter and sugar. Press onto the bottom of prepared pan.

3. In a large bowl, beat cream cheese, sugar, sour cream, buttermilk, cocoa and vanilla until smooth. Add eggs; beat on low speed just until combined. Stir in food coloring. Pour over crust. Place springform pan in a large baking pan; add 1 in. hot water to the larger pan.

4. Bake until the center is just set and top appears dull, 60-70 minutes. Remove springform pan from water bath. Cool on a wire rack for 10 minutes. Carefully run a knife around inside edge of pan to loosen the rim; cool for 1 hour longer. Refrigerate overnight, covering when completely cooled. Remove sides of pan.

5. For frosting, in a small bowl, beat cream cheese and butter until fluffy. Add confectioners' sugar and vanilla; beat until smooth. Frost top of cheesecake. Refrigerate until serving.

1 PIECE: 463 cal., 29g fat (17g sat. fat), 131mg chol., 276mg sod., 46g carb. (39g sugars, 1g fiber), 7g pro.

GRANDMA'S SECRET

After filling your pan, tap it gently on the countertop a couple of times to remove any air bubbles. Batter that is smooth, with very little air in it, makes the creamiest, best cheesecake.

PEACH COBBLER

PEACH COBBLER

I created this peach cobbler recipe myself with a few tips from my mom and grandma.
Because it's so quick and easy, it can be made in minutes to suit any occasion.
I've used it as a breakfast fruit dish, a dinner dessert and a light snack.
—*Martha Betten, North Manchester, IN*

PREP: 15 MIN. • **BAKE:** 20 MIN. • **MAKES:** 8 SERVINGS

½ cup butter, melted
1 can (15¼ oz.) sliced
  peaches, drained
1¼ cups sugar, divided
1 cup all-purpose flour
2 tsp. baking powder
¼ tsp. salt
1 cup 2% milk
  Whipped cream, optional

Preheat oven to 400°. Pour butter into a shallow 2-qt. baking dish; set aside. Drain peaches, reserving ¼ cup juice. In a saucepan, bring peaches and reserved ¼ cup juice just to a boil. Meanwhile, in a bowl, combine 1 cup sugar, the flour, baking powder and salt. Stir in milk; mix well. Pour over butter in baking dish. Spoon hot peaches over batter. Sprinkle with the remaining ¼ cup sugar. Bake until bubbly and golden, 20-25 minutes. Serve warm and, if desired, with whipped cream.

¾ CUP: 328 cal., 13g fat (8g sat. fat), 34mg chol., 282mg sod., 52g carb. (40g sugars, 1g fiber), 3g pro.

THELMA'S CHOCOLATE ECLAIR

I love eclairs, but making the actual pastry is difficult, so I came up with this recipe
as a substitute. It still satisfies my cravings with the same wonderful flavors.
—*Thelma Beam, Esbon, KS*

PREP: 20 MIN. + CHILLING • **MAKES:** 15 SERVINGS

14 to 15 whole
  graham crackers
3½ cups 2% milk
2 pkg. (3.4 oz. each) instant
  vanilla pudding mix
1 carton (8 oz.) frozen
  whipped topping, thawed

TOPPING
2 oz. semisweet chocolate
2 Tbsp. butter
1½ cups confectioners' sugar
3 Tbsp. 2% milk
1 tsp. light corn syrup
1 tsp. vanilla extract

1. Line a 13x9-in. dish with half the graham crackers, breaking crackers to fit as needed.

2. Whisk milk and pudding mix for 2 minutes; let stand until soft-set, about 2 minutes. Fold in whipped topping. Spread mixture evenly over crackers. Top with remaining crackers.

3. In a microwave-safe bowl, microwave chocolate and butter until melted; stir until blended. Stir in remaining ingredients. Spread over top. Refrigerate, covered, 8 hours or overnight.

1 PIECE: 238 cal., 8g fat (5g sat. fat), 12mg chol., 229mg sod., 38g carb. (26g sugars, 1g fiber), 3g pro.

FROZEN CHRISTMAS SALAD

My mom's use of red and green cherries to decorate dishes at Christmastime inspired me to create this holiday gelatin mold. It's cool, creamy and fun to serve guests.
—*Pat Habiger, Spearville, KS*

PREP: 25 MIN. + FREEZING • MAKES: 10 SERVINGS

1 can (20 oz.) crushed pineapple, drained
2 cups miniature marshmallows
1 pkg. (8 oz.) cream cheese, softened
½ cup mayonnaise
12 red maraschino cherries, chopped and patted dry
12 green maraschino cherries, chopped and patted dry
½ cup chopped walnuts
1 cup heavy whipping cream

1. In a small bowl, combine the pineapple and marshmallows. Set aside until marshmallows are softened, about 15 minutes.

2. Meanwhile, in a small bowl, beat the cream cheese and mayonnaise until smooth. Stir into marshmallow mixture. Fold in cherries and walnuts.

3. In a small bowl, beat cream until soft peaks form. Fold into the marshmallow mixture. Spoon into a 6-cup mold; freeze overnight. Let stand at room temperature for 15-20 minutes; unmold onto a serving plate.

1 SERVING: 371 cal., 28g fat (12g sat. fat), 51mg chol., 142mg sod., 29g carb. (24g sugars, 1g fiber), 3g pro.

CHERRY RHUBARB CRUNCH

My husband's grandmother gave me this recipe, along with a bundle of rhubarb, when we were first married. I had never cared for rhubarb, but after trying this dessert, I changed my mind. Now my children dig in, too!
—*Sharon Wasikowski, Middleville, MI*

PREP: 20 MIN. • BAKE: 40 MIN. • MAKES: 15 SERVINGS

1 cup rolled oats
1 cup packed brown sugar
1 cup all-purpose flour
¼ tsp. salt
½ cup cold butter, cubed
4 cups diced rhubarb
1 cup sugar
2 Tbsp. cornstarch
1 cup water
1 tsp. almond extract
1 can (21 oz.) cherry pie filling
½ cup finely chopped walnuts
Vanilla ice cream, optional

1. Preheat oven to 350°. In a large bowl, combine oats, brown sugar, flour and salt; stir well. Cut in butter until crumbly. Pat 2 cups mixture into a greased 13x9-in. baking dish; cover with diced rhubarb. Set aside remaining crumb mixture.

2. In a saucepan, combine sugar and cornstarch. Stir in water; cook until thickened and clear. Stir in almond extract and cherry pie filling; spoon over rhubarb. Combine nuts with the 2 cups reserved crumb mixture; sprinkle over cherries.

3. Bake until filling is bubbly and topping is lightly browned, 40-45 minutes. If desired, serve with ice cream.

1 PIECE: 294 cal., 9g fat (4g sat. fat), 16mg chol., 116mg sod., 52g carb. (38g sugars, 2g fiber), 3g pro.

OLD-FASHIONED CHOCOLATE PUDDING

One of the nice things about this easy pudding is you don't have to stand and stir it. It's a must for my family year-round! I also make it into a pie with a graham cracker crust that our grandchildren love.
—*Amber Sampson, Somonauk, IL*

PREP: 10 MIN. • COOK: 30 MIN. + CHILLING • MAKES: 4 SERVINGS

2 **cups whole milk**	⅓ **cup all-purpose flour**
2 **Tbsp. butter**	¼ **tsp. salt**
2 **oz. unsweetened chocolate, chopped**	2 **large egg yolks, beaten**
⅔ **cup sugar**	½ **tsp. vanilla extract**
	Whipped cream, optional

1. In a double boiler or metal bowl over simmering water, heat milk, butter and chocolate until chocolate is melted (chocolate may appear curdled).

2. Combine sugar, flour and salt. Sprinkle over chocolate mixture (do not stir). Cover and continue to cook in the double boiler over medium-low heat, 20 minutes. With a wooden spoon, stir until smooth. Remove from the heat.

3. Stir a small amount of the hot mixture into the egg yolks; return all to the pan, stirring constantly. Cook and stir until mixture is thickened and a thermometer reads 160°. Remove from heat; stir in vanilla. Cool for 15 minutes, stirring occasionally. Transfer to dessert dishes.

4. Cover and refrigerate for 1 hour. If desired, top individual servings with whipped cream.

⅔ CUP: 413 cal., 20g fat (11g sat. fat), 120mg chol., 254mg sod., 52g carb. (40g sugars, 3g fiber), 8g pro.

CHEESECAKE STRAWBERRY TRIFLE

The only drawback to this lovely dessert is that there are never any leftovers. For a patriotic look, replace one of the layers of strawberry pie filling with blueberry—or use whatever filling you prefer.
—*Lori Thorp, Frazee, MN*

TAKES: 20 MIN. • MAKES: 16 SERVINGS

1 pkg. (8 oz.) cream cheese, softened
1 cup sour cream
½ cup cold whole milk
1 pkg. (3.4 oz.) instant vanilla pudding mix
1 carton (12 oz.) frozen whipped topping, thawed
1½ cups crushed butter-flavored crackers (about 38 crackers)
¼ cup butter, melted
2 cans (21 oz. each) strawberry pie filling

1. In a large bowl, beat the cream cheese until smooth. Beat in sour cream; mix well. In a small bowl, beat milk and pudding mix on low speed for 2 minutes. Stir into the cream cheese mixture. Fold in whipped topping. In another small bowl, combine the crackers and butter.

2. In a 2½-qt. trifle bowl, layer half each of the cream cheese mixture, the crumb mixture and the pie filling. Repeat layers. Refrigerate until serving.

1 SERVING: 369 cal., 22g fat (14g sat. fat), 46mg chol., 333mg sod., 37g carb. (21g sugars, 1g fiber), 4g pro.

BAKED CUSTARD WITH CINNAMON

Mother used to make this comforting custard when I was growing up on the farm. It was a wonderful welcome-home treat after a chilly evening of doing chores. Now I fix it for my husband and four sons.
—*Mary Kay Morris, Cokato, MN*

PREP: 10 MIN. • BAKE: 50 MIN. + COOLING • MAKES: 4 SERVINGS

2 large eggs, room temperature
2 cups whole milk
⅓ cup sugar
¼ tsp. salt
Dash ground cinnamon
Dash ground nutmeg

1. Preheat oven to 350°. In a small bowl, whisk eggs, milk, sugar and salt. Pour into 4 ungreased 8-oz. custard cups; sprinkle with cinnamon and nutmeg.

2. Place custard cups in a 13x9-in. baking pan; pour hot water in pan to a depth of ¾ in. Bake, uncovered, until a knife inserted in the center comes out clean, 50-55 minutes. Remove cups to a wire rack to cool. Serve warm or chilled. Store in the refrigerator.

1 CUSTARD: 177 cal., 7g fat (3g sat. fat), 123mg chol., 239mg sod., 23g carb. (22g sugars, 0 fiber), 7g pro.

CHEESECAKE
STRAWBERRY TRIFLE

GRANDMA'S SECRET
Dried fruit absorbs moisture. To make your pudding even richer, first plump your raisins. Pour hot water over the raisins to cover, let sit for 10-15 minutes, then drain and use them in the recipe as directed.

STEAMED CARROT PUDDING

This recipe, passed down from my Canadian grandmother, has been in my family for at least three generations. It's been a favorite wintertime dessert for us and is always served for Easter and other holiday meals.
—*Ann Searcey, Kettering, OH*

PREP: 20 MIN. • **COOK:** 1¼ HOURS • **MAKES:** 8 SERVINGS

½ cup butter, softened
½ cup sugar
2 large eggs,
  room temperature,
  lightly beaten
1 tsp. vanilla extract
1 cup all-purpose flour
1 tsp. baking powder
1 tsp. baking soda
1 tsp. salt
1 tsp. ground cinnamon
½ tsp. ground nutmeg
¼ tsp. ground cloves
1 cup shredded
  peeled carrots
1 cup shredded uncooked
  peeled potatoes
1 cup each raisins,
  chopped dates and nuts

VANILLA SAUCE
½ cup sugar
2 Tbsp. cornstarch
¼ tsp. salt
2 cups cold water
¼ cup butter, cubed
2½ tsp. vanilla extract
  Dash ground nutmeg

1. In a large bowl, cream butter and sugar until light and fluffy, 5-7 minutes. Beat in eggs and vanilla. Combine dry ingredients and spices; gradually add to the creamed mixture. Stir in carrots, potatoes, raisins, dates and nuts.

2. Pour mixture into a well-greased 6-cup pudding mold or metal gelatin mold. Cover with foil. Place on a rack in a stockpot. Add 1 in. boiling water to stockpot; cover and boil gently for 1¼-1½ hours or until a toothpick inserted in the center comes out clean, replacing water as needed. Let stand for 5 minutes before unmolding.

3. Meanwhile, in a small saucepan, combine sugar, cornstarch and salt. Stir in water until smooth. Bring to a boil over medium heat; cook and stir for 1-2 minutes or until thickened. Remove from heat. Stir in the butter, vanilla and nutmeg. Serve sauce with warm pudding.

1 PIECE WITH ¼ CUP SAUCE: 570 cal., 28g fat (12g sat. fat), 92mg chol., 760mg sod., 75g carb. (49g sugars, 5g fiber), 9g pro.

MINI CHERRY CHEESECAKES

These little cheesecakes make a fun dessert that's just right for cooks who don't have a lot of time for fussy recipes. Plus, you get to eat a whole mini cheesecake yourself!
—*Kay Keller, Morenci, MI*

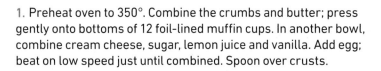

PREP: 20 MIN. + CHILLING • **BAKE:** 15 MIN. + COOLING • **MAKES:** 12 SERVINGS

1 cup crushed vanilla wafers (about 30 wafers)
3 Tbsp. butter, melted
1 pkg. (8 oz.) cream cheese, softened
⅓ cup sugar
2 tsp. lemon juice
1½ tsp. vanilla extract
1 large egg, room temperature, lightly beaten

TOPPING
1 lb. pitted canned or frozen tart red cherries
½ cup sugar
1 Tbsp. cornstarch
Red food coloring, optional

1. Preheat oven to 350°. Combine the crumbs and butter; press gently onto bottoms of 12 foil-lined muffin cups. In another bowl, combine cream cheese, sugar, lemon juice and vanilla. Add egg; beat on low speed just until combined. Spoon over crusts.

2. Bake until centers are almost set, 12-15 minutes. Cool completely in pans.

3. For topping, drain cherries, reserving ½ cup juice in a saucepan; discard the remaining juice. To reserved juice, add cherries, sugar, cornstarch and, if desired, food coloring. Bring to a boil; cook until thickened, about 1 minute. Cool; spoon over cheesecakes. Refrigerate, covered, for at least 2 hours.

1 MINI CHEESECAKE: 213 cal., 12g fat (6g sat. fat), 44mg chol., 127mg sod., 26g carb. (21g sugars, 1g fiber), 2g pro.

FROM GRANDMA'S KITCHEN: To give these a sweet-salty spin, use crushed pretzels instead of vanilla wafers. You can also substitute strawberries for the cherries—an especially tasty option when they're in season and you can buy locally-grown berries.

PRESSURE-COOKER
CHOCOLATE-APRICOT DUMP CAKE

Years ago, I used to prepare a version of this dessert in the oven. Oh, it was so good! I converted the recipe to my pressure cooker, and now we can enjoy it quickly. Try it also with white cake mix and blueberry pie filling. It's best served warm with ice cream or whipped cream.
—*Joan Hallford, North Richland Hills, TX*

PREP: 10 MIN. • **COOK:** 35 MIN. + STANDING • **MAKES:** 8 SERVINGS

1 can (21 oz.) apricot or peach pie filling
2 cups devil's food cake mix
½ cup chopped pecans, toasted
½ cup miniature semisweet chocolate chips, optional
½ cup butter, cubed
Vanilla ice cream, optional

1. Spread pie filling in the bottom of a greased 1½-qt. baking dish. Sprinkle with cake mix, pecans and, if desired, chocolate chips. Dot with butter. Cover baking dish with foil.

2. Place trivet insert and 1 cup water in a 6-qt. electric pressure cooker. Fold an 18x12-in. piece of foil lengthwise into thirds, making a sling. Use the sling to lower the baking dish onto the trivet. Lock lid; close pressure-release valve. Adjust to pressure-cook on high for 35 minutes.

3. Quick-release pressure. Using foil sling, carefully remove baking dish. Let stand 10 minutes. If desired, serve warm cake with ice cream.

1 SERVING: 360 cal., 18g fat (9g sat. fat), 31mg chol., 436mg sod., 49g carb. (26g sugars, 1g fiber), 2g pro.

CARAMEL PEAR PUDDING

Don't expect this old-fashioned dessert to last long. The delicate pears and irresistible caramel topping make it a winner whenever I serve it. It's nice to have a tempting fall cake that puts the season's best pears to excellent use.
—*Sharon Mensing, Greenfield, IA*

PREP: 15 MIN. • **BAKE:** 45 MIN. • **MAKES:** 8 SERVINGS

1 cup all-purpose flour
⅔ cup sugar
1½ tsp. baking powder
½ tsp. ground cinnamon
¼ tsp. salt
Pinch ground cloves
½ cup whole milk
4 medium pears, peeled and cut into ½-in. cubes
½ cup chopped pecans
¾ cup packed brown sugar
¼ cup butter
¾ cup boiling water
Optional: Vanilla ice cream or whipped cream

1. Preheat oven to at 375°. In a large bowl, combine the first 6 ingredients; beat in milk until smooth. Stir in pears and pecans. Spoon mixture into an ungreased 2-qt. baking dish.

2. In another bowl, combine the brown sugar, butter and water; pour over batter. Bake, uncovered, for 45-50 minutes. Serve warm, with ice cream or whipped cream if desired.

1 SERVING: 359 cal., 12g fat (4g sat. fat), 17mg chol., 223mg sod., 63g carb. (46g sugars, 3g fiber), 3g pro.

CARAMEL-APPLE SKILLET BUCKLE

My grandma used to bake a version of this for me when I was a little girl.
She would make it using fresh apples from her tree in the backyard. I've adapted
her recipe because I love the combination of apples, pecans and caramel.

—Emily Hobbs, Springfield, MO

PREP: 35 MIN. • **BAKE:** 1 HOUR + STANDING • **MAKES:** 12 SERVINGS

½ cup butter, softened
¾ cup sugar
2 large eggs,
   room temperature
1 tsp. vanilla extract
2 cups all-purpose flour
2½ tsp. baking powder
1¾ tsp. ground cinnamon
½ tsp. ground ginger
¼ tsp. salt
1½ cups buttermilk

TOPPING
⅔ cup packed brown sugar
½ cup all-purpose flour
¼ cup cold butter
¾ cup finely chopped
   pecans
½ cup old-fashioned oats
6 cups thinly sliced peeled
   Gala or other sweet
   apples (about 6 medium)
18 caramels, unwrapped
1 Tbsp. buttermilk
   Optional: Vanilla
   ice cream, whipped
   cream, additional
   chopped pecans and
   ground cinnamon

1. Preheat oven to 350°. In a large bowl, cream butter and sugar until light and fluffy, 5-7 minutes. Add eggs, 1 at a time, beating well after each addition. Beat in vanilla. In another bowl, whisk the flour, baking powder, cinnamon, ginger and salt; add to the creamed mixture alternately with the buttermilk, beating well after each addition. Pour batter into a greased 12-in. cast-iron or other ovenproof skillet.

2. For topping, in a small bowl, mix brown sugar and flour; cut in butter until crumbly. Stir in pecans and oats; sprinkle over batter. Top with apples. Bake until apples are golden brown, 60-70 minutes. Cool in pan on a wire rack.

3. In a microwave, melt the caramels with buttermilk; stir until smooth. Drizzle over cake. Let stand until set. Serve with toppings as desired.

1 PIECE: 462 cal., 19g fat (9g sat. fat), 64mg chol., 354mg sod., 68g carb. (42g sugars, 3g fiber), 7g pro.

"Very good way to use up several ripe apples! As soon as it came out of the oven, I covered the whole thing with caramel topping (I had jarred caramel topping, so I used it liberally). The caramel melted right into the apples and the cake, giving it a beautiful appearance and making for a delicious cake. Next time, I think I will put the apples on top of the batter and then cover with the streusel."
—GRAMMY DEBBIE, TASTEOFHOME.COM

PEACH BAVARIAN

PEACH BAVARIAN

Fruit molds are my specialty. This one, with its refreshing peach taste, makes a colorful salad or dessert.
—*Adeline Piscitelli, Sayreville, NJ*

PREP: 15 MIN. + CHILLING • MAKES: 8 SERVINGS

1 can (15¼ oz.) sliced
  peaches
2 pkg. (3 oz. each) peach or
  apricot gelatin
½ cup sugar
2 cups boiling water
1 tsp. almond extract
1 carton (8 oz.) frozen
  whipped topping, thawed
  Additional sliced
  peaches, optional

1. Drain peaches, reserving ⅔ cup juice. Chop peaches into small pieces; set aside.

2. In a large bowl, dissolve gelatin and sugar in boiling water. Stir in the reserved juice. Chill until slightly thickened. Stir extract into whipped topping; gently fold in gelatin mixture. Fold in peaches.

3. Pour into an oiled 6-cup mold. Chill overnight. Unmold onto a serving platter; garnish with additional peaches if desired.

1 PIECE: 249 cal., 5g fat (5g sat. fat), 0 chol., 53mg sod., 47g carb. (47g sugars, 0 fiber), 2g pro.

ANGEL STRAWBERRY DESSERT

This is a wonderful treat when fresh strawberries are readily available.
Every time I make this pretty dessert, someone asks for the recipe.
—*Theresa Mathis, Tucker, GA*

PREP: 30 MIN. + CHILLING • MAKES: 16 SERVINGS

1½ cups sugar
5 Tbsp. cornstarch
1 pkg. (3 oz.)
  strawberry gelatin
2 cups water
2 lbs. fresh strawberries,
  hulled, divided
1 pkg. (8 oz.) cream cheese,
  softened
1 can (14 oz.) sweetened
  condensed milk
1 carton (12 oz.) frozen
  whipped topping, thawed
1 prepared angel food
  cake (8 to 10 oz.),
  cut into 1-in. cubes

1. For glaze, in a large saucepan, combine the sugar, cornstarch and gelatin. Add water and stir until smooth. Cook and stir over medium-high heat until mixture begins to boil. Cook and stir 1-2 minutes longer or until thickened. Remove from the heat; cool completely. Cut half the strawberries into quarters; fold into the glaze.

2. In a small bowl, beat cream cheese until smooth. Beat in condensed milk until blended. Fold in whipped topping.

3. In a 4-qt. clear glass bowl, layer half the cake cubes, glaze and cream mixture. Repeat layers. Cut remaining strawberries in half and arrange over the top. Cover and refrigerate for at least 2 hours or overnight.

1 SERVING: 344 cal., 11g fat (8g sat. fat), 24mg chol., 202mg sod., 57g carb. (43g sugars, 1g fiber), 5g pro.

STATE FAIR CREAM PUFFS

The Wisconsin Bakers Association has been serving these treats at the Wisconsin State Fair since 1924. In recent years, more than 300,000 are sold annually!
—*Ruth Jungbluth, Dodgeville, WI*

PREP: 25 MIN. • **BAKE:** 30 MIN. + COOLING • **MAKES:** 10 SERVINGS

1 cup water
½ cup butter
¼ tsp. salt
1 cup all-purpose flour
4 large eggs,
 room temperature
2 Tbsp. 2% milk
1 large egg yolk,
 lightly beaten
2 cups heavy
 whipping cream
¼ cup confectioners' sugar
½ tsp. vanilla extract
 Additional confectioners'
 sugar

GRANDMA'S SECRET

When baking cream puffs, be sure to leave about 3 inches of space around each one on the baking sheet. The dough needs space to expand, and the steam that makes them rise needs room to evaporate.

1. Preheat oven to 400°. In a large saucepan, bring water, butter and salt to a boil over medium heat. Add flour all at once; stir until a smooth ball forms. Remove from heat; let stand for 5 minutes. Add eggs, 1 at a time, beating well after each addition. Continue beating until mixture is smooth and shiny.

2. Drop by ¼ cupfuls 3 in. apart onto greased baking sheets. Combine milk and egg yolk; brush over puffs. Bake until golden brown, 30-35 minutes. Remove to wire racks. Immediately cut a slit in each for steam to escape; let cool.

3. In a large bowl, beat cream until it begins to thicken. Add sugar and vanilla; beat until almost stiff. Split cream puffs; discard soft dough from inside. Fill the cream puffs just before serving. Dust with confectioners' sugar. Refrigerate leftovers.

1 CREAM PUFF: 340 cal., 29g fat (17g sat. fat), 196mg chol., 197mg sod., 14g carb. (5g sugars, 0 fiber), 5g pro.

STRAWBERRY CREAM PUFFS: Omit whipped cream filling. In a small mixing bowl, beat 2 packages (8 oz. each) softened cream cheese and 1 cup sugar until fluffy. Fold in 4 cups whipped cream and 3 cups coarsely chopped strawberries. Fill as directed.

VANILLA CREAM PUFFS: Omit whipped cream filling. In a bowl, whisk 1½ cups milk, 1 package (5.1 oz.) instant pudding mix and ½ tsp. almond extract for 2 minutes. Let stand for 2 minutes or until soft-set. Fold in 4 cups whipped cream. Fill as directed.

CHOCOLATE GLAZE FOR CREAM PUFFS: In a heavy saucepan, melt 6 Tbsp. semisweet chocolate chips, 1½ tsp. shortening and ¾ tsp. corn syrup over low heat, stirring until smooth. Drizzle over cream puffs.

SLOW-COOKER BANANAS FOSTER

The flavors of caramel, rum and walnut naturally complement fresh bananas in this version of a dessert classic. It's my go-to choice for any family get-together.
—*Crystal Jo Bruns, Iliff, CO*

PREP: 10 MIN. • COOK: 2 HOURS • MAKES: 5 SERVINGS

5 medium firm bananas	⅓ cup chopped walnuts
1 cup packed brown sugar	⅓ cup sweetened
¼ cup butter, melted	shredded coconut
¼ cup rum	Optional: Vanilla
1 tsp. vanilla extract	ice cream or
½ tsp. ground cinnamon	sliced pound cake

1. Cut bananas in half lengthwise, then widthwise; layer in the bottom of a 1½-qt. slow cooker. Combine the brown sugar, butter, rum, vanilla and cinnamon; pour over bananas. Cover and cook on low for 1½ hours or until heated through.

2. Sprinkle with walnuts and coconut; cook 30 minutes longer. Serve with ice cream or pound cake.

1 SERVING: 462 cal., 17g fat (8g sat. fat), 24mg chol., 99mg sod., 74g carb. (59g sugars, 4g fiber), 3g pro.

FIGGY APPLE BRIE TART

Our holiday gatherings often included baked Brie. I transformed it into a dessert that's both savory and sweet. It makes a wonderful appetizer, too.
—*Kristie Schley, Severna Park, MD*

PREP: 25 MIN. • BAKE: 15 MIN. • MAKES: 8 SERVINGS

3 Tbsp. butter, softened
¾ cup sugar
2 large apples
1 cup dried figs, halved
½ lb. Brie cheese, rind removed, sliced
1 sheet refrigerated pie crust

1. Preheat oven to 425°. Spread butter over bottom of a 10-in. ovenproof skillet; sprinkle evenly with sugar.

2. Peel, quarter and core apples; arrange in a circular pattern over sugar, rounded side down. Place figs around apples. Place skillet over medium heat; cook until sugar is caramelized and apples have softened slightly, 10-12 minutes. Remove from heat; top with cheese.

3. Unroll pie crust; place over fruit and cheese, tucking under edges. Place skillet in oven on an upper rack; bake until crust is golden brown, 15-18 minutes. Let cool in skillet 5 minutes. Carefully invert onto a serving plate; serve warm.

1 PIECE: 394 cal., 19g fat (11g sat. fat), 45mg chol., 315mg sod., 50g carb. (33g sugars, 2g fiber), 8g pro.

STICKY TOFFEE RICE PUDDING WITH CARAMEL CREAM

Simple rice pudding gets a makeover with this upscale recipe. It has just the right thickness to soak up a hot caramel topping.
—*Janice Elder, Charlotte, NC*

PREP: 45 MIN. • **BAKE:** 35 MIN. + COOLING • **MAKES:** 16 SERVINGS

3 cups water
1 cup uncooked medium grain rice
¼ tsp. salt
3 cups pitted dates, chopped
3 cups 2% milk
2 tsp. vanilla extract
1 cup packed brown sugar
1½ cups heavy whipping cream, divided
¼ cup butter, cubed
½ cup sour cream
¼ cup hot caramel ice cream topping

1. In a large saucepan, bring the water, rice and salt to a boil. Reduce heat; cover and simmer for 12-15 minutes or until rice is tender. Add dates and milk; cook and stir for 10 minutes. Remove from the heat; stir in vanilla. Set aside.

2. Preheat oven to 350°. In a small saucepan, combine brown sugar, 1 cup cream and the butter. Bring to a boil. Reduce heat; simmer, uncovered, for 2 minutes, stirring constantly. Stir into rice mixture. Transfer to a greased 13x9-in. baking dish. Bake, uncovered, until bubbly, 35-40 minutes. Cool for 15 minutes.

3. Meanwhile, in a small bowl, beat the sour cream, caramel topping and remaining cream until slightly thickened. Serve with warm rice pudding. Refrigerate leftovers.

½ CUP RICE PUDDING WITH 1 TBSP. TOPPING: 329 cal., 14g fat (8g sat. fat), 38mg chol., 112mg sod., 50g carb. (37g sugars, 2g fiber), 4g pro.

GRANDMA'S ORANGE MILK SHERBET

My dear grandma made this sherbet for my birthday party in the 1930s. She squeezed whole oranges to get the juice for it. I often double the recipe since it's so refreshing on a hot summer day.
—*Marilynn Engelbrecht, Harrisonville, MO*

PREP: 20 MIN. + FREEZING • **MAKES:** ABOUT 2 QT.

3 cups whole milk
1½ cups orange juice
¾ cup sugar
2 cans (8 oz. each) unsweetened crushed pineapple

1. In a large saucepan, heat milk over medium heat until bubbles form around sides of pan. Set aside to cool.

2. In a large bowl, combine orange juice and sugar thoroughly. Stir in milk. Transfer to an 11x7-in. dish; freeze until mushy.

3. Transfer mixture to a bowl and whip. Add pineapple and juices. Return mixture to dish and freeze.

½ CUP: 97 cal., 2g fat (1g sat. fat), 6mg chol., 23mg sod., 20g carb. (19g sugars, 0 fiber), 2g pro.

STICKY TOFFEE RICE PUDDING
WITH CARAMEL CREAM

ROASTED BANANA & PECAN CHEESECAKE

We always keep bananas on hand, but with just two of us in the house, they usually ripen
faster than we can eat them. That makes them perfect for roasting and
baking into this cheesecake with a nutty crust.
—*Patricia Harmon, Baden, PA*

PREP: 45 MIN. + COOLING • BAKE: 45 MIN. + CHILLING • MAKES: 12 SERVINGS

3 medium ripe bananas,
  unpeeled
1¾ cups crushed pecan
  shortbread cookies
3 Tbsp. butter, melted

FILLING
2 pkg. (8 oz. each)
  cream cheese, softened
1 pkg. (8 oz.) reduced-fat
  cream cheese
½ cup sugar
¼ cup plus 2 Tbsp. packed
  brown sugar, divided
1 tsp. vanilla extract
2 Tbsp. spiced rum,
  optional
4 large eggs, lightly beaten
½ cup chopped pecans
½ tsp. ground cinnamon
12 pecan halves, toasted
  Chocolate syrup

1. Preheat oven to 400°. Place the unpeeled bananas in an
8-in. square baking dish. Bake until banana peels are black,
10-12 minutes. Cool to room temperature. Reduce oven
setting to 325°.

2. Place a greased 9-in. springform pan on a double thickness
of heavy-duty foil (about 18 in. square). Wrap foil securely around
the pan. Place on a baking sheet.

3. In a small bowl, mix cookie crumbs and melted butter. Press
onto bottom and 1 in. up sides of prepared springform pan. Bake
until set, 8-10 minutes. Cool on a wire rack.

4. In a large bowl, beat cream cheese, sugar and ¼ cup brown
sugar until smooth. Beat in vanilla and, if desired, rum. Add
eggs; beat on low speed just until blended. Remove ½ cup
cream cheese mixture to a small bowl. Pour the remaining
filling into crust.

5. Peel and place roasted bananas in a food processor; process
until smooth. Add to the ½ cup reserved cream cheese mixture;
stir in chopped pecans, cinnamon and remaining 2 Tbsp. brown
sugar. Pour over the plain cream cheese mixture. Cut through
filling with a knife to swirl.

6. Place springform pan in a larger baking pan; add 1 in. hot water
to the larger pan. Bake until the center is just set and top appears
dull, 45-55 minutes. Remove springform pan from water bath.
Cool on a wire rack for 10 minutes, then run a knife around
the edge of the cake to loosen it from the pan; remove the foil.
Cool for 1 hour longer. Refrigerate overnight, covering when
completely cooled.

7. Remove rim from pan. Top cheesecake with pecan halves;
drizzle with chocolate syrup.

NOTE: To toast nuts, bake in a shallow pan in a 350° oven for
5-10 minutes or cook in a skillet over low heat until lightly
browned, stirring occasionally.

1 PIECE: 430 cal., 30g fat (14g sat. fat), 126mg chol., 308mg sod.,
33g carb. (24g sugars, 2g fiber), 8g pro.

BUTTERSCOTCH PECAN DESSERT

Light and creamy, this terrific treat never lasts long after I serve it. The fluffy cream cheese layer topped with cool butterscotch pudding is a lip-smacking combination.

—*Becky Harrison, Albion, IL*

PREP: 15 MIN. + CHILLING • **BAKE:** 20 MIN. + COOLING • **MAKES:** 20 SERVINGS

- ½ cup cold butter, cubed
- 1 cup all-purpose flour
- ¾ cup chopped pecans, divided
- 1 pkg. (8 oz.) cream cheese, softened
- 1 cup confectioners' sugar
- 1 carton (8 oz.) frozen whipped topping, thawed, divided
- 3½ cups cold 2% milk
- 2 pkg. (3.4 or 3.5 oz. each) instant butterscotch or vanilla pudding mix

1. Preheat oven to 350°. In a small bowl, cut the butter into the flour until crumbly; stir in ½ cup pecans. Press into an ungreased 13x9-in. baking dish. Bake until lightly browned, 20 minutes. Cool.

2. In a small bowl, beat cream cheese and sugar until fluffy. Fold in 1 cup whipped topping; spread over crust.

3. In a large bowl, whisk milk and pudding mix for 2 minutes. Let stand for 2 minutes or until soft-set; pour over the cream cheese layer. Refrigerate until set, 15-20 minutes. Top with remaining whipped topping and remaining ¼ cup pecans. Refrigerate for 1-2 hours.

1 PIECE: 242 cal., 14g fat (8g sat. fat), 27mg chol., 247mg sod., 23g carb. (18g sugars, 1g fiber), 3g pro.

PEACH CRISP PARFAIT POPS

My little ones love fruit crisps and ice pops. I created a healthy and delicious treat that combines the two. For a sweet addition, use cinnamon sticks in place of the wooden pop sticks.
—Carmell Childs, Orangeville, UT

PREP: 15 MIN. + FREEZING • MAKES: 8 SERVINGS

2 cartons (5.3 oz. each) fat-free vanilla Greek yogurt
2 tsp. brown sugar
¼ tsp. ground cinnamon
Pinch ground nutmeg
1 cup granola without raisins
8 freezer pop molds or paper cups (3 oz. each) and wooden pop sticks
1 can (15 oz.) sliced peaches in extra-light syrup or juice, drained and chopped

In a small bowl, combine yogurt, brown sugar, cinnamon and nutmeg; fold in granola. Divide half the yogurt mixture among molds or paper cups. Top with half the peaches; repeat layers. Top molds with holders. If using cups, top with foil and insert sticks through foil. Freeze until firm.

1 POP: 167 cal., 3g fat (0 sat. fat), 0 chol., 40mg sod., 28g carb. (15g sugars, 5g fiber), 10g pro. DIABETIC EXCHANGES: 1½ starch, ½ fat-free milk.

BANANA SPLIT DESSERT

Here's a mouthwatering make-ahead dessert that looks scrumptious and tastes as good as it looks!
—Elmer Thorsheim, Radcliffe, IA

PREP: 30 MIN. + FREEZING • MAKES: 25 SERVINGS

3½ cups graham cracker crumbs
⅔ cup butter, melted
4 to 5 medium bananas
½ gallon Neapolitan ice cream (block carton)
1 cup chopped walnuts
1 cup chocolate chips
½ cup butter
1 pint heavy whipping cream

1. In a small bowl, combine crumbs and melted butter. Set aside ½ cup; press the remaining crumbs into a 15x10x1-in. pan. Slice bananas widthwise and layer over crust. Cut ice cream widthwise into 10 slices; place over bananas. Spread the edges of the ice cream slices to cover the bananas and form a smooth layer. Sprinkle with nuts. Cover and freeze until firm.

2. In a large saucepan, melt chocolate chips and butter; stir until smooth. Pour over ice cream and nuts; freeze until firm.

3. In a large bowl, whip cream until stiff peaks form; spread over chocolate layer. Top with the reserved ½ cup crumbs. Store in freezer (will keep for several weeks). Remove from freezer about 10 minutes before serving.

1 PIECE: 406 cal., 26g fat (14g sat. fat), 66mg chol., 204mg sod., 41g carb. (20g sugars, 1g fiber), 5g pro.

FROM GRANDMA'S KITCHEN: For the easiest cutting, purchase a rectangle-shaped package of ice cream in the flavor of your choice.

CARAMEL APPLE STRUDEL

My father, who was born and raised in Vienna, Austria, would tell us stories about how his mother covered all of the kitchen counters with dough whenever she made apple strudel. This recipe is a modern, delicious way to carry on part of my family's heritage.
—*Sarah Haengel, Bowie, MD*

PREP: 35 MIN. + COOLING • BAKE: 25 MIN. • MAKES: 8 SERVINGS

5 medium apples, peeled and chopped (5 cups)
¾ cup apple cider or juice
¼ cup sugar
½ tsp. ground cinnamon
¼ tsp. ground allspice
¼ tsp. ground cloves
1 frozen puff pastry sheet, thawed
¼ cup fat-free caramel ice cream topping
1 large egg
1 Tbsp. water
1 Tbsp. coarse sugar
Optional: Sweetened whipped cream and additional caramel ice cream topping

1. Preheat oven to 375°. In a large saucepan, combine the first 6 ingredients. Bring to a boil. Reduce heat; simmer, uncovered, 15-20 minutes or until apples are tender, stirring occasionally. Cool completely.

2. Unfold puff pastry onto a large sheet of parchment; roll into a 16x12-in. rectangle. Transfer parchment and pastry to a baking sheet, placing a short side of the rectangle facing you. Using a slotted spoon, arrange apples on the bottom half of pastry to within 1 in. of edges. Drizzle apples with caramel topping. Roll up jelly-roll style, starting with the bottom side. Pinch seams to seal, and tuck ends under.

3. In a small bowl, whisk egg with water; brush over the pastry. Sprinkle with coarse sugar. Cut slits in top. Bake 25-30 minutes or until golden brown. If desired, serve with whipped cream and additional caramel topping.

1 SLICE: 270 cal., 9g fat (2g sat. fat), 26mg chol., 140mg sod., 46g carb. (24g sugars, 4g fiber), 3g pro.

"Soooo gooood! This recipe is a keeper. I prefer to put the caramel on top instead of inside so everyone can choose how much they want. I made a couple of these babies and put them in the freezer to pull out for the holidays."
—JMFORGACS, TASTEOFHOME.COM

CHOCOLATE-COVERED
STRAWBERRY COBBLER

CHOCOLATE-COVERED STRAWBERRY COBBLER

This cobbler came about because I love chocolate-covered strawberries.
Top it with whipped cream, either plain or with a little chocolate syrup stirred in.
—*Andrea Bolden, Unionville, TN*

PREP: 15 MIN. • BAKE: 35 MIN. + STANDING • MAKES: 12 SERVINGS

1 cup butter, cubed
1½ cups self-rising flour
2¼ cups sugar, divided
¾ cup 2% milk
1 tsp. vanilla extract
⅓ cup baking cocoa
4 cups fresh strawberries, quartered
2 cups boiling water
Whipped cream and additional strawberries

1. Preheat oven to 350°. Place butter in a 13x9-in. baking pan; heat pan in oven 3-5 minutes or until the butter is melted. Meanwhile, in a large bowl, combine flour, 1¼ cups sugar, the milk and vanilla until well blended. In a small bowl, mix cocoa and the remaining 1 cup sugar.

2. Remove baking pan from oven; add batter. Sprinkle with strawberries and the cocoa mixture; pour boiling water evenly over top (do not stir). Bake 35-40 minutes or until a toothpick inserted into cake portion comes out clean. Let stand 10 minutes. Serve warm with whipped cream and additional strawberries.

1 SERVING: 368 cal., 16g fat (10g sat. fat), 42mg chol., 316mg sod., 55g carb. (41g sugars, 2g fiber), 3g pro.

CARAMEL PECAN ICE CREAM DESSERT

My mother made sure to share this old-fashioned recipe with me because
she knew I'd want to make it. I love desserts, especially this one!
—*Mary Wright, Morriston, ON*

PREP: 35 MIN. + FREEZING • MAKES: 15 SERVINGS

1¾ cups all-purpose flour
1 cup quick-cooking oats
1 cup chopped pecans
1 cup packed brown sugar
1 cup butter, melted
1½ cups caramel ice cream topping
2 qt. vanilla ice cream, softened

1. Preheat oven to 400°. In a large bowl, combine the flour, oats, pecans and brown sugar. Add butter; mix well. Spread in a thin layer in a 15x10x1-in. baking pan. Bake for 15 minutes or until golden, stirring occasionally. Crumble while warm; cool.

2. Press half the crumb mixture into a 13x9-in. dish. Drizzle with half the caramel sauce; spread with ice cream. Top with the remaining caramel sauce and crumb mixture. Cover and freeze until firm. Remove from the freezer 10 minutes before serving.

1 PIECE: 515 cal., 26g fat (13g sat. fat), 64mg chol., 300mg sod., 68g carb. (48g sugars, 2g fiber), 6g pro.

LEMON PANNA COTTA WITH BERRIES

Cool, creamy and pretty as a picture, this luscious Italian dessert is elegant
enough for the fanciest dinner party. It goes especially well with coffee.
—*Mariela Petroski, Helena, MT*

PREP: 25 MIN. + CHILLING • **MAKES: 7 SERVINGS**

1 envelope
  unflavored gelatin
1⅓ cups half-and-half cream
2 cups heavy
  whipping cream
⅓ cup honey
1 tsp. grated lemon zest
  Dash salt
⅔ cup each fresh
  blackberries, blueberries
  and raspberries
2 Tbsp. sugar
2 Tbsp. lemon juice
1 Tbsp. amaretto, optional

1. In a small saucepan, sprinkle gelatin over half-and-half;
let stand for 1 minute. Heat over low heat, stirring until gelatin
is completely dissolved. Stir in the whipping cream, honey,
lemon zest and salt. Cook and stir until blended. Pour into
seven 6-oz. ramekins or custard cups.

2. Cover and refrigerate for at least 5 hours or until set. In a
small bowl, combine berries, sugar, lemon juice and, if desired,
amaretto. Cover and refrigerate for at least 30 minutes. Unmold
panna cotta onto dessert plates; serve with berry mixture.

1 SERVING: 382 cal., 30g fat (19g sat. fat), 116mg chol., 73mg sod.,
25g carb. (21g sugars, 2g fiber), 4g pro.

DOWN EAST BLUEBERRY BUCKLE

This buckle won a contest at my daughter's college. They shipped us four
lobsters, but the real prize was seeing the smile on our daughter's face.
—*Dianne Van Der Veen, Plymouth, MA*

PREP: 15 MIN. • **BAKE:** 30 MIN. • **MAKES: 9 SERVINGS**

2 cups all-purpose flour
¾ cup sugar
2½ tsp. baking powder
¼ tsp. salt
1 large egg,
  room temperature
¾ cup 2% milk
¼ cup butter, melted
2 cups fresh or
  frozen blueberries

TOPPING
½ cup sugar
⅓ cup all-purpose flour
½ tsp. ground cinnamon
¼ cup butter, softened

1. Preheat oven to 375°. In a large bowl, whisk the flour, sugar,
baking powder and salt. In another bowl, whisk egg, milk and
melted butter until blended. Add to the flour mixture; stir just
until moistened. Fold in blueberries. Transfer to a greased
9-in. square baking pan.

2. For topping, in a small bowl, mix sugar, flour and cinnamon.
Using a fork, stir in softened butter until mixture is crumbly.
Sprinkle over batter.

3. Bake until a toothpick inserted in center comes out clean,
30-35 minutes (do not overbake) . Cool in pan on a wire rack.
Serve warm or at room temperature.

NOTE: If using frozen blueberries, use without thawing to avoid
discoloring the batter.

1 PIECE: 354 cal., 12g fat (7g sat. fat), 49mg chol., 277mg sod.,
59g carb. (32g sugars, 2g fiber), 5g pro.

COOKIE SWIRL COBBLER

An extra-rich chocolate chip cookie dough and crescent roll topping provide a tasty twist on a classic cherry cobbler. Serve it with a scoop of vanilla ice cream.

—Jeanne Holt, St. Paul, MN

PREP: 20 MIN. • BAKE: 25 MIN. + COOLING • MAKES: 12 SERVINGS

1 cup (about 8 oz.) refrigerated chocolate chip cookie dough, softened
2 Tbsp. brown sugar
⅓ cup white baking chips
¼ cup plus 2 Tbsp. toasted sliced almonds, divided
1 can (21 oz.) cherry pie filling
½ tsp. almond extract, divided

2 cups fresh or frozen unsweetened raspberries
1 tube (8 oz.) refrigerated crescent rolls
¾ cup confectioners' sugar
3 to 4 tsp. 2% milk
Vanilla ice cream, optional

1. Preheat oven to 350°. Combine cookie dough, brown sugar, baking chips and ¼ cup almonds. Set aside. In a large saucepan, heat cherry pie filling over medium heat until bubbly. Remove from heat; stir in ¼ tsp. almond extract. Fold in raspberries. Transfer to a greased 13x9-in. baking dish.

2. Unroll crescent dough into a long rectangle; press perforations to seal. Drop small spoonfuls of the cookie dough mixture over top; spread gently to cover. Roll up jelly-roll style, starting with a long side; pinch seam to seal. Cut crosswise into 12 slices; arrange cut side up on cherry mixture.

3. Bake until golden brown, 25-30 minutes. Cool 10 minutes. Meanwhile, combine confectioners' sugar, remaining almond extract and enough milk to make a medium-thick glaze. Drizzle the rolls with glaze; sprinkle with remaining 2 Tbsp. toasted almonds. Serve warm, with ice cream if desired.

NOTE: To toast nuts, bake in a shallow pan in a 350° oven for 5-10 minutes or cook in a skillet over low heat until lightly browned, stirring occasionally.

1 SERVING: 308 cal., 11g fat (4g sat. fat), 2mg chol., 224mg sod., 49g carb. (22g sugars, 2g fiber), 3g pro.

SWEET & TART LEMON JELL-O

With its sunny lemon color, this gelatin mold brightens up any table.
I usually make two molds for parties because it disappears so quickly.
—*Patricia Ryzow, Thousand Oaks, CA*

PREP: 15 MIN. + CHILLING • COOK: 5 MIN. • MAKES: 12 SERVINGS

1 envelope
  unflavored gelatin
1 cup cold water
2 cups boiling water
2 pkg. (3 oz. each)
  lemon gelatin
1 can (12 oz.) frozen
  limeade concentrate,
  thawed
2 cups heavy
  whipping cream
3 Tbsp. confectioners'
  sugar
  Quartered fresh
  strawberries and
  fresh mint

1. In a small saucepan, sprinkle unflavored gelatin over cold water; let stand 1 minute. Heat and stir over low heat until the gelatin is completely dissolved. Remove from heat.

2. In a large bowl, add boiling water to lemon gelatin; stir for 2 minutes to completely dissolve. Stir in unflavored gelatin mixture and limeade concentrate. Refrigerate until slightly thickened.

3. Beat cream until it begins to thicken. Add confectioners' sugar; beat until soft peaks form. Beat gelatin mixture until frothy; fold in whipped cream. Transfer to an 8-cup ring mold coated with cooking spray. Refrigerate, covered, until set.

4. To serve, unmold onto a large plate. Serve with strawberries and mint.

1 SERVING: 252 cal., 15g fat (9g sat. fat), 45mg chol., 46mg sod., 29g carb. (28g sugars, 0 fiber), 3g pro.

GRANDMA'S BUTTERSCOTCH CANDY

The recipe for this wonderfully buttery candy was handed down from my grandma.
My brothers, sisters and I love it now as much as we did when we were
little, and so do our families. It has become a cherished tradition.
—*Catherine Rothermel, Columbus, OH*

PREP: 5 MIN. • COOK: 30 MIN. + COOLING • MAKES: ABOUT ¾ LB.

2 cups sugar
⅔ cup water
¼ tsp. cream of tartar
2 Tbsp. butter
1 tsp. vanilla extract

1. Butter a 13x9-in. pan; set aside. In a heavy saucepan, combine the sugar, water and cream of tartar. Bring to a boil, without stirring, over medium heat until a candy thermometer reads 300° (hard-crack stage). Syrup will turn a golden color.

2. Remove from the heat; stir in butter and vanilla. Return to heat. Cook and stir until thermometer returns to 300°. Pour into prepared pan. Cool. Break into pieces.

½ OZ. CANDY: 73 cal., 1g fat (1g sat. fat), 3mg chol., 10mg sod., 17g carb. (16g sugars, 0 fiber), 0 pro.

GRANDMA'S SECRET
To make a healthier version, fold in 4 cups whipped topping instead of the sweetened whipped cream to save 75 calories and 10g fat per serving.

MOM'S BEST PUMPKIN CHEESECAKE

Swirls of pumpkin don't just turn this fall cheesecake into a
showstopper—they also make it even more delicious!
—*Jami Geittmann, Greendale, WI*

PREP: 35 MIN. • BAKE: 55 MIN. + CHILLING • MAKES: 12 SERVINGS

1½ cups graham cracker
crumbs
¼ cup sugar
⅓ cup butter, melted

FILLING
4 pkg. (8 oz. each)
cream cheese, softened
1½ cups sugar
2 Tbsp. cornstarch
2 tsp. vanilla extract
4 large eggs,
room temperature,
lightly beaten
1 cup canned pumpkin
2 tsp. ground cinnamon
1½ tsp. ground nutmeg

TOPPINGS
Optional: Whipped
cream, additional
ground cinnamon
and caramel syrup

1. Preheat oven to 325°. Place a greased 9-in. springform pan on a double thickness of heavy-duty foil (about 18 in. square). Securely wrap foil around pan.

2. Combine crumbs and ¼ cup sugar; stir in butter. Press onto bottom and 1½ in. up the sides of prepared pan. Place on a baking sheet. Bake until set, 10-15 minutes. Cool on a wire rack.

3. For filling, beat 1 package cream cheese, ½ cup sugar and cornstarch until smooth, about 2 minutes. Beat in the remaining 3 packages of cream cheese, 1 package at a time, until smooth. Beat in the remaining 1 cup sugar and the vanilla. Add eggs; beat on low speed just until combined. Place 2 cups filling in a small bowl; stir in pumpkin, cinnamon and nutmeg.

4. Pour half the plain filling over crust; dollop with half the pumpkin filling. Cut through with a knife to swirl. Repeat layers and swirling.

5. Place springform pan in a large baking pan; add 1 in. hot water to the larger pan. Bake until center is just set and top appears dull, 55-65 minutes. Remove springform pan from water bath. Cool on a wire rack 10 minutes. Carefully run a knife around the inside edge of pan to loosen; cool 1 hour longer. Refrigerate overnight, covering when completely cooled. Remove rim from the pan. If desired, top with whipped cream and cinnamon or caramel sauce.

1 PIECE: 518 cal., 34g fat (19g sat. fat), 152mg chol., 361mg sod., 47g carb. (36g sugars, 1g fiber), 8g pro.

RECIPE INDEX